Mathematics in the Primary School

A sense of progression

Third edition

**Sandy Pepperell, Christine Hopkins,
Sue Gifford and Peter Tallant**

Routledge
Taylor & Francis Group

LONDON AND NEW YORK

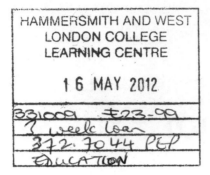
First edition published 1996, reprinted 1996, 1997 and 1998
Second edition published in Great Britain by David Fulton Publishers 1999

Third edition published 2009
by Routledge
2 Park Square, Milton Park, Abingdon, Oxon OX14 4RN

Simultaneously published in the USA and Canada
by Routledge
711 Third Avenue, New York, NY 10017

Routledge is an imprint of the Taylor & Francis Group, an informa business

© 2009 Sandy Pepperell, Christine Hopkins, Sue Gifford and Peter Tallant

Typeset in Bembo by HWA Text and Data Management Ltd, London

British Library Cataloguing in Publication Data
A catalogue record for this book is available from the British Library

Library of Congress Catalogin- in-Publication Data
Mathematics in the primary school : a sense of progression / Sandy Pepperell ...
[et al.]. — 3rd ed.
    p. cm.
  Includes bibliographical references and index.
  1. Mathematics—Study and teaching (Primary) I. Pepperell, Sandy.
  QA135.5.M36934 2009
  372.7'044--dc22   2008044875

ISBN 10: 0-415-48879-6 (pbk)
ISBN 13: 978-0-415-48879-2 (pbk)

ISBN 10: 0-415-48880-X (hbk)
ISBN 13: 978-0-415-4880-8 (hbk)

Contents

Acknowledgements

We would like to thank all the teachers, children and students who have contributed ideas and material to this book; in particular our thanks to the teachers and children at: All Saints' Church of England First School, Merton; Abelour House, Banffshire; Bishop Gilpin School, Merton; Charles Dickens School, Southwark; Cypress Infant School, Croydon; Fairchildes Primary School, Croydon; Kingsley Infant School, Croydon; Sheringdale School, Wandsworth; St Mark's Church of England Primary School, Kingston; St Matthew's Church of England Primary School, Kingston; Surbiton Hill Nursery School, Kingston. Further material contributed by Suzanne Cowan, Jon Kurta, Penny Latham, Valerie Newman and Sue Pope.

In addition we should like to recognize the contribution of more recent members of the maths team at Roehampton: Julie Alderton, Barbara Allebone and Freda Rockliffe.

Preface to the third edition

In preparing the book for its third edition the editors have taken account of general developments in some areas of primary teaching in England, while continuing to write with a view wider than any one national curriculum. So we now use the term 'Foundation Stage' as well as the 'early years' to recognise that Nursery and Reception classes in England are officially referred to in this way. While the content of the earlier edition of our book remains topical, we have also included explicit consideration of planning for talk in mathematics to reflect a growing emphasis on the need to engage children more actively in learning mathematics. In addition, we have added a new section on mathematical difficulties to reflect the team's interest in developing strategies to support those who are being identified as having particular needs in learning mathematics. Both of these are current priorities for mathematics teaching in England (for example as addressed in the Report by Sir Peter Williams for the DCFS, 2008) as well as having wider relevance.

An expert teacher working with a class of children can make teaching look easy, but the background preparation needed to reach this stage is substantial. Not only does the primary teacher need to have a grasp of the general principles of children's learning and of a range of curriculum subjects but also of the approaches and emphases which will make those subjects come alive. All teachers know that events in the classroom do not always turn out as they expect and that constant reflection and adaptation is required to provide appropriate learning experiences for the children.

This book is concerned with just one aspect of the primary curriculum: mathematics. We have tried to identify important principles which might inform mathematics teaching and hope that this will be useful both to students preparing to be teachers and also to teachers re-examining their approach to mathematics teaching as a part of the continual process of professional updating.

In preparing to teach mathematics effectively we suggest that there are nine key principles to consider:

- Teachers have responsibility for generating positive attitudes towards mathematics in the face of some negative views held generally about the subject. Reflecting on their own experiences as learners may help develop awareness of feelings and attitudes to teaching and learning mathematics. Teachers need to address, and seek answers to, questions such as: What is mathematics really about? Why do I feel the way I do about it? Understanding how they have reached their own positions will influence the experiences offered to pupils and the attitudes pupils will develop.
- Teachers need to have a confident grasp of the mathematics they teach and of the ways in which children learn mathematics.
- This means teachers need to read up on key aspects of mathematical content, including the concepts and skills children need to develop, in order to plan appropriate experiences. Some understanding of common misconceptions and difficulties is also essential in planning for children to encounter and deal with potential areas of confusion.
- Children should have the opportunity to challenge, explore and create in mathematics as in any other curriculum area. Teachers therefore need to build a bank of starting points, problems, stories and apparatus which will stimulate mathematical thinking and encourage children to discover and test rules and patterns.
- Children will benefit from being aware of what they are learning and how it fits into an overall idea

of what mathematics is and of its applications. Teachers can help children to gain confidence in working mathematically by encouraging them to reflect on their learning and involving them in setting targets for learning.

- Teachers need to develop interactive approaches, which encourage children to share and explain their methods for working in mathematics with each other as well as with their teachers. Productive 'talk' is a crucial ingredient in learning and teaching. Teachers need to use questioning to encourage generalising and abstract thinking.
- The range of teaching and organisational approaches needs to be varied to meet particular aims.
- Interactive whole class teaching might set the context and pace of learning, and allow children to share strategies and benefit from the ideas of others. Children also need time to work on solving problems or to consolidate learning in groups, in pairs or as individuals. Teachers will also need to interact with children in smaller groups to teach and to assess understanding. This will depend on skills in planning independent activities and teaching children to work together on tasks.
- The teaching of mathematics can be enhanced by team planning. Teachers generally benefit from sharing ideas and expertise and evaluating together. Often it is in these contexts that teachers can discuss with colleagues the really successful moment or the misconception that needs addressing. Supportive group planning encouraged by the head teacher and mathematics specialist can draw on the strengths of individuals to increase the quality of the learning experience of all children in the school.

We hope that this book will contribute to the professional development needed to implement confidently such an approach to primary mathematics.

Sandy Pepperell, Christine Hopkins, Sue Gifford and Peter Tallant
Roehampton, December 2008

Using and applying mathematics

MATHEMATICAL THINKING

Whether or not we articulate them, the answers we have to questions such as, '*What is mathematics really about?*' and '*What is mathematics for?*', provide the basis for our approach, as teachers, to the teaching and learning of mathematics. Our answers to these and similar questions will depend on our own experiences as learners and these experiences will have been generated from the views of those who taught *us*. Put another way, our opinions are formed from what and how we were required to learn and the reasons for doing so that we were given (or not!). If the major emphasis was placed on the acquisition of facts and the need to memorise and to make use of rules unthinkingly, then this is what we will bring first to our teaching. This is what we will view mathematics to be about. We will think of it as simply school mathematics – something we merely pick up and put down and this solely in the context of the classroom. If this is the nature of our experience, there is also the danger that we have suffered the anxiety over mathematics which Williams (2008) reported is still a significant factor in our society. If the way in which we were taught, however, has challenged us to view mathematics as an area of learning which is stimulating, rewarding and something which touches us personally, if our focus is on making connections and enjoying mathematics' potential for being a means of interpreting and understanding the world, then these will be the views we bring and to which our children will be exposed.

As a prelude to teaching mathematics, therefore, the first task for teachers is to reflect on and to analyse their experiences of learning it. Teachers must assess the quality and nature of their experiences and seek ways to ensure that the 'messages' about mathematics that are given to children are appropriate in that they stimulate engagement, enthusiasm and deep thought. Children should work with teachers who are committed to the idea that the acquisition of knowledge and skills is important. Equally, however, children must have the opportunity to learn with teachers who recognise that knowledge and skills are of limited value as end products. It is in the addressing of Using and Applying mathematics that children can begin to get to the heart of mathematics and find purpose and fulfillment in learning about it. What Using and Applying mathematics involves, and how it can be addressed in the classroom, is discussed in detail below.

1.1 WHY DO CHILDREN LEARN MATHEMATICS IN SCHOOL?

Responses to this question usually include:

- the need to solve practical everyday problems;
- to use mathematics in other areas of learning;
- to learn to reason logically;
- to gain some satisfaction and enjoyment from exploring this area of human knowledge.

These basic reasons lead naturally to an emphasis on mathematical thinking. It is of little use if a child can correctly complete pages and pages of calculations but does not know how to get started when faced with an unfamiliar problem or a task presented in a practical rather than a written form. It is harder for children to relate the mathematics they do in one situation to that required by another than is sometimes assumed. We need to encourage children to generalise and abstract from particular situations and experiences, so they can move from concrete to abstract and back again. Moving in this way, from concrete to abstract and vice versa, involves children in modelling, in representing things in different ways. This relates to the essential nature of mathematics as the discovery and application of numerical and spatial relationships. Generalising is therefore involved both in the process of abstraction and in the transfer of mathematical ideas from one context to another.

An approach to the teaching and learning of mathematics which develops the skills needed to tackle unfamiliar problems and the processes involved in doing mathematics needs to focus on generalising mathematical relationships. However, this central aspect of mathematics is perhaps the most difficult to develop. Because of this, it is the one concentrated on in this section and is a recurring theme throughout the book.

Three aspects involved in mathematical thinking – reasoning mathematically, mathematical communication and solving problems – underpin much of the discussion in this book.

Reasoning mathematically: reasoning mathematically involves children in:

- searching for patterns and relationships within their mathematical work;
- moving from particular examples to general statements about mathematical ideas and vice versa
- ;thinking logically in a mathematical situation.

Mathematical communication: mathematical reasoning also depends on mathematical communication; this involves encouraging children to articulate their thinking and to move towards using more abstract language, symbols and representations. This means children need opportunities for:

- talking about the mathematics:
  - listening, reflecting and responding;
  - explaining why a method works;
  - posing their own mathematical questions;
- using mathematical language/terminology;
- using a range of representational forms (modelling).

Solving problems: this involves children in exploring relationships within mathematics and also using mathematics with understanding in a variety of contexts. This means children need opportunities for seeing mathematical similarities in apparently different situations and for mathematical decision making. This includes:

- making their own decisions about appropriate mathematical ideas and operations;
- drawing upon a variety of strategies;
- choosing tools and materials (for example number line, calculator, cubes, squared paper);
- making links between different aspects of mathematics and between mathematics and other subjects.

It is important to say here that, in trying to find solutions in mathematics, children will also have the important experience of discovering what does _not_ work. They will try things which are not obviously successful. Children may find this discouraging, initially. They may feel that they have 'done it wrong'. Here, the role of the teacher is to address the vitally important affective factors which influence children when they are learning. Part of thinking mathematically is a willingness to pursue a line of enquiry, to explore, to be open to possibilities. Anxiety concerning our ability to succeed restricts our ability to think, to consider possibilities, to 'have a go'. Negative attitudes can lead to unwillingness even to engage with a task or merely to a desire to find a solution quickly; perhaps in order to demonstrate that we can 'do it' or simply to allow us to move on to something else. If the children's attempts to solve a problem do not yield success then negative attitudes may be created or reinforced. Sensitive and appropriately-timed interaction with the children is vital, therefore. How a teacher reacts to children pursuing an idea which does not generate an immediate solution is crucial. Indeed, her reaction to children's efforts will not only influence their experience with the specific situation but also, potentially, have a profound effect on their general view of mathematics and what it involves. It is the role of the teacher to explore, with the children, how an apparently unsuccessful attempt to solve the problem can contribute to an eventual solution. This can be brought about through careful discussion of the children's ideas in order to draw out what has indeed been achieved. In short, the teacher might say, '*Okay, that hasn't worked, try something else*' or, alternatively, she could respond with, '*Now that really helps. If it can't be that … then what do you think it* could *be?*'. If the teacher models this response consistently then the children will learn to incorporate it into their approach and to recognise that their efforts are of real potential value, even if they do not produce an immediate solution. In other words, if we know what does not work, then we can be on the way to discovering what does. Another aspect of what the children can describe as 'failure', is 'getting stuck'. Once again, the teacher's response is crucial in sustaining children's involvement and maintaining positive attitudes and her role is to support and at the same time challenge the children. One strategy for achieving this is by prompting the children to try to think of something they have done before which might help. Another is to ask them to talk through what they have done so far in order to help them to generate an overview of the problem. There are other strategies available and many of them rest on the high-level, professional skill of questioning for more of which see below.

When planning children's work, these three themes of *reasoning mathematically*, *mathematical communication* and *solving problems* should act as a checklist for judging the value of all of the mathematical activities in which the children engage.

Having set up opportunities for the children, the teacher's role is to develop and sustain the children's thinking. Case studies are used throughout the book to give some indication of how the teaching principles identified might influence classroom practice. The case studies are in different schools with children of different ages, but it will become apparent that similar questions are used to extend the children's thinking.

Key questions

The thoughtful use of certain key questions by the teacher can encourage mathematical reasoning by the children. In practice it is not the questions alone which support the problem-solving but all aspects of the verbal and non-verbal interaction between the teacher and the children. By showing interest, puzzled looks and body language the teacher sustains the children's thinking, while the tone of voice in which the questions are posed shows the teacher's involvement with the problem. If the teacher poses these questions in many different situations, then the children have the opportunity to internalise the questions and develop as independent thinkers.

The questions serve to encourage different ways of reasoning. It should be noted that most of them are 'open', in other words they require an extended response:

- *Looking for patterns and relationships*:
  - What is your prediction … ?
  - How many different … ?
  - What will happen if … ?

- *Moving to general statements*:
  - Are they the same … ?
  - Is it true that … ?

- *Thinking logically*:
  - What makes you think that … ?
  - How do you know that … ?

- How can you be sure … ?
- Why does it not work … ?

- *Drawing conclusions and testing them out*:
  - So that means that …
  - If we are right then …
  - If that is true then what about …

Case study: *Rosanne Posner*

How can we develop reasoning at Key Stage 1?

Here is a 'Maths morning' in a Year 1 class, where the majority of the children are five years old. By looking closely at the activities in which the children are involved, we can identify teaching strategies for promoting the children's mathematical reasoning. So what might this look like in the Year 1 classroom? At first sight, it looks like a typical group work session with different groups working on different tasks set up by the teacher. However, all the tasks are related in that they have arisen from the theme of 'Pairs', taken from Kerslake *et al.* (1992).

The morning begins with 'Maths talk time', where the teacher sits with the whole class gathered together on the carpet and encourages them to work out how many children are in their class today. This is a small example of a *real life problem,* in the context of completing the register. The numbers are entered by the teacher in the dinner register in full view of the children. She also shows them and comments on the day and the date displayed on the class calendar board, so there is an expectation that mathematical ideas can be the subjects of discussion. '*Twenty-seven children are here today*', Misha points out. Asking Misha to explain to everyone how she worked that out is one way of supporting the development of her mathematical reasoning.

When the teacher introduces the class to their tasks for the morning, she asks them if they think they have enough sky and water yet in the Noah's Ark role play area that they are creating by painting and building in one corner of the room. (This is to be their 'boat corner' where the animals will go in two by two!)

Asking the children this as well as how much more they think they need to paint encourages them to make a decision about a practical problem involving measuring and estimating. Getting children to think about the purpose of their work gives them a focus for their reasoning. Sharing with them clear expectations for how they will work and what they will have achieved by the end of the time available also supports their attempts at reasoning by showing them the parameters within which they can make their own decisions about the problems to be solved.

Some children are playing the 'Sock Game'; this entails moving counters around a sock-shaped board, and then covering the small sock pictures they land on with any matching sock cards that they are holding. The use of a spinner with numbers on it tells the players how many spaces to move their counters. The aim of the game is to be the first to place all your cards on the board. The children have to start by checking that they each have the same number of cards to ensure that the game will be fair. As in many board or card games, the children may start to predict, and the teacher can encourage this prediction using questions such as *'What will happen if you spin a 4 on your next go?'*. The children are beginning to think about issues of probability and odds and evens, and are being encouraged to consider different possible outcomes. These are early examples of reasoning in the form of prediction, which is important because it involves thinking ahead and is related to the beginnings of abstract thought. Later, the children pass on the instructions for how to play the game to other children, which ensures that they articulate the thinking involved.

Another group are exploring whether their own feet are the same size or different sizes. Kayleigh says that she does not think that hers are the same size. This prompts her teacher to ask *'What makes you think that?'* in order to explore the child's reasoning. Kayleigh then tests her estimation by measuring. The teacher has put out a selection of materials for the group to use, including string, scissors, rulers, plain and squared paper. *'What do you think your feet will measure?'* the teacher asks them. One child uses the markings on a ruler to count without reading the actual numbers. Others count squares in order to compare the area of each foot. Asking them why they have chosen these particular materials and methods gives the children another opportunity to explain their reasoning.

At the end of the morning, the teacher gathers the whole class back onto the carpet. Adam reports to the other children, *'When I was doing my foot work, I measured to see if my feet were the same ...'*. His group has been testing predictions about the size of their feet, and now they are explaining their reasoning to other children who have been engaged in other different activities. The teacher shows genuine interest in the children's thinking to encourage them to share what is going on in their heads. She can ask further prompting and probing questions such as *'Why?'* or *'How do you know that?'*. This gives high status to the mathematical reasoning that has been going on and helps to build an atmosphere of mathematical curiosity in the room.

As far as the development of mathematical reasoning is concerned, we have seen this being implemented in this Year 1 classroom in many different ways. The children have been using and applying mathematical ideas in practical tasks, in relevant and realistic problem-solving situations, and to investigate within mathematics itself. They have also had opportunities to explain their thinking which will support the development of their reasoning.

The teacher helped to make this happen by:

- setting up interesting and rich *activities;*
- providing access to appropriate *resources;*
- using the classroom *space* effectively;
- using *time* creatively and efficiently;
- *grouping* and regrouping the children flexibly;
- *intervening* skilfully and supportively, mainly through the use of prompting and probing questions.

How can we develop reasoning at Key Stage 2?

An afternoon in a Year 6 class reveals opportunities for further development of the children's mathematical reasoning.

We can see in the following account how the children are reasoning mathematically. Some of them (Tammy, Della, Billy, Lorraine, Michelle and Emma) are working on an exploration called 'Using weights' from the *HBJ Mathematics* scheme's 'True or false?' theme (see Figure 1.1):

There are five weights:

1 ounce;
2 ounces;
4 ounces;
8 ounces;
16 ounces (or 1 lb).

Is it true that these could be used to weigh any item up to 31 ounces? What if there is also a 32 ounce weight? What weights could be made with these? What weights could not be made?

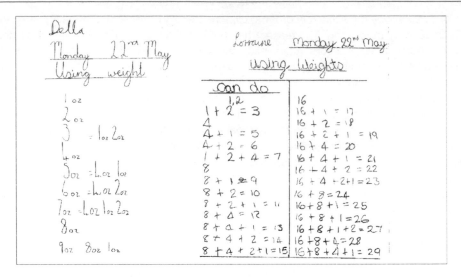

Figure 1.1 Della and Lorraine's work on the 'Using weights' problem

The following snippets of conversation both between the children seated around the table and with their teacher show not only how the pupils are explaining their reasoning but also how the teacher is prompting and probing their thinking by observing closely, listening carefully and intervening skilfully. As we shall see, she even uses a tactical 'no response' as one of her strategies.

The children embark on their exploration into the possible ways of combining the values of the five weights by making (and recording) an initial prediction that can then be tested:

Teacher: *'What's your prediction?'*
Child: *'Is a prediction like an estimate, Miss?'*

For the teacher, this is an opportunity to discuss the meaning of some mathematical terminology with the child. Billy does not believe that it is possible to make up all the other weights using those provided. He is happy to venture his opinion because he knows the teacher will not scold him if it turns out to be inaccurate. Indeed, she positively encourages a questioning and conjecturing atmosphere by her reassuring yet thought-provoking interactions with the class.

The children are used to working in an investigative way and they set about the task with noticeable commitment, diligently exploring the possibilities for combining the weights and systematically recording their results. With no prompting from their teacher, they begin to add the values of the weights together effortlessly in order to investigate the 'Is it true that ...?' statement in the wording of the exploration:

Emma: *'Miss Sandell, can you do take-aways?'*
Child: *'Don't be so stupid, of course you can't!'*

The teacher appears to let this go unnoticed but she has made a mental note of Emma's question. Undaunted, Emma continues creating the addition sums that are enabling her and the others to proceed with their exploration:

Child: *'Once you get past 16 you use 16 all the time.'* This child is searching for a pattern in the results, as is the next one ...
Child: (looking perplexed) *'It should go "1 plus 1 equals 2, 2 plus 2 equals 4 ..."'*
Teacher: *'Why doesn't it do that?'*

Child: *'Because you can't do any one of them twice.'*

This is an example of children explaining reasons and of mathematical reasoning itself, prompted by the teacher's skilful use of questioning:

Child: *'You could make 63 if you added a 32 ounce weight.'* We know that this child is predicting and conjecturing (speculating) because she is thinking aloud about a possibility that has not yet been tried.'

Teacher: *'Is that all? Are there any other possibilities?'*

Child: *'Yes.'*

Teacher: *'How do you know that there are?'*

The teacher is probing the child's thinking here in order to prompt further reasoning.

After working on the task for a while, one child makes a general statement while looking at the results already obtained:

Child: *'If you had the numbers 1 to 10 you could go on forever.'*

Teacher: *'You would need to work it out, perhaps by recording it systematically, in order to prove this.'*

Child: (with a look of excitement on his face) *'Can you do 47?'*

Child: *'You can't do it.'*

Teacher: *'What exactly is it that you can't do?'*

Here the teacher is probing the child's thinking to provoke him into identifying for himself where the obstacle he perceives lies and what form it takes. This is instead of blocking the child's thinking by telling him that he is either right or wrong.

On another occasion, a child searches for and spots a pattern in the results:

Child: *'So when you get to 47 you start using the number 16 in the middle instead of at the beginning.'*

Earlier, Emma had asked if they could do 'take-aways' (as well as adding), so later, the teacher rejoins the group to demonstrate the use of balance scales to get the children thinking about the numerical differences between the values of the weights. The teacher encourages the children to work out the results there and then, so there is a great deal of quick calculation in the form of mental, finger and pencil and paper methods happening. The teacher is also able to discuss with the children the special meaning in mathematical language of a term like 'difference between' in a context where it matters to them.

The group can now make up weights in new ways because they can use the differences as well as the totals. For example, a 12 ounce parcel can be weighed by placing a 4 ounce weight alongside the parcel and a 16 ounce weight on the other side.

Following the discussion about using the differences between the values of the weights as a method of weighing more items than have been possible before, an interesting thought occurs to one of the children:

Child: *'What if you timesed them now, Miss Sandell?'*

This child's idea of changing the operation involved shows that responsibility is being taken for extending the task by suggesting an alternative method. Unfortunately, classroom time is running out by this stage, but the child is left with an intriguing self-made puzzle to take away and mull over.

The afternoon ends with these children reporting their exploratory work to another group which has not been involved in this particular activity. This has the effect of consolidating their recent mathematical reasoning by making them re-present their ideas explicitly in order to communicate effectively with a new audience. Opportunities for them to receive and answer questions from the listeners serve to extend their reasoning even further.

The exploratory nature of this activity, in which the children are required to make decisions for themselves, provides many opportunities for the using and applying of mathematics and for mathematical reasoning in particular. The teacher's expectation and acceptance that the children will both communicate with each other and be in charge of organising and extending their work also makes this happen. In addition to this, she gives them scope to devise and refine their own ways of recording. Finally, the teacher's interventions serve to keep the children's thinking momentum going rather than interfering with it or stifling it. Overall, what we have seen in this Year 6 classroom is a mixture of opportunities to use and apply mathematics in practical tasks and within mathematics itself.

Glossary

This section is intended as a reference for teachers, to support subject knowledge and underpin planning, and not all of the terms need be used directly with children.

Generalisation: a generalisation in mathematics draws on the evidence of specific cases to suggest a general property (for example, noticing that $3 + 5 = 8$, $1 + 7 = 8$, $7 + 3 = 10$) and after testing out lots of combinations of odd numbers a child suggests the generalisation that *'If you add two odd numbers you get an even number.'*

Hypothesis: the generalisation may also be described as an hypothesis; it is a guess based on the evidence. An hypothesis may be shown to be true or shown to be false.

Tammy (see Figure 1.2) disproves the hypothesis: *'The longer your legs the faster you can run'* with a single counter example. The statement is not true in *all* cases although there may be a general correlation.

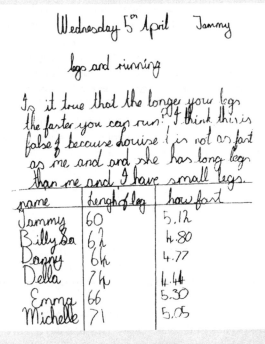

Figure 1.2 True or false?

Modelling: representing ideas in different ways.

Proof: a proof in mathematics is a series of logical statements to convince you that an hypothesis is always true, that it *must be* true. Children can be encouraged to move towards proof and logical reasoning by questions such as: *'Are you sure? Why do you think that? Can you explain? But what if …?'*. Tammy above disproves a statement with an example which does not fit (disproving by counter example). Another type of proof is *proof by exhaustion*, for example it can be shown that there are only a certain number of totals obtainable from throwing two dice by pairing each number on one dice with each on the other.

Number

2.1 INTRODUCTION – THE TEACHING OF NUMBER

Having identified the themes of reasoning, communication and solving problems as applying across all areas of mathematics teaching, we turn now to the content area of number. The primary number curriculum can be seen as a cycle of learning about the number system whilst using and applying that knowledge. In the early years children are learning to count and beginning to use and apply their counting with simple calculations. Counting develops through an understanding of the place value system which enables very large numbers to be named. A further cycle begins when children extend their understanding of numbers to include negative numbers and fractions of numbers.

Since Victorian times criticisms by inspectors of the teaching of mathematics in schools have focused on children being given too much practice of skills without understanding, without meaningful contexts and without attention to mathematical patterns and relationships. What teaching approaches will enable children to become confident and expert in applying their knowledge of number to familiar and unfamiliar situations? The current emphasis is on flexibility, confidence and the use of a variety of resources and methods, including mental methods and a variety of methods of recording, appropriate to the mathematical problem being tackled.

If teachers are to help children become confident and expert, they need:

- to understand the structure of the number system and the calculations on which the children are working;
- to be aware of common misconceptions;
- to encourage children to explain their methods – and to build on the children's answers in their teaching;
- to find the appropriate balance in the use of practical apparatus, mental mathematics, published schemes and calculators and computers.

Since mental mathematics underpins and drives all other methods, teachers can greatly increase children's confidence by explicitly working on and developing skills at working with numbers 'in the head'. There are differing views on the balance between written algorithms and the use of calculators and these are explored in Section 2.3.

2.2 NUMBER IN THE EARLY YEARS

This section on Number is arranged in chronological order to give a sense of progression. Some recurring themes are reasoning, encouraging mental strategies for calculations and creating a number environment in the classroom through language and display.

Strands can be found as follows:

- developing an understanding of place value and extending the number system (see Sections 2.2, 2.3 and 2.4);
- understanding relations between numbers and calculations (see Sections 2.2, 2.3 and 2.5);
- solving numerical problems (see Section 2.6).

Learning to count

A range of different kinds of knowledge and skills have to be acquired in order for children to learn to count. Schaeffer et al. (1974) for instance, suggested that children go through the following stages:

- Recognising small numbers like 1, 2 or 3 without counting but just by looking (sometimes called 'subitising'; we do this when we recognise numbers on a dice).
- Being able to compare more and less when two sets are paired up.
- Being able to recite the number names in order (ordinal aspect of number):
  - 1 to 12. These numbers must be learnt by rote; there is no pattern to help.
  - 13 to 19. Here the numbers from 3 to 9 are repeated, though not exactly; 'thir' is not quite 'three'. Each number is followed by 'teen' for 10, though the children will need to learn that thirteen is written 13 with the 1 representing the ten before the 3.
  - 20 to 99. Quite a lot of pattern spotting has gone on for children to count past 20: they have to combine two patterns, the 1 to 9 pattern and the 20, 30, 40 … pattern. You can see children grappling with these two patterns by watching when they get stuck, which is usually at a 9 (for example 29) or a 10s number (for example 40). By reciting the sequence of number names past 30 children are beginning to learn about the decimal structure of our number system.
- Being able to say one number for each object (one to one correspondence). To accomplish this task successfully, children need to synchronise touching an object and saying the next number word in the sequence. In the learning stages children can be observed to say two numbers for one object, skip an object or lose track of which things they have counted. It seems to help if they count things arranged in a line and actually move the things as they count them, as on an abacus, rather than counting static things like pictures, which is more challenging.
- Knowing the last number you say is the number of the whole collection. This is the cardinal aspect of numbers. If you ask children how many things there are after they have counted, say, five objects, they may say, 'eight' or 'three'! A child who understands cardinality is likely to be able to fetch you five pencils when asked, rather than bringing back a whole handful. Asking children to 'get me five', is a key assessment of whether they realise the significance of the final number and understand the purpose of counting.
- In addition, children need to understand that objects can be counted from any object in the set. As long as each object is counted only once using the repeatable order of number names, the order of counting the objects does not matter. This is called 'order-irrelevance'.
- Being able to compare and estimate numbers. Using counting in order to compare two groups, for instance to check fair shares, shows a sophisticated confidence in counting. Knowing which numbers are bigger than which, for all the numbers up to 10, seems to be the last aspect of counting that children grasp. For young children it is not obvious that the counting numbers are each worth one more than the one before (see Figure 2.1) and that the counting sequence indicates the increasing value of numbers, enabling us to calculate using the number line. Understanding the relative value of numbers, shown by the ability to compare numbers and to estimate, underpins the development of children's 'number sense', according to researchers in the USA (Gersten *et al.* 2005).

Some aspects of learning about number are now receiving less emphasis than previously. For instance, the relevance of ideas emphasised by Piaget, such as sorting, ordering and one-to-one matching (or one-to-one correspondence) is being questioned. Although interesting in terms of children's number understanding, they are not prerequisites for this. The work of Vygotsky (1978), a Russian psychologist, has proved influential in focusing attention on what children can achieve with assistance.

Other aspects of young children's understanding of numbers are now receiving more attention. Close observation of what children do know about numbers has made it clear that some young children have a range of informal and individual strategies for solving problems. Some very young children can count verbally to high numbers and write numerals, perhaps because someone does this with them at home. Hughes (1986) found that most young children can write a label for a box containing a small

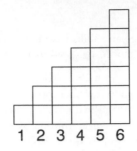

1 2 3 4 5 6

Figure 2.1 Staircase – each number is one more than and includes the previous one

number of objects, by drawing tallies (see Figure 2.2). He also found that three year olds could add and subtract mentally with very small numbers, in the context of a game with bricks being added to or taken away from some hidden in a box. Close observation of young children reveals that their number knowledge is developing on several fronts at once; they may be able to count verbally to quite high numbers while still learning the cardinal value of small numbers. At the same time they may be moving from tallying to understanding the meaning of numerals. They can also compare, estimate, add, subtract and share small numbers of objects. What is interesting to observe is how children solve these kinds of problems; do they use fingers, visualise or count aloud?

It is clear that what we do not need to do is protect young children from big numbers; they seem to be naturally interested and excited by them. Some will just want to talk about big numbers but a small proportion of three and four year olds will know quite a lot about them. We need to be sure that we allow children to show us what they know, and that we do not put a ceiling on our expectations. However there is a vast difference in the number experiences of children before the age of four, and some may know very little about number values or counting. Through observing individual children in everyday activities we should be able to comfortably challenge all of them at an appropriate level, and provide unpressured but stimulating experiences to develop their skills and understanding.

Most children enjoy acquiring counting skills. They may have been taught by relatives at home, with daily counting routines involving their favourite activities and allowing them to count to high numbers, for instance by counting skips or kicks. What children may need help with is seeing the point of counting; they need to see purposes for counting, like comparing amounts or laying the table, and they need to be encouraged to put their counting skills to use, for instance by checking no scissors have gone missing when tidying up. Since the many examples of numerals which children meet in everyday life – for instance on buses, telephones or birthday cards – often do not clearly represent a number

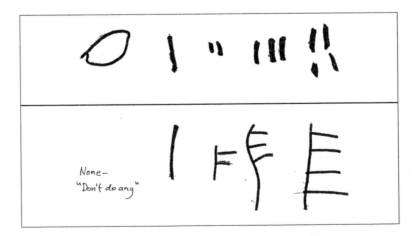

Figure 2.2 How many objects are in the box?

of things, but are used more as a code or label, children also need help in recognising the meaning of written numbers.

What activities help children to count and learn about numbers and numerals?

Research in New Zealand (Young Loveridge 1987) found that five year old children's expertise in number was associated with a family focus on number which included counting while preparing food, attention to money, lots of game playing including card games and bingo, and especially discussions related to time. Using the calendar to count down to birthdays and other events and pointing out times on the clock seemed to be particularly significant. Discussing numerals wherever they occurred was also important, for instance when playing with calculators, watching Sesame Street, reading distances on signposts or the speedometer in the car. It is interesting that in the past we would have considered some of these experiences too difficult for very young children; it seems that some three and four year olds are *number experts*, who because of repeated experience, are beginning to tell the time, interpret speedometers and even attempt the same sums as their older siblings. The *number novices* in this study, who had not had these kinds of experiences and who did not see their parents using numbers to solve problems in everyday life, were less competent with numbers. It therefore seems important that in school we replicate and build on these kinds of experiences, but we may need to organise more regular group activities, so that we are sure that all children benefit and so we can monitor this systematically.

Activities for counting

- Discussing ages, birthdays, cards, badges and candles; counting down to birthdays and other events; using a calendar; discussing times of the day, 'how many minutes to', relating to different clocks.
- Counting when preparing food or equipment, 'How many do we need?'
- Making lists or using recipes that include numbers.
- Counting children for dinners and registers and recording these.
- Playing games which involve counting objects or actions, for example skittles or hopping.
- Encouraging children to record scores of games in their own way with easels or clipboards.
- Putting out number apparatus and charts for children to refer to as they need to, with numbers up to 100 or beyond!
- Reading and making number books.
- Discussing numbers in books and magazines, including page numbers, prices in catalogues and brochures.
- Labelling things with numbers, so you know how many there should be when tidying up 'How many are missing?'.
- Using computers and calculators.
- Providing objects with numerals on and demonstrating their use: scales, height charts and rulers, tape recorders, video and washing machines, thermometers, timers.
- Having numerals conspicuous in role play areas, on clocks, telephones, calculators, appointment books, till and price labels, tickets, dials on cars, trains, planes.

Number rhymes and action songs

Rhymes like *five little ducks* or *ten currant buns* help children to become familiar with the number names and, if they are acted out or linked to pictures, help children to learn the cardinal values of the numbers. Spoken numbers can be linked to displays of symbolic numerals and to numbers of fingers. Rhymes are also important for demonstrating the important fact that each number in the counting sequence is worth one more than the one before, which means that when a duck swims away or a bun gets eaten, you can predict how many are left simply by counting backwards. In this way children can begin to learn about addition and subtraction and to calculate mentally. Rhymes can be adapted to provide extra challenge, for instance by eating two buns at a time.

Case study: *Sue Gifford*

A nursery shopping game

I was visiting the nursery school, and wanted to take an activity which would engage the children and allow them to show me what they knew about numbers. I decided on a miniature shop, with a dice to decide how much money you had to spend. Although this introduced a turn-taking element involving waiting, in my experience this is more bearable with miniature shop games because children can spend time inspecting their purchases, counting their money and deciding what to buy next, as well as checking that others are playing correctly. It would also allow me to focus on one child at a time, while working with a group.

I hoped this activity would show me:

* how the children counted, and whether they understood cardinality;
* whether they could compare numbers:
  * add or subtract in a practical way;
  * recognise numbers of dots without counting, or numerals;
  * represent numbers by tallying or writing numerals.

I set up shop with five teddy bears (one large shopkeeper and four small shoppers, each with a miniature shopping basket) and miniature grocery boxes from the local toy shop, which I arranged in a tray with sections labelled with prices from 1p to 4p. I also had a container of real one penny coins, a box for a till and a numeral and spots dice, numbered 1 to 6. In reserve I had another dice numbered 5 to 10 and, for those who had trouble counting the little spots on the dice, six beans coloured blue on one side, which could be thrown instead of a dice and the blue sides counted. I also had other coins, felt tips, blank labels and Post-its. I was all set to assess the children's number knowledge, or so I thought.

I started off with Sanyu and the two coloured beans. However, since she did not pay any attention to whether the beans came up blue or white, but insisted on counting all six beans each time, despite my reminders, and matched six pennies to six beans, I changed to the numeral and dots dice.

Sanyu threw a 2, asked where the two pence coins were and was perplexed as to what to do, until I suggested getting two pennies. Next time she threw a 5 and immediately got five pennies, recognising the numeral on the dice and counting the pennies. She then looked for something costing five pennies and seemed unhappy about buying things for less, which suggested that she was not confident either about shopping or about the relative values. When I encouraged her to buy something from the section of items priced at three pence, she wanted to take three of them, as did the other children who had joined the game. I then felt totally confused as to what this showed about the children's understanding: presumably they did not see the price label as an indicator of cost or value, but as a label directing them as to which items they should buy. Presumably for some children of this age the idea of exchanging money for goods is complex enough, without the added complication that some things cost more than others. I have noticed that when children as old as five or six play shops, they tend to just hand over any number of coins in exchange for items bought, without paying attention to actual prices or relative values, so this may be a much more sophisticated idea. However, just when I was thinking it was too difficult for her, Sanyu got the hang of the rules and started instructing the other children, getting boxes back out of the pockets of over eager shoppers. After a few goes, as she was shouting at the children as to what to do, and to 'up' the pace of the game, I made her shopkeeper instead of the large teddy and she managed this with apparent satisfaction. When some children could not read the numerals on the price labels, I drew some circles to stand for the number of pennies on them: one child commented, 'Ohs', presumably seeing the circles as letters. Wishing I had put sticky coins under the numerals to illustrate their value, I decided to put the labels away and have everything costing one penny, as the many for one relationship still seemed to create a problem for several children and put too many steps between throwing the dice and getting purchases in the basket. This worked fine, and the game still gave plenty of opportunities to count and recognise numbers.

The children had enjoyed the role play between the teddies ('Good morning, what would you like?' 'Thank you!') and the children carefully put pennies into the paw of the shopkeeper. Some were engaged by making their teddy do the shopping, and tried to get it to hold the basket, which was too big; others found fitting the teddy into the baskets more satisfying, or making it fall on the floor, and then comforting it. Most children held the teddies, some commented on the shopping and decisions about what they would buy (sweets for the kids' tea), and opened and closed the boxes while waiting for turns. It was interesting how much more some children were engaged by the role playing and story element than others. This made the turns and waiting longer, and yet could obviously be beneficially developed further. This is a tension I have often felt with mathematics and shop role play; insisting on the counting and prices often seems to interrupt equally valuable imaginative play. I wondered whether it would be better to separate the two and make the game more tightly focused on dice and money for goods exchange without any story-line of the teddies. But then were the teddies not attracting some children and giving the mathematics and money a softer and more comforting image? Or on the other hand, was it me and the staff, rather than the children, who needed to make the counting cuddly? Perhaps the children just needed to have their attention drawn to each others' turns a little more.

Most children could read the numerals or count the dots on the dice. The group with me just before 'fruit time' could all read numerals to 6 confidently. At fruit time they counted round the group of 16 children. The teacher and some of the children counted up to 27 pieces of fruit, so I decided to see if they could use a 5 to 10 dot and numeral dice. Most children needed help with this, but several in the group could recognise the numerals, or count the dots, and all seemed happy to be helped to count the dots, or be told, and then count out the money, sometimes with help. This seemed a comfortable level of challenge, which surprised their teacher.

I showed the children who were less expert how to count by arranging the coins in a line and moving them as they (or the teddy) counted them. Fadilah would check the number of coins, usually being one out with numbers up to 5, but adjusting this completely by herself. Tom could not count nine pennies accurately without encouragement to check, but then would do this, arranging his pennies in a line by himself and moving them to count. Several other children spontaneously attempted to do this after I had shown them. I was interested that Tom, and most of the others, although they estimated a handful for numbers over 6, were often only two pennies out. Tom was interested in the number he had left, for example when he had nine pennies and spent six, he counted the three left. Did this show an awareness of subtraction? I would need to ask him some hypothetical questions about spending, preferably with small numbers, to get a better idea of his understanding. With the higher number dice, the children accumulated several coins which gave opportunities to count higher numbers, as did the large baskets of groceries.

There were interesting variations in the children's awareness of having to pay for groceries. Sean was identified by his teacher as interested in numbers. He took the wooden numerals and went off and laid them in a line on the floor grouping identical numbers together, and pointed this out to me insistently and with satisfaction. He started off as identifying 6 as 9, and maintained this, despite my inviting him to look at, and then count, the dots. He could recognise 10 on the dice. Does his teacher mean he is interested in numerals rather than counting or numbers in general?

When Sean became the shopkeeper, the rule of one penny per object, which Sanyu had enforced, became varied. Some children would fill up their basket at one go, or have one or a few things, and Sean requested apparently arbitrary amounts from one to seven pennies, unrelated to the amount of shopping, and more to how much money individual children had. However, once when I asked if he was sure, when he had asked for five pennies (all that the child had) for one box, he reasoned that there might be problems when we ran out of groceries. (However the children suggested putting everything back and starting again, 'or doing something else'.) Sean certainly seemed to understand that one item could cost several coins, but did not seem to have an idea that there might be a reason for this in terms of varying value.

Early on, I got out more boxes, when we ran out, and invited the children to write price labels on Post-its. Sanyu wrote 4 confidently, and Tom's 4 was less conventional. Sanyu wrote 2 and a reversed 2, which she distinguished confidently, and stuck both on as 'price labels', but we did not use them to pay for things. Perhaps because I had already introduced numerals on labels, this was what the children did. Dawn said she could not write 3 so I got out the wooden numerals and she and Tom copied this (Tom wanted to draw round it, but I asked him to copy it, which he attempted). He repeatedly held up 2 back to front and said it looked like 5. Dawn then did 7 and said, 'Denny is going to be this' (a sibling with approaching birthday?). Tom said, 'I am going to do 10, no 20' (jokingly, as though aware this was a ridiculously high price) and finally said it was nine. This seemed to show quite a lot of knowledge of and interest in numbers and numerals amongst the children.

The activity seemed generally successful, with some children staying five minutes and some, like Tom, an hour. They seemed interested in the dice and the boxes and money, so I judged I would miss out the teddies the next time, but would definitely play the game again with this age group. Some of the three year olds were more interested in throwing the dice and filling their baskets with as many boxes as they could, rather than attending to numbers or counting pennies and goods, but they were enjoying playing at playing the game. They were all careful with the money, and were more interested in pocketing the boxes if anything!

I had found out quite a lot about the children's counting and number recognition, although as I did not know the children, I found it hard to remember who had done what unless I managed to note their names and jot something down. Some of this had surprised the teacher and raised her expectations for this age group: for instance, that Tom could count to nine and several four year olds enjoyed working out the numbers 5 to 10 on a numeral and dots dice. I could try cards like this on a future occasion. Obviously I would need to see what they did another time in a different context to make any hard and fast assessments, but I had some clues. With hindsight I realised that I tended to assume quite quickly that the children did not understand or that something was too hard for them, when given time they grasped the situation and adjusted their behaviour; or if shown how, learned how to do things quite quickly, like counting objects by moving them one at a time. Again, I would need to see what they did on another occasion to say they had really learned something. What I was not sure about was the children's understanding about shopping and transactions with coins. What do they think is going on? What do they understand about the different coins and why we have them? I would have to ask them.

Revised version of the game

- start with everything costing one penny;
- use dot and numeral dice to 6, keeping 5 to 10 in reserve;
- have extra boxes in reserve, to stimulate rearrangement of rules;
- have a till to pay into, and possibly smaller baskets for the teddies.

Extensions

- everything costs three pence;
- ask the children to price the things, using objects more obviously differing in value, and then read the labels when shopping;
- introduce labels with different prices and sticky money illustrations.

Starting to calculate

A Year 2 class were doing some mental arithmetic in the few minutes before dinner time. Nobody could do '20 take away 6' and the teacher suggested they count back six on their fingers. This was tricky, as the children had to keep track of how many they had counted back as well as actually counting backwards. It is also quite a slow method. The children could have counted out 20 blocks of course, but this still leaves the problem of how children get from counting blocks to calculating mentally, which is what we want them to do for small numbers like this. There will be some children who are still not calculating mentally by Year 5 or 6, and have to get out the blocks or do complicated things with their fingers, to do sums like '42 subtract 17'.

So how do children move from practical to mental addition and subtraction? It is easy to train classes of very young children to do sums on paper; they read the numbers, count the bricks, add or subtract them, then count again and write the answer. They may have got the idea of putting two lots together for add, and taking some away for minus, but they are not yet able to calculate.

Martin Hughes (1986) asked some three year olds to work out how many bricks would be hidden in a box containing, say, three bricks if two were taken away. He did other addition and subtraction problems with small numbers in the context of a game where children could see the number of bricks in the box to start with, and how many bricks were being added or taken away, but not the resulting number. He found that many three year olds could solve these problems, either mentally or by using their fingers. Some children just knew the answer and others seemed to be visualising the bricks. What is important here is that very young children are already capable of mental calculation with very small numbers, if they have something to think with. Hughes found that this did not mean that the activity always had to be practical; if he asked the children hypothetical problems involving, say, imagining sweets, they could also answer. If, however, he asked them problems using just abstract numbers, like 'three take away two', they usually could not answer. Some could, however, using their fingers. Fingers seem to be potentially very important in helping children generalise from one context to another; if they realise that they can represent two bricks or two sweets or two anything with two fingers, they are well on the way to abstracting relationships between numbers. It seems therefore that we can build on this capacity for mental arithmetic with young children by providing problems in meaningful contexts, such as games, and by encouraging them to visualise and to use their fingers to solve the problems.

Developing subitising skills and helping children to recognise dot patterns for numbers, as on dice, can familiarise them with some addition facts almost subliminally. For instance, in recognising eight in

Figure 2.3, you may see two fours or even four twos: this involves the important idea that numbers are made up of other numbers or *part whole* relationships. This key idea helps in recognising that addition and subtraction are linked, and that because four and four make eight, four removed from eight leaves four. Dot patterns with doubles seem easiest to learn first (see Figure 2.3), and can be connected to finger patterns on two hands: other patterns can be developed from these, for example '*How many ways can you show me eight fingers?*'

Figure 2.3 Other patterns illustrate how visual representations can help with counting and addition

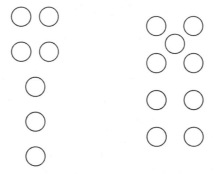

Figure 2.4 Seven is displayed as four and three dots. Nine is displayed as five and four

There is often a progression in the way that children solve problems with bigger numbers. When adding two numbers, children begin by counting all their bricks or fingers; for instance, for 3 + 5 they get 3, then 5, then count all 8 from the beginning. Later children will just count on from the 3 to get 8. Later still, they will reverse the numbers (commutativity) to count on from the larger one, so they count from 5, 3 more to get 8. This, the commutative principle, seems to be discovered spontaneously by children. Finally, children will just know the answer without having to think about it, or they will have instant recall. These strategies need to be made explicit to children and the teacher's role is to move children on to more efficient ones as appropriate. As children begin to add longer strings of numbers, associativity is another general arithmetic rule that is helpful. To add 5 + 7 + 3, for example, knowing you can add 7 and 3 first and then add on 5 means you can use a number bond for 10. This will give the same answer as adding 5 + 7 first and might be easier.

Counting on and back have been seen as important strategies to bridge the gap between having to count all and having recall of number facts, and this has led to an emphasis on number lines in helping children to visualise this process.

Another strategy which some children use spontaneously is recomposing numbers. For instance, a child may add 3 and 4 (near double) by thinking of a related fact, like 3 and 3 making 6 (double), and therefore adding one more to get 7. The child is using a derived fact, by adapting one which is well known. (The doubles, for example 3 + 3 = 6, 4 + 4 = 8, seem to be easily learned and need to be drawn to children's attention.) Another child may use their fingers to think of a number like 8 as made up of 5 and 3. This helps when adding numbers like 6 and 8, which can be thought of as 5 and 1 and 5 and 3, so the two 5s are added to make 10 and the 1 and 3 added to make 4, giving 14 altogether. Although this sounds long-winded, the visualising may be done in a flash. This child is using the ability to recompose numbers using 5, which fits in well with using fingers to represent numbers from an early stage. When children are very familiar with number bonds for 10, they can use this to look for 10 complements when adding; with 6 and 8, they can quickly see they need to take 2 from the 6 to make 8 into 10, leaving 4 more to make 14 (sometimes known as 'bridging through 10'). Both strategies are also useful when subtracting; if 7 from 15 is seen as taking 5 from 15, then 2 more from 10, the answer should be instantly recognised as 8. These strategies have an advantage over counting on and back, in that they are quicker, and less susceptible to errors due to losing track. They are also generalisable to bigger numbers, where counting on and back becomes even more problematic.

When the children are waiting for their dinner they can be encouraged to recall the number bonds to 10, and to look for ways of recomposing numbers like 20 as 10 and 10. Of course a lot of experience is required in splitting up numbers in different ways, with a variety of apparatus, as well as using fingers, before children can calculate mentally in fast and effective ways. It is interesting to note that Japanese and Korean schools, whose children do very well in number in international tests, put a lot of emphasis on finding patterns in number bonds for small numbers, and on recomposing numbers with 5 and 10, encouraging the use of fingers at this stage. It is the encouragement to visualise, to look for patterns, and to look for ways of recomposing numbers which seem to be the important elements in developing mental calculations.

The following is a summary of ways to encourage mental calculation:

- use meaningful contexts, for example from situations in the classroom, stories, money problems;
- encourage and emphasise:
  - representation of problems with fingers;
  - adding or subtracting 1 or 2 to start with;
  - learning the doubles facts;
  - recomposing numbers to 5 and something and 10 and something;
  - the bonds for 10;
  - spotting complements to 10 when adding or subtracting;
  - number facts for all the numbers up to 10 and up to 20;
  - looking for patterns;
  - looking for ways of turning unfriendly numbers into friendly numbers.

Children's number stories

Making up number stories is an activity which can provide a variety of learning opportunities. A group of children can be asked to draw pictures illustrating number bonds to 10 (see Figure 2.5) or to make up a story involving numbers. As well as being able to calculate, children need to be able to decide what kind of operation is required to solve a particular problem. They need to be able to relate abstract sums on paper or on the calculator to a problem set in a context. Asking children to make up stories to match sums is another way of helping children to relate abstract symbols to meaningful contexts. In the following example the children were asked to make up a number story, and this shows the children developing a flexible feel for the composition of numbers, and playing around with addition and subtraction. They might then go on to replicate their story on a calculator. The story is quite complicated (see Figure 2.6) and requires careful reading!

Some activities

How many ways? – to gain familiarity with number bonds

Provide children with lots of apparatus so they can show all the ways of making:

- Multilink models with five cubes;
- Unifix towers of 10 using two colours;
- plates of six biscuits using two kinds;
- cakes with seven candles using two colours;
- trains of Cuisenaire worth nine using different rods;

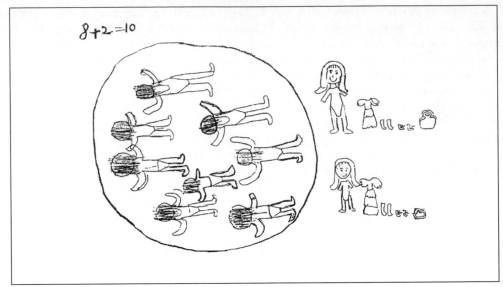

$8+2=10$

Figure 2.5 A picture for 8 + 2 = 10

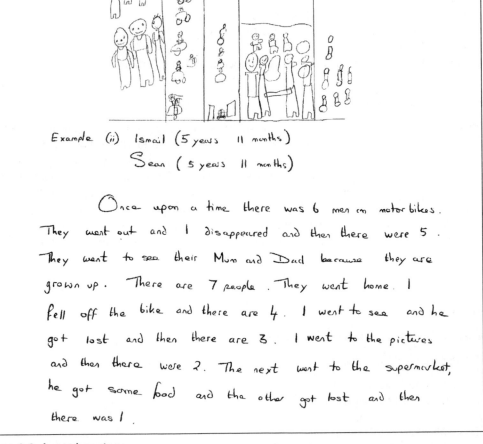

Example (ii) Ismail (5 years 11 months)

Sean (5 years 11 months)

Once upon a time there was 6 men on motor bikes. They went out and 1 disappeared and then there were 5. They went to see their Mum and Dad because they are grown up. There are 7 people. They went home. 1 fell off the bike and there are 4. I went to see and he got lost and then there are 3. I went to the pictures and then there were 2. The next went to the supermarket, he got some food and the other got lost and then there was 1.

Figure 2.6 A number story

- dominoes with eight spots altogether;
- baskets of five eggs using two colours;
- 10p using different coins;
- different sets of 10 beans sprayed blue on one side.

Then they can record using pictures and numbers, spot patterns in the number bonds (for example 1 and 9, 2 and 8, 3 and 7) and investigate the number of combinations for each total (see Figures 2.7 to 2.10).

The child was given cardboard ladybirds and counters and asked to give each ladybird eight spots.

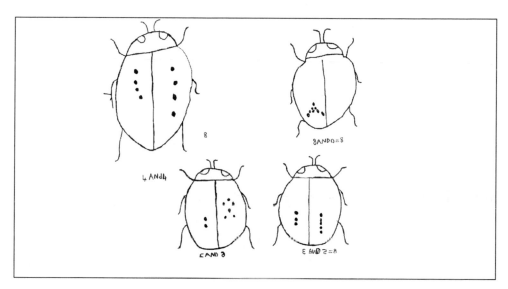

Figure 2.7 Ladybirds with eight spots

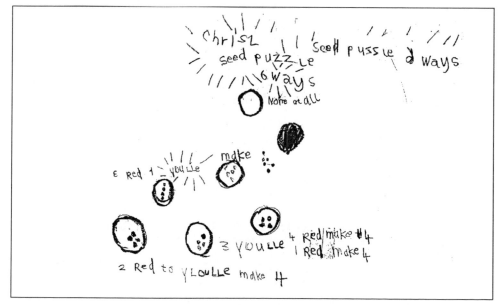

Figure 2.8 Seed puzzle . The child was given red and yellow counters and some pots. The task was to put four counters in each pot in as many different ways as possible. Here the child finds all five combinations (for example 3 red and 1 yellow, 4 red, etc.) but intriguingly includes 'none at all'.

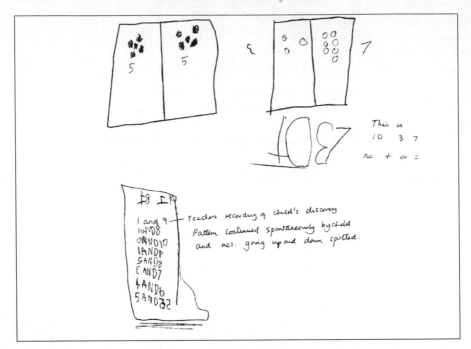

Figure 2.9 Ten counters on a divided baseboard (child's work annotated by the teacher)

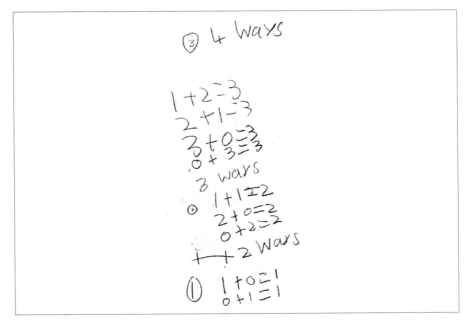

Figure 2.10 How many ways are there to make 3?. The child continued the patterns to find systematically how many ways to make two and then one.

Yoghurt pots – to learn faster recall of number bonds

Take a set number of counters and put them under an upturned pot. Take some out and challenge the children to tell you (by holding up their fingers) how many are still under the pot. It is interesting to see how the children work this out. Do they:

- visualise, or count the hidden counters?
- use their fingers in some way?
- consult number lines on the wall nearby?
- just know?

Children can play this in pairs, putting some counters on top of the pot and leaving some hidden underneath. It is interesting to see how they record the possibilities in their own way. Figure 2.11 shows a child's recording for six counters.

Board games

Board games can be adapted, so that two dice are used, and the scores added, subtracted or doubled. This is more challenging if dice numbered 1 to 9 are used.

2.3 DEVELOPING A FEEL FOR NUMBER

A skilful early years teacher draws on skills similar to those used by child psychologists in trying to analyse what is involved in activities such as learning to count. To do this the teacher will need to observe children and their responses to a range of different kinds of questioning. Gradually, an activity which seemed straightforward is seen as involving a whole range of skills and understandings. The need for this insight into what is involved in an activity continues in working with older children and the teacher will also need deeper understanding of the mathematical ideas. Whatever activity the children are involved in, the teacher will need a grasp of the ideas on which the activity depends together with a sense of direction, of what comes next. It is this sense of direction which enables a teacher to intervene successfully to encourage learning.

Figure 2.11 Six counters and a pot

Understanding place value

The base 10 system of numerals which children learn to use, called the Hindu-Arabic system, has important features and regularities which, once mastered, enable us to write larger and larger numbers. Built into this way of naming and writing numbers is the idea of grouping and counting in tens and using the position of a digit within a number to indicate its value. In this system a two-digit number like 44 is interpreted by saying that the numeral 4 on the left is worth four 10s and the numeral 4 on the right four units. Adults learning the names for numbers in another language such as French can gain some insight into the difficulty of memorising the numbers with non-standard names (for example onze, douze, treize, quatorze, quinze, etc.) and the pleasure of realising that vingt et un, vingt-deux, vingt-trois, etc. have easy standard names. In some classes there will be a range of languages spoken and children can learn from each other. Children can repeat the numbers in a language they know and listen for patterns in languages spoken by other children. Some with more regular patterns such as Cantonese or Mandarin, where 11, 12, 13 are constructed as ten-one, ten-two, ten-three and so on, may make learning to count more accessible than the irregular patterns found in English. It has also been suggested that the structure of the numbers in these Chinese languages helps also with calculation in that the groupings in ones, tens and hundreds are clearer in the way that numbers are said.

Once they have grasped the patterns in the place value system, especially past the second decade (11–19) children can carry on saying larger and larger numbers. Writing the numbers down, however, presents some difficulties. Common errors for children learning to write numbers in the 'teens' are to reverse the digits, perhaps to match the order of pronunciation, as in writing 31 for 13. Larger numbers, such as 24, are written as they sound, 20 followed by 4 giving 204 rather than 24. In the following section ways of working on the links between spoken and written numbers are considered.

The classroom may provide an environment which helps children to appreciate the structure of the number system. A large number square with the numbers from 1 to 100 set out in rows of ten can act as a reference point (Wigley 1994), showing patterns of counting in ones horizontally and adding on tens vertically.

Additionally, a large clear number line always visible on the classroom wall can help to develop a strong image of the progression of the numbers. Number lines marked in tens and blank number lines for the children to work on provide familiar images to which the children and their teacher can turn when working on problems. Caleb Gattegno emphasised the value of a place value chart (see Figure 2.12). As the teacher points to the number the child says the number. Initially this helps to connect the words with the numbers; for example, 'four hundred' and the symbols 400. Later the teacher can point in turn to 400 and 30 and 5 and teach the condensed way of writing this. Place value means that the position occupied by an individual digit within a number indicates how much the digit is worth:

- without place value we would have to write 4 hundreds and 3 tens and 5;
- with place value we can write 435.

Sets of number cards showing hundreds, tens and ones, which can be placed on top of each other to show the condensed way of writing numbers, provide a useful image of the information 'hidden' in a number (Figure 2.13, from BEAM publications, see Resources section below). The number system condenses a great deal of information; this makes it powerful but also explains some of the difficulties children experience later with algorithms for subtraction and multiplication. Lots of varied experience

1	2	3	4	5	6	7	8	9
10	20	30	40	50	60	70	80	90
100	200	300	400	500	600	700	800	900

Figure 2.12 Gattegno whole number chart

with counting and writing and problems with numbers will provide a sound basis for later learning. Hundred squares in different scripts (for example Bengali, Chinese) will give children opportunities to see patterns of tens and ones in a variety of systems from different cultures.

Activities

- Using the calculator to 'count' by using the constant function can help a child who has spotted the tens and ones pattern in verbal counting to relate this to the way numbers are written. On most calculators using the constant function to count in ones is done by pressing + 1 =, then pressing = repeatedly.
- Placing numbers on number lines in different ranges (starting at 100 and going up in tens, starting at 800 and going up in hundreds or starting from zero and going up in tenths).
- Placing a random set of two digit numbers or three digit numbers on a blank line. Challenges can be set so that some numbers are closer together as these appear to be harder to order than those that are further apart.
- Making jigsaws of the 100 square and fitting these together helps children use the patterns of tens and ones (see Figure 2.14).
- Dienes apparatus can be used for activities and games which require children to think of numbers in terms of numbers of tens and ones. (Dienes apparatus provides a physical model of the number

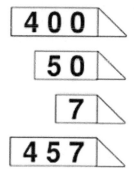

Figure 2.13 Stacking number cards for place value

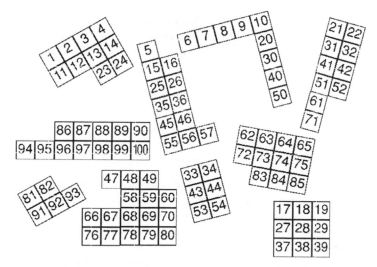

Figure 2.14 Jigsaw of a hundred square

system. It consists of single cubes, sets of cubes joined in a line to make a 'long' representing 10, sets of longs joined to make a 'flat' representing 100 and sets of ten flats joined to make a cube representing 1000.)

- 'Guessing how many things are in the jar' can be a daily event, with the counting done by grouping in tens. The number of objects can be varied to help children gain a feeling for estimating large numbers. If the objects are pegs, placing them on ten by ten pegboards can give a clear image of lines of tens and squares of hundreds.
- Investigating the system of metric measures gives a practical context for work on place value. Finding how many 10 cm rods make a metre, how many 100 gm weights make a kilo, or how many 100 ml measures make a litre, and calibrating a scale on a bottle, together with practice in reading measures, can help children in visualising relationships between numbers.

Mental mathematics

Mathematics happens inside people's heads; paper or computer screens are used to record the reasoning and to help the memory. The separation of the thinking and reasoning which goes on in the head from the written recording can be helpful in realising the importance of encouraging mental mathematics. The term 'mental arithmetic' is a narrower one sometimes associated with 10 questions to be answered quickly in a test situation. 'Mental mathematics' is used to emphasise the importance of what goes on inside the head in all aspects of mathematics. It is where mental models and flexibility are developed. Ways of developing mental strategies for addition and subtraction were considered earlier in this Section, looking at helping children to recall and derive facts and to apply the arithmetic laws, such as commutativity. Older children will continue to need to develop confident recall but also to build new facts from those already known for example, by extending patterns with single digit numbers to larger numbers and to fractions and decimals.

Examples of this are:

$$3 + 2 = 5$$
$$13 + 2 = 15$$
$$23 + 2 = 25, \text{etc.}$$
$$30 + 20 = 50$$
$$300 + 200 = 500$$
$$3000 + 2000 = 5000$$
$$0.2 + 0.3 = 0.5$$

In this section a further law of arithmetic (distributivity) will also be discussed in developing methods for multiplication and division especially with the extended range of numbers. Mental mathematics focusing on number can involve children in:

- carrying out a calculation and describing how they did it;
- a calculator game designed so that lots of possibilities have to be tried out in the head before a move is made;
- saying number rhymes or counting backwards in threes;
- mathematical discussion led by the teacher with a group or the whole class;
- becoming skilled with operations on simple numbers 'in the head'.

The last item, particularly the learning of tables, is often emphasised in public discussion of children's number skills and the need for understanding rather than rote learning alone is sometimes missed. For the teacher, tables or multiplication facts are just one part of confident mental calculation which involves many other aspects of number, including addition facts and the important realisation that subtraction is the opposite of addition whilst division is the opposite of multiplication. Communication with parents and enlisting their help in developing children's mathematics is, however, very important so the informal term 'tables' is used here.

Multiplication and division

Learning multiplication facts is important; it gives children confidence to tackle numerical problems if they can easily recall the answer to 7×8 for example. It is probably a myth that at some point children stopped learning their tables; what did happen is that teachers, becoming more aware of how often children felt humiliated by the process of public testing, found other ways to motivate the learning of these facts and to assess the children's learning. It is important to realise that the inverse operation of finding factors is even more useful than the multiplication facts (for example the understanding that if 6×7 is 42 then 7 divides into 42 six times). Questions such as, 'Is 49 a square number?' or 'Can you find a number that is a factor of 64 and also of 40?' will seem impossible to children who have to chant their tables to work out the answers. Children need to do more than learn their tables – they need to learn 'to be friendly with' (in other words, confident with) all the numbers from 1 to 100. Conceptual understanding and seeing pattern will support the deriving of facts from those that are recalled. For example, nine nines could be worked out from the knowledge of ten nines, if it is understood that the pattern builds by repeated addition so that subtracting 9 from 90 will give the desired result.

If familiarity with all the numbers to 100 seems very demanding then a comparison with spelling may help. Children learn to spell hundreds of words, many of them non-standard ones, but there are only 100 basic multiplication facts. A junior school child who feels bogged down by tables can be encouraged to take a multiplication square and to cross off all the ones that seem easy (twos, threes, fives and tens perhaps). There is a way of doing the nine times table on the fingers which takes care of the nines (see Case study later in this section) – leaving just a core of obstinate facts to be learnt. Identifying patterns in a 10 by 10 multiplication square can also help with memorising and deriving facts. For example, all multiples of 4 are double the multiples of 2. All multiples of 5 have 0 or 5 in the units position. Children should be encouraged to explore these patterns for themselves and also to notice that the square is divided in half by the square numbers (1×1, 2×2, 3×3, etc.) along the diagonal from the top left hand to bottom right hand corner (1 to 100) with multiples mirrored on each side because of commutativity (for example find 6×3 and 3×6).

Children's experiences of multiplication

Learning tables, or knowing multiplication facts, and being able to apply them begins in the early years with children learning to count pairs of things. This is quite a leap in terms of being able to think of numbers of numbers rather than numbers of individual items. Learning the totals of double numbers, like 2 and 2 and 3 and 3, will similarly begin at an early age. Children need to practise counting groups of things and to build a familiarity with the number sequences of counting in twos, threes, fives and tens. This can be done in practical ways, with objects and pictures, for instance by counting:

- pairs of eyes, shoes, gloves, wheels on bikes, 2p coins;
- threes in Multilink or Cuisenaire rods, tricycle wheels or segments of fingers;
- fours with legs on animals or tables, sides of squares or rectangles;
- fives with hands, 5p coins, petals on flowers, groups of children in PE;
- sixes with hexagons, egg boxes, legs on minibeasts, chairs round tables;
- sevens with heptagons, spots on ladybirds;
- eights with spider legs and octopi, octagons.

If children build up a staircase pattern physically with shapes, rods or other apparatus, they can record this with numbers and relate to the pattern made by circling these on a number line or number square (see Figure 2.15).

Children may need help in counting verbally in twos and threes. It is useful to practise counting in which the multiples of 3 are said loudly whilst the in-between numbers are whispered. Later the children can just 'think' the in-between numbers:

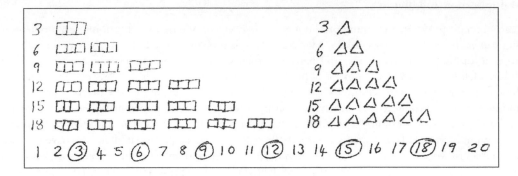

Figure 2.15 A 'staircase' pattern of threes made with Multilink or triangles made out of sticks. The pattern is circled on a number line

1, 2, **3**, 4, 5, **6**, 7, 8, **9** ...

The multiples can then be represented as steps along a number line to demonstrate counting in steps other than ones.

While building up these patterns children can relate the multiplication facts to division and begin to look at the factors of numbers in a practical and visual way. For instance they can take, say, 24 blocks and see if they can count them in twos, threes, fours, fives and tens, recording which ways work with none left over. A powerful image is that of the array (or rectangle) – setting out the number in rows and columns to also show commutativity (5 x 2 or 2 x 5):

```
* * * * *
* * * * *
```

These sorts of activities help children to think of recomposing numbers in different ways, and to develop a flexible feel for numbers, while appreciating the interrelationships between numbers and operations. As well as learning the number facts from practical activities and investigations, children need activities which help develop speed of recall and situations and stories which require their application.

A third multiplication structure (to be added to ideas of repeated addition and the array) is that of scaling. This is where a quantity is 'x times as big' for example, so 12 is three times as big as 4:

```
* * * *
* * * * * * * * * * * *
```

A practical example of this can be found in Section 3 (making boxes twice or half size requiring the doubling or halving of all the dimensions in proportion).

Mathematical language

Many different words are used to describe the same operation in different contexts. Just a few of the possibilities are:

+ add, sum, total, more than, plus, and;
– take away, subtract, minus, less than;
× times, multiply, lots of, product;
÷ share, divide, equal groups of;
= equals, is equivalent to, makes, is the same as.

When working on mental mathematics it is possible for the teacher to vary the language used and to listen to the children's language. New vocabulary will be introduced by the teacher to extend children's thinking. Some of this new vocabulary will need distinguishing from everyday usage (for example, times, product). Questions and problems need to be provided which use these various words for operations and reflect the different models of the operations represented. For example, 'share' and 'group', which both refer to division, are associated with different language patterns and models of the operation. Sharing a quantity refers to a situation where the number of sets is already known but the number in each set is calculated. Grouping relates to knowing the number in each set and the number of sets is calculated. Skills in carrying out operations are of little use if children cannot identify the appropriate operation to use when a problem is encountered.

Common misconceptions

Learning is more effective when common misconceptions are addressed, exposed and discussed in teaching (Ofsted 1995).

Studies with large numbers of children have revealed some very common misunderstandings. By introducing these difficult ideas and discussing children's views, teachers can help children to clarify their ideas.

Misconception 1: To multiply by 10 you add a zero

This misconception arises from over-generalising a pattern that is true for whole numbers:

    20 × 10 = 200
    400 × 10 = 4000
    but 0.2 × 10 is not 0.20

Teachers can help to avoid the misconception by talking about what digits represent in a number, for example 20 × 10, the 2 no longer represents two tens but two hundreds. When children start to work with decimals, asking what they expect 0.2 × 10 to be and then trying it out on a calculator will get a discussion started.

Misconception 2: 0.25 is bigger than 0.3

Again, early experience leads to the correct conclusion that for whole numbers a longer number is always larger than a shorter number; for example, 273 is larger than 99.

It seems likely that this mistake is more likely to arise if the numbers are read as zero point twenty-five and zero point three. With that way of reading, twenty-five sounds larger than three. The correct way to read the numbers is 'zero point two five' and 'zero point three'. Unlike large numbers, where the place value is integral to the number word, small numbers are read as digit-lists. To help reinforce place value 0.3 could be spoken of as 'three tenths' and 0.25 as 'two tenths, five hundredths'. This way of reading, together with work on number lines and scales, can help to make clear that the numbers to the right of the decimal point represent smaller and smaller divisions. This is also important when reading calculator displays; 1.333 (which could be read as 1.3 recurring) needs to be interpreted as between 1.3 and 1.4 (see Figure 2.16).

Calculator work is very useful for emphasising that a long number is not necessarily a large number.

A complication is that in working with money we do read £4.25 as four pounds twenty-five. Measurement is a useful bridge with children encouraged to verbalise and notice the difference between:

4 m 25 cm which is read as four metres twenty-five centimetres, and
4.25 m which is read as four point two five metres.

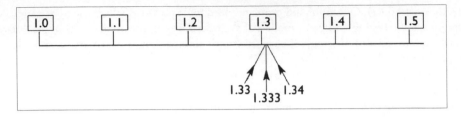

Figure 2.16 Finding 1.333 on a number line

Misconception 3: If you cannot take a large number from a smaller one then taking the small one from the large one will do

        34
      − 17
        23

Putting the calculation in a context in which the answer has to make sense can help to make clear why this does not work. For example, 34 children in the class, 17 children go to singing, this would seem to leave 23 children in the classroom. But 17 children singing and 23 in the classroom is 40 children altogether – something has gone wrong. The teacher may also choose to present another similar problem in which the mistake is more obvious because of the size of the numbers. For example, 34 – 7 = 33 uses the smaller from larger misconception to give an answer which clearly cannot be true. It needs skilful teaching, firstly to identify the error and then to help the child to understand why the method does not work but with support the problem can be recognised and a correct method identified. Computer programmers never expect programs to work first time – they expect to perform many trials and to 'de-bug' the program. The idea of finding the 'bugs' in a piece of mathematics can be used rather as the idea of editing is used to work on and polish a piece of writing. One of the reasons for this misconception is the '7 from 4, you can't do' argument rather than 7 from 4 is -3 (in other words, 3 less than zero), 10 from 30 is 20, so 20 less 3 is 17. In fact, a calculation like the one shown is best represented horizontally (34 – 17), when children are more likely to do the calculation mentally. When children need to use pencil and paper methods because the numbers are too difficult to hold in the head, they can be introduced to standard algorithms, based on confident mental methods, numerical knowledge and a secure understanding of place value (see the comments on standard algorithms later in this section).

Case study: Shirley Lee

Circle game

The work was carried out with a Year 6 class in a mixed ability group. The introductory activity was a circle game, a simplified version of an activity developed by Adrian Pinel. Its purpose was to practise and to develop confidence in recalling number facts and in mental calculation.

On this occasion the children sat on the carpet and I sat with them. The activity works just as well with the children sitting at their tables or desks. They each had a card on which there was an answer at the top of the card and a question written below the answer.

I started off the game by asking the question written on my card (see Figure 2.17). I knew someone was holding a card with the answer 6; it was Jane. She called out six. I then instructed Jane to read out the question on her card. 'Six nines?' she asked. There was a bit of a pause. I suggested: 'Just have a look at the cards of the people near you. Give the person who has the answer a gentle nudge if they haven't noticed it's their turn.' There were smiles all round at this. By making it clear that it was okay to help each other my intention was to remove any anxieties about making a mistake in public and at the same time I wanted to make it clear that everyone was expected to keep on task, even if their turn had gone. (Everyone had at least one card but several children had two.) Robert had the card with 54 at the top and so the game continued until the last question: 'Double 12' instructed Gemma. The answer, 24, was on my card – the first card of the game. We had completed the circle.

Figure 2.17 The first card

The children loved it and asked to play again. Some children wanted to keep their cards, others wanted to 'swap'. Negotiations were completed quickly and we played one more time. I jotted down those calculations at which there was some hesitation for my future reference. This introductory activity contained fairly straightforward table facts and my intention was to make sure those facts which caused some difficulty were highlighted and reintroduced in other activities.

I wanted to make sure the children knew the value of such an activity. When asked, they offered:

'You have to listen all the time.'
'You do lots of calculations in your head.'
'You have to work out every answer.'
'It's tables practice.'
'It's fun.'

I suggested the children really practised ways of recalling number facts and quick ways of calculating numbers which worked well for them. This led to a discussion about the children's preferred strategies for recalling their table facts. They acknowledged that there really was not time to 'count on in ones' when playing a game. You needed to either know the answer or have a quick method of finding it out.

'Six times nine' was one question we discussed. The children offered these favourite strategies for finding the answer:

'*I* know 6 tens, so then it's easy to find 6 nines.'

'*I* find the nine times table easy because of the pattern the nines make. Look it's 9, 18, 27, 36, 45, 54.'

'*I* always work out times 5 and add on from there, so if I need 6 nines, I do 5 times 9 (which is the same as 9 times 5) and add on another 9.'

'*I* know my square numbers, so I know that 6 × 6 is 36 and I need another 3 sixes which is 18 and I do it that way.'

Paul had a finger method taught to him by his uncle which he demonstrated to the rest of the group. The children helped each other to practise Paul's method (see Figure 2.18).

The boy in the figure below is demonstrating 9 × 7 = 63 by folding down the seventh finger. This leaves six fingers standing up on the left and three fingers standing up on the right, so the answer can be read off as 9 × 7 is 63. In the same way, 5 × 9 can be read off by folding down the fifth finger, etc.

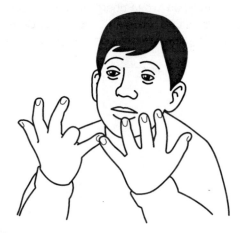

Figure 2.18 9 × 7 = 63

The group was intrigued to find their friends worked things out in so many different ways. It reminded me once again of the importance of listening to the children's explanations of how they think and also of the futility of insisting that one algorithm has merit over all others. These particular children had not only experienced a rich variety of number activities, they had clearly been encouraged to see possible links between them, for example developing square numbers. Visualising them and learning them had given one child easy access to the table facts he found difficult to learn.

Following the introductory activity, I moved to the main activity which was to make a circular card game. The purpose of the activity was to develop logical thinking and to encourage an awareness of the links between number operations.

I told the children they were going to make their own version of the game to play in a small group, on their own or at home. They worked in groups of four or five. Tim, a child with Down's Syndrome, worked in a pair with his carer but participated with the whole group for the introductory activity and for the feedback session.

Each group played a mini-version of the circle game. They then set to work to produce a game themselves. Where children found it difficult to get going, I intervened by first playing the practice game with the children and then setting out the cards which made the completed circle on the table (see Figure 2.19). I then removed one card, inviting them to suggest possible questions which could complete the circle if the card had been lost. They soon got the idea and began to offer a range of possible answers to fill the gap, showing not only that they understand how to proceed with making the game but that they had a growing awareness that the same answer could be obtained by a variety of methods. Some children went on to:

- 'patent' their own set of cards by putting a logo on the back to identify their games;
- realise they needed to mark those cards which belonged together in a set with a symbol or letter;
- mix the operations, use decimals, fractions and measurement.

Tim had been working on change from 10p. His classroom assistant worked with him to produce sets of cards in this context. When the class reassembled on the carpet to discuss their version of the game, Tim's version was of considerable interest. Nobody else had thought of doing a money game and Tim was clearly pleased at the positive response he received.

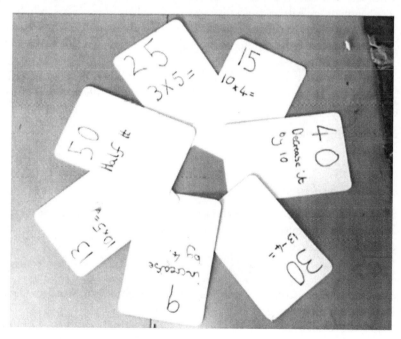

Figure 2.19 A completed loop of cards

A range of methods for calculating

Calculators

The main arguments used for and against calculator use are as follows:

- For:
  - they are widely used in adult life;
  - there is evidence that children using calculators learn more rapidly about large numbers, decimals and estimation;
  - they enable more complex problems to be tackled, using 'real' data;
  - the skills involved in using calculators effectively need to be learnt;
- Against:
  - children are observed using calculators for very simple calculations instead of developing mental methods;
  - facility with pencil and paper algorithms for multiplication and division may be reduced.

As is often the case with polarised arguments, these positions often become self-fulfilling prophecies. That is, where a teacher values the use of calculators they are used effectively and appropriately; where a teacher feels strongly that calculators make children lazy, the children accept this view and prefer pencil and paper methods. A balanced view is most likely where there is a carefully thought out school policy which emphasises calculator activities that make children think. The essential element in an effective calculator policy is the corresponding emphasis on mental mathematics and developing conceptual understanding of procedures.

If calculators are to be used effectively then teachers and children need to be clear about the purposes of calculator use. It can be helpful to distinguish two quite different ways of using them in the classroom:

- calculators as a learning device;
- calculators as a tool.

(1) Calculators as a learning device

The teacher decides that some aspect of the children's understanding can be developed through the use of a calculator activity. The calculator may be used to provide rapid feedback or to generate lots of examples from which the children can deduce a pattern.

ACTIVITY 1

Teacher's decision: the teacher identified a group of children as needing to work on place value. This task was chosen to assist their learning.

Reason for using the calculator: to provide rapid and accurate feedback about the number system.

Children's role: thinking and learning about the value of each digit in a number.

Children work in pairs. Each child puts a three digit number less than 500 into the calculator without showing the other child. They then ask each other for one of the numbers from 1 to 9, thus:

First child: 'Do you have any threes digits?'

The second child has 238 on her calculator and so must say, 'Yes you can have 30'. The first then adds 30 to her total and the second child takes 30 away from 238. The game continues until one child's total is reduced to zero, or when an agreed target – say 700 – is reached. (The game works better if the target is not too large as throughout the game the sum of the children's numbers remains the same and, if the target is too large, the game only ends when one child reaches zero.) The main learning point of the activity is in seeing that taking 30 away from 238 wipes out the 'tens' leaving 208; similarly subtracting 200 would wipe out the hundreds.

ACTIVITY 2

Teacher's decision: an open-ended activity is required which enables children to demonstrate their understanding of number.

Reason for using the calculator: to encourage the children to experiment and explore number relationships.

Children's role: to be imaginative in their exploration, to reason and to make sense of the number operations.

One of the findings of the Calculator Aware Number Project (PRIME 1991), a major project on the use of calculators, was that a small number of open-ended activities could be used repeatedly to explore the number system. A useful activity involves drawing three blobs joined with arrows (see Figure 2.20). A number is put in the first blob and an operation on the first arrow.

This gives the number in the second blob and an operation can be chosen to give the number in the third blob. So far the calculator has been doing all the work but now the child must find an operation to bring them back to the number in the first blob – this is where the thinking occurs (see Figure 2.21). In practice children rapidly learn to look ahead and choose their early numbers and operations to make it possible to complete the circle. Their choices give information to the teacher on the level of their mathematical understanding. Once the activity is familiar, children can return to it to try out more and more complicated ideas.

(2) Calculators as a tool

When faced with a problem involving calculations, such as working out how much money the class should have brought in for the school trip, the child needs to:

Step 1: consider the problem and decide which type of calculation is needed.
Step 2: choose whether to use head, calculator or pencil and paper.
Step 3: calculate.
Step 4: check reasonableness of the answer.
Step 5: loop back to Step 1 if working on a substantial or open problem.

An over-emphasis on Step 3, involving the practice of standard algorithms, may result in children lacking skills in the essential Step 1, deciding which type of calculation to perform. If a calculator is used to work on a practical problem then Step 1 is essential because of the need to decide which button to press.

For Step 2, deciding which method to use, children need to be encouraged to take some degree of personal responsibility in deciding what sums they can more sensibly do in their head.

Figure 2.20 Blobs and arrows

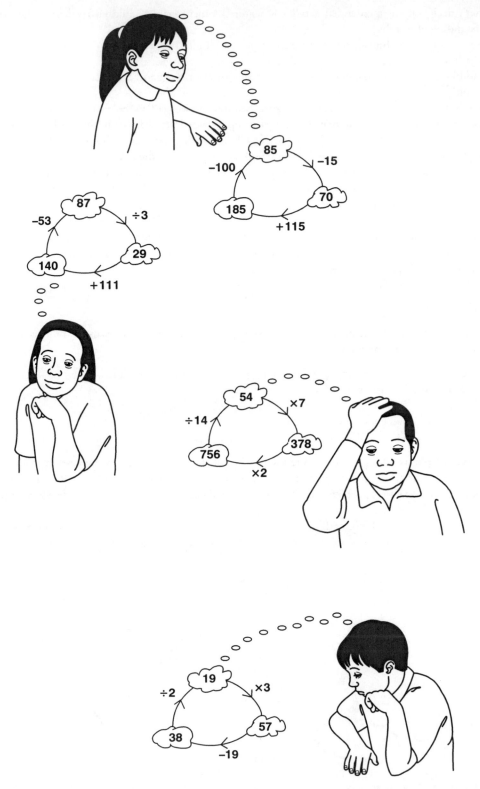

Figure 2.21 Children thinking

Step 4, checking the reasonableness of the answer, is the essential skill required if children are to make effective practical use of their mathematical calculations. It is only possible if children have developed skills in mental mathematics and are able to see when their answers make no sense.

Informal written methods and standard algorithms

Algorithms are step by step procedures such as those used to multiply large numbers. There are some important decisions for schools to make about approaches and timing. Here are two very different possible approaches:

- Analysing into small steps:
    - practise simple algorithms;
    - introduce problems leading to simple algorithms;
    - practise harder algorithms;
    - practise word problems leading to harder algorithms.
- Analysing into substantial elements:
    - develop children's mental mathematical skills;
    - introduce problems and encourage children to discuss the problems and develop their own methods;
    - work on estimation and a 'feel' for the size of the answer;
    - introduce standard methods, building on children's own effective non-standard methods;
    - practise problems leading to harder algorithms.

The second approach is more likely to lead to the 'confidence and intellectual flexibility' (Ofsted 2008: 21) needed to tackle new problems using well understood strategies and develop new ones. Some people argue that children who learn simple vertical algorithms (see Figure 2.22) first, tend to generalise inappropriate methods: for instance, by subtracting the smaller unit from the larger no matter where its position because this has always been the case in the easy examples.

When children meet the harder subtraction, they continue to take the smaller digit away from the larger, because this is what they have been doing in all the previous examples.

It could be argued that using the written algorithm for easy two digit subtractions, like 89 – 53 is like using a sledgehammer to crack a nut, since these can easily be done in the head as indeed we should be expecting children to do. It would make more sense to introduce a written method only when there is a need for it – that is, when the calculation becomes difficult to do mentally. Mental calculation, it is argued, is more likely to require the child to understand what they are doing. Children can complete written algorithms by memorising 'tricks' without understanding, or make mistakes by not remembering the procedures correctly, having no sensible means of reconstructing the procedure. In either case, of course, it is important that children are encouraged to check by another method, so they have a fallback strategy available.

Introducing vertical algorithms for addition and subtraction

It seems logical that children should not be introduced to the sophisticated, standard vertical written methods of computation until they have some basic mental skills, number knowledge and understanding. If you check to ensure children have these, there should be no danger of them completing two digit

$$
\begin{array}{rr}
89 & 83 \\
-53 & -59 \\
\hline
36 & 36
\end{array}
$$

Figure 2.22 Generalising an inappropriate method: always take the smaller from the larger number

calculations by having to count cubes or secretly drawing lots of tallies as some children do. They should also have experience of informal methods of recording mental calculation (informal jottings), which demonstrate the steps taken. The image of the empty number line (unnumbered), along which steps in working out can be recorded has gained ground from its origin in the Netherlands mathematics curriculum (see Rousham (2003) on its introduction to the primary curriculum in the UK). For 38 + 29, this could be carried out in a number of ways but one example might be counting up from 38 in jumps of 2, 20 and 7 (see Figure 2.23):

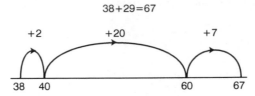

Figure 2.23 One way of adding 38 and 29 on the empty number lines

Here are two examples of subtracting 39 from 63 (Figures 2.24 and 2.25)

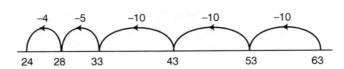

Figure 2.24 Counting back from 63 in jumps of 10, 10, 10, 5 and 4

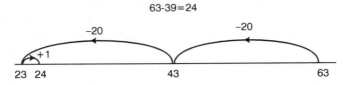

Figure 2.25 Counting back two jumps of 20 results in subtracting 40. Then 1 must be added to compensate for subtracting too much

Before they are introduced to

$$\begin{array}{r} 38 \\ +29 \\ \hline 67 \end{array}$$

children should, for instance:

- know 9 and 8 is 17;
- know 29 is 20 and 9;
- be able to add 34 and 22 without counting in ones (by adding tens and units separately and by counting on in tens from 34, then adding the 2).

Then an informal vertical method could be used where the lines are expanded to show more clearly the partitioning of the number:

$$38 + 29 = 30 + 20 + 8 + 9$$
$$50$$
$$+\ \underline{17}$$

With the standard method (Figure 2.26) children could then be asked to do some detective work to see what is going on. In this way, they are being asked to make sense of the algorithm and explain how it works, rather than being taught to memorise a procedure with fragile understanding.

$$38$$
$$+2\,_19$$
$$\overline{67}$$

Figure 2.26 A formal written algorithm for addition

Similarly, children should be asked to spot what is going on with the following (see Figure 2.27):

$$53$$
$$-29$$
$$\overline{24}$$

Figure 2.27 What is going on in this calcution?

and they should already have some mental strategies to check the answer. They need to:

- know bonds to 10;
- be able to count on in tens from 29;
- and then add on the units to get to 53.

They should also be encouraged to look for ways of making 'unfriendly numbers' friendlier. For instance, in working out 53 – 29, they might notice that 29 is 1 less than 30 and, by adding one on to both 53 and 29, make the easier calculation of 54 – 30.

When they understand the method of computation, children can try harder numbers where they cannot work out the answer easily in their heads. Then they will need to be encouraged to check, using strategies like looking at the final digits and approximating the size of the answer.

Children also need to be encouraged to explain methods and share them, and to develop a flexibility in expressing numbers in different ways, by splitting them up or recomposing them and thinking of relationships with other numbers. For instance when adding 8 + 9 children might:

- think of complements to 10 – make the 9 up to 10 by taking 1 from 8 giving 10 and 7 or 17
- use the nearest double – 8 add 8 is 16 and 1 more is 17.

If they are encouraged to make and look for patterns, they will know that 18 + 9 and 28 + 39 will also end with 7.

Informal and formal methods for multiplication

Evidence that very few adults used the formal methods which they had been taught at school has led to an interest in methods which, whilst they involve some paper recording, were developed by the children themselves. Teachers can explore these strategies by asking children to explain how they have worked out a calculation. In this example the child is trying to work out 16 × 15. She has noticed that

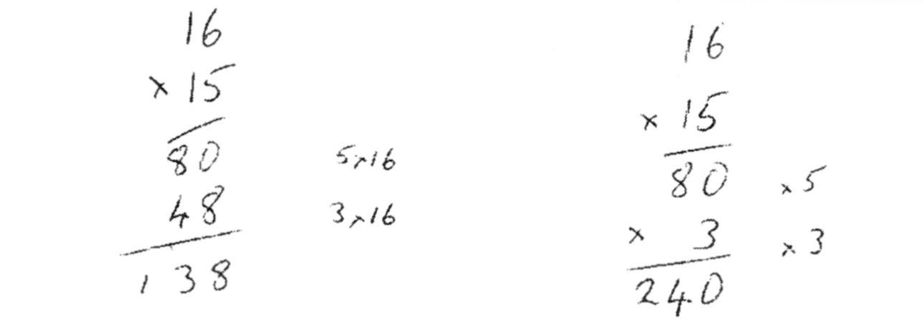

Figure 2.28 First and second attempts – can you follow the child's reasoning?

15 is five times three. After her first attempt she said, 'I see what I need to do, I must multiply the top line not add it.' This method relies on knowing how to use the factors of 15 (see Figure 2.28).

This same child was also able to do the calculation in a number of other ways , including the more conventional (see Figure 2.29), which requires understanding that 16 × 15 can be dealt with by splitting 15 into 10 and 5, multiplying 16 by 10, then by 5 and adding the two answers (16 × 15 = (10 × 16) + (5 × 16)). This is known as the distributive law.

$$
\begin{array}{ll}
16 & \\
\times\ 15 & \\
\hline
80 & \times 5 \\
1\ 60 & \times 10 \\
\hline
240 &
\end{array}
\qquad
\begin{array}{ll}
16 & \\
\times\ 15 & \\
\hline
160 & \times 10 \\
80 & \times 5 \\
\hline
240 &
\end{array}
\qquad
\begin{array}{l}
5 \times 16 = 80 \\
10 \times 16 = 160 \\
15 \times 16 = 240
\end{array}
$$

Figure 2.29 More than one way to multiply

A method which quite clearly illustrates this is setting out a long multiplication in a rectangular form (see Figure 2.30); for example, for 46 × 23, showing the way in which the numbers are split into tens and units to make smaller calculations the results of which can then be totalled.

Problems requiring several similar calculations give children a chance to hone their methods:

- The problem. Using 6, 8 and 5, work out 68 × 5.
- Then try other multiplications using the same digits.
- Which way gives the largest answer?

Figure 2.31 shows a child's response to this question which demonstrates a robust, effective non-standard method for 2-digit by 1-digit multiplication using repeated addition.

Figure 2.32 gives a child's method showing a more compact form of recording and an explanation demonstrating an understanding of the distributive law.

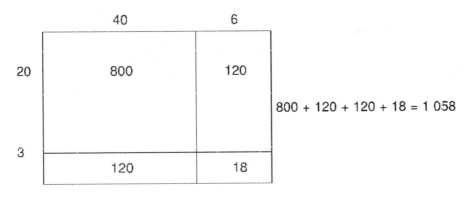

Figure 2.30 Grid multiplication method for 46 × 23

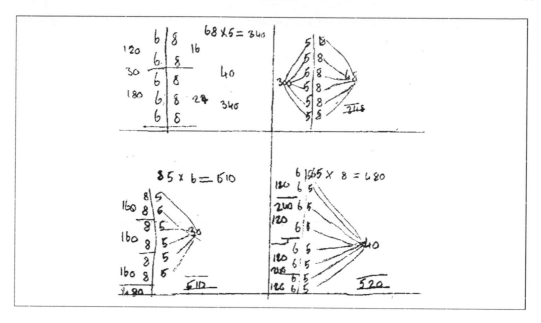

Figure 2.31 68 × 5 by a robust, non-standard method

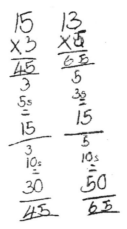

Figure 2.32 A near formal method

Children's experiences of division

(1) Children will encounter division in a variety of forms and be expected to make a variety of responses

SHARING

Children need to learn that sharing in a mathematical context means equal shares. Sharing in a family context is a much more complicated idea: consider sharing out the potatoes for lunch; sharing your teddy with your baby brother.

'Here are 12 sweets, let's share them between these four teddies'. One response is a physical dealing out: one for you, one for you, etc. Then you count up to see how many sweets each teddy has. Alternative responses might be to sweep the sweets into four piles, or for larger numbers to count them out two at a time.

(In a sharing problem you know how many groups to form and are trying to find out how many will be in each group.)

GROUPING

'There are 28 children here today; can you get into groups of three.' The expected response is to join hands in threes and then look round to see how many groups of three have been formed.

(In a grouping problem you know how many in each group and are trying to find out how many groups can be formed.)

'Take a handful of cubes and see how many groups of three you can make.' The expected response is to take groups of three until there are no cubes left, then count the number of groups.

Fractions, decimals, percentages and division

Find a third of nine counters. The expected response is to partition into three equal sets (to find one third you divide by 3, Figure 2.33). What is 1 divided by 10? This can be expressed as $^1/_{10}$ or 0.1. Find 1% as dividing the whole by 100 to give a one-hundredth part of a whole.

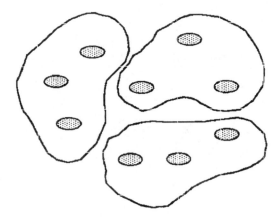

Figure 2.33 Find a third of nine counters

DIVISION AS THE INVERSE OF MULTIPLICATION

    4 multiplied by 3 = 12
    means 12 divided by 4 = 3
    and 12 divided by 3 = 4.

DIVISION BUTTON ON A CALCULATOR

Planning events offers real life problems: 'This six-pack of cola costs £2.60 – is it a good buy? How much is that for one can?' The child needs first to interpret the problem as division, then to enter in the correct order 2.60 divided by 6 and finally to interpret the result 0.4333333.

(2) Children will also be exposed to a variety of language styles

FORMAL WRITTEN LANGUAGE

How many sets of 2 make 8? Share 6 sweets equally between 2.

SPOKEN LANGUAGE OF PARENTS AND OLDER BROTHERS AND SISTERS

'How many twos in eight?' 'Twos into six?'

SPOKEN LANGUAGE IN THE CLASSROOM

Which is likely to contain elements of both formal and informal phrases: '*share equally*', '*share between*', '*share by*', '*into*'.

CHILD'S INFORMAL WRITTEN RECORDING

'*Take a handful of cubes, count to see how many you've got. Can you group them in threes and write something down to show me how you worked it out?*'

- counting the cubes, for example 37 cubes;
- splitting up in some way, such as:
  - 10 lots of 3 are 30;
  - 2 lots of 3 are 6;
  - and 1 left over.

WRITTEN RECORDING

The very compact standard written method for dividing larger numbers (long division) is complex and requires much other knowledge and understanding to execute with confidence. Some alternative approaches which provide robust non-standard but efficient ways of dividing larger numbers involve the idea of 'chunking' (repeatedly subtracting larger amounts until zero is reached or counting up in chunks to the required total). See Figure 2.34 for examples (smaller numbers are used to illustrate):

$$
\begin{aligned}
&44 \\
&\underline{-30} \ (10 \times 3) \\
&14 \\
&\underline{-12} \ (4 \times 3) \\
&\ \ 2 \text{ left over}
\end{aligned}
$$

⎫ that makes 14 lots of 3

Figure 2.34 44 divided by 3 chunking method

10 x 3 (30) + 4 x 3 (12) = 42
Add another 2 reaches the target of 44
So 10 + 4 lots of 3 and 2 more equals 44

(3) Images offered to help understanding of division

These include:

- objects such as counters, in piles;
- drawings of rectangular arrays (see Figure 2.35);

Figure 2.35 Array

- structured apparatus of unit cubes, strips of ten cubes and blocks of 100;
- all the mental images built up in earlier number work (see Sections 2.2 and 2.3);
- counting in twos, threes, etc.;
- multiplication square used to find factors;
- Gattegno chart to emphasise multiplying and dividing by 10.

To chart a course though all these variations the teacher will need a clear sense of direction. When a child approaches the teacher saying: 'I don't understand', a teacher will typically pause for only one or two seconds before replying. In that time she will need to have decided:

- What is the purpose of this exercise?
- What do I know about this child's previous experience and understanding?
- What language or image shall I use in my response?

In making this assessment in order to allow learning to progress, the teacher may draw on these principles:

- crucial ideas underpinning division are: the knowledge of multiplication and division facts, particularly multiplying by 10; the ability to split up and recombine numbers in a variety of ways;
- estimation makes more sense when the problem is in some context (see Sections 3.3 and Section 4); a context is also needed for making sense of remainders.

In practice this may well mean establishing some activities which can become part of the classroom ritual to be worked on several times a week for short periods. These familiar activities, the images shared by teacher and children, can be referred to when the children are having difficulties.

ACTIVITY 1: TOWERS

This provides a useful image for sharing problems. You will need Multilink cubes and a variety of cardboard shapes – equilateral triangles, squares, regular pentagons and hexagons.

The child takes a handful of Multilink cubes, counts them and selects a shape. The task is to build a tower at each corner of the shape. The towers must be of the same height, any left over cubes are placed in the middle. So if 16 cubes are taken and towers built on the triangular mat, there will be 5 cubes in each tower and 1 left over (see Figure 2.36). The children can be encouraged to predict the remainder, to try to find a mat where there is no remainder. (See the Count Me In games for a version using scoring (Mosley 1986).)

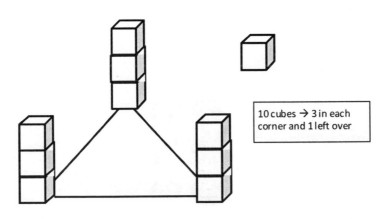

10 cubes → 3 in each corner and 1 left over

Figure 2.36 Towers

ACTIVITY 2

A collection of calculator activities selecting numbers which will multiply to reach a target number (see Section 2.4).

ACTIVITY 3: 'SPOTTING DIVISION'

The first hurdle in extracting meaning from word problems seems to be in identifying that the problem is a division one without clear verbal clues:

- The exchange rate is 1.1 euros to the pound (general information).
- A menu costs 30 euros (specific information).
- How much is that in pounds? (a question that does not specify division).
- As opposed to a problem with clear verbal clues:

- Suzy shared some sweets with her friends. She had 24 sweets and there were four people including Suzy. How many sweets did each get? (to address this problem the key vocabulary of 'sharing' would be identified to signify division).

The solving of word problems can lead to very narrow, procedural approaches rather than encouraging thinking. An emphasis on underlining key numbers or vocabulary rather than tackling meaning through discussion can detract from independent reasoning, a concern highlighted in an Ofsted report (2008) in relation to the apparent increase in this type of task in English primary schools.

Helpful tactic 1: Estimation If the first problem is changed to an exchange rate of 10 euros to the pound, the success rate shoots up. Many children will answer £3 immediately and can then see that what they did was work out 30 divided by 10. They can then tackle the harder problem of working out 30 divided by 1.1 and can at least get started.

Helpful tactic 2: Familiarity at identifying the operation A local map is placed on the classroom wall with the scale clearly marked. A route for a walk is measured using a piece of string:

- Scale is 4 cm to 1 kilometre (general information).
- The walk is 17 cm on the map (specific information).
- How far is that? (a question that does not specify division).

The activity can be repeated, changing the walk and/or the map, linked perhaps to the work on geography or history, until identifying the operation becomes familiar. Similar activities involving conversion from one currency to another can be based around a euro-corner in which information on the culture of another country includes numerical information to be interpreted. Such classroom displays provide a parallel for older children to the home corner full of numerals which supports mathematics in the early years.

ACTIVITY 4

Real-life problems such as planning an event will provide further contexts in which a variety of operations are needed (see Section 2.6). Activities involving checking for 'Value for money' are particularly useful for division. A collection of varying sizes of packages for tea, coffee, cereal, etc., marked with prices, is a useful resource.

Children need to experience a wide variety of problems rather than a diet of routine word problems in order to develop mathematical thinking and use skills such as estimation as well as applying numerical knowledge.

Estimation

Whatever method of calculation is chosen, it is essential that when the calculation is complete the child takes notice of the answer. 'Is this a reasonable answer?' is the essential question that needs to be internalised.

How can a child learn to answer this question? A crucial factor in estimating is to have something to compare with. To decide whether a bookcase will go through a door, you need to see both the bookcase and the door. To decide if 27 is a reasonable answer to 13 times 14, you need to be able to compare the answer with a familiar benchmark such as 10 times 10 is 100 – so 27 is far too small. A collection of familiar benchmarks can be used to make judgements:

- For calculations: $10 \times 10 = 100$, $20 \times 20 = 400$, a thousand times a thousand is a million.
- For ratios: three quarters is 75%, which is 0.75, which is a half plus a quarter.
- For heights: my height is 1 metre 20 cm, my sister is 1 metre 40 cm.
- For measures: a bag of sugar weighs a kilo, which is about 2.2 pounds (2.2 lbs).
- For numbers: the number of children in the class, the school, the number of people in the city, town or village in which the children live.

Children can be encouraged to develop their own set of benchmarks or to make a display of significant benchmarks.

Rounding

More formal methods of estimating use rounding. Using a calculator to find out how many 43p cans of soup can be bought for £4.00 gives an answer of 9.30232. This must be rounded down to give 9 cans and some change.

Using a calculator to find out how many coaches are needed to take 400 children on a trip when each coach takes 43 children gives the same answer of 9.30232, which this time must be rounded up to give 10 coaches if some children are not to be left behind.

The decision to round up or down is taken by considering the sense of the question.

There are two formal systems of rounding: by decimal places and by significant figures (see Figure 2.37):

With both these formal systems the convention is to round up if the digit is 5 or above but the overriding consideration is to give an answer that makes sense in the context of the question.

> To one decimal place   3.92   is 3.9
>   4.090 is 4.1
> To one significant figure 3.92   is 4
>   357   is 400

Figure 2.37 Rounding

2.4 EXTENDING THE NUMBER SYSTEM

The process of learning to count, which begins with the counting numbers 1, 2, 3 … and proceeds with an ever more confident grasp of how to count on and on, is the beginning of an exploration of number. With increased acceptance of calculator use children are beginning to use larger numbers, negative numbers and decimals at an earlier age.

Really large numbers

There seems to be a certain pleasure in using numbers larger than you have ever used before. The moment of counting on beyond 20 for the first time, or beyond 100, can be very satisfying. Children need to continue to develop their counting skills just as they continue to develop their reading skills. Calculators can be used to explore large numbers and children encouraged to read out the numbers, for example four thousand nine hundred and ninety-nine, and then to predict what number will be obtained by adding 2.

Children can be encouraged to invent their own problems using numbers as large as they please. A million is sometimes used to mean 'an amazingly large number', a number so big it is hard to imagine. So why not try to imagine it; suppose you did have a million of your favourite chocolate bar – what would that look like? would it fill a suitcase? or the classroom? or the school? (A word of warning: one class decided to collect a million empty drink cans and found they had taken on far more than they bargained for!)

Working with really large numbers involves opportunities for considering the most effective means of recording them. Thinking about 100 as 10^2, for example, can lead to ideas of indices and (much later) to Standard Form.

A really large number called the 'googol' was invented by a physicist George Cranow for his daughter; it has become accepted and appears in reference books. It is reported that 'Google' (the search engine) was a misspelling of this number.

A googol is 1 followed by 100 zeros:

10 000 000 000 000 000 000 000 000 000 000 000 000 000 000 000 000 000 000 000 000 000 000 000 000 000 000 000 000 000 000 000 000 000 000

Figure 2.38 A googol

Activities involving large numbers

Have you been alive for 1,000,000 seconds?

What is the distance round the equator? Make a poster that helps to make sense of this distance by comparing it with more familiar distances – for example, the distance between two familiar cities, the distance run in a marathon, or the distance you can walk in an hour.

What is the largest number you can find in the newspaper?

Links with science – how far away are the Sun and the planets from Earth?

Developing and extending the number line – one way of thinking about the progression in children's understanding of number is to think of gradually developing a more and more complicated idea of the number line:

- an early number line of large numbers on the floor or in the playground which children can walk along or jump along two steps at a time;
- number lines with the numbers 10, 20, 30 ... emphasising the pattern of counting in tens;
- number lines with space to put in 2½ and 4¼ (see Figure 2.39);
- number lines going up in really large steps to a million (see Figure 2.40);
- and then there is the negative number line ...

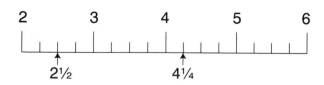

Figure 2.39 Fractions on a number line

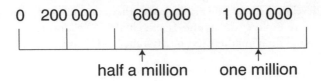

Figure 2.40 A number line with very large steps

Glossary

(There are further glossaries for Number after the sections 'Introducing negative numbers', 'Fractions, decimals and percentages', 'Properties of numbers' and at the end of Section 2.)

This section is intended as a reference for teachers, to support subject knowledge and underpin planning, and not all of the terms need to be used directly with children.

Associativity: to add or multiply three numbers you must decide whether you will find the sum or product of the first pair of numbers or the last pair first. Then add or multiply the result by the third number, for example 3 + 4 + 5 can be tackled as (3 + 4) + 5 or 3 + (4 + 5).

Commutativity: in adding or multiplying two numbers, the order does not matter. This enables choice about easier calculations, for example 9 + 3 might be easier than 3 + 9.

Distributivity: in multiplication you can partition a number to make the process easier, for example 5 × 16. Partition 16 into 10 and 6 and multiply each by 5. Then add the two answers. 5 × 16 = 5 × (10 + 6) = (5 × 10) + (5 × 6). This will also work with subtraction, for example 5 × 19 can be tackled as 5 × (20 − 1) = (5 × 20) − (5 × 1).

Indices: also referred to as index notation, this is a shorthand way of writing numbers using powers. This can be applied to any number base, but in base ten (our place value system) multiples of 10 are represented by positive powers and fractional parts by negative powers:

$10 \times 10 = 100 \ (10^2)$
$10 \times 10 \times 10 = 1\ 000 \ (10^3)$
$10 \times 10 \times 10 \times 10 = 10\ 000 \ (10^4)$
$10^1 = 10 \times 1$

$10^{-1} = 1/10 = 0.1$
$10^{-2} = 1/100 = 1/10^2 = 0.01$
$10^{-3} = 1/1,000 = 1/10^3 = 0.001$

Standard form: also called scientific notation; this is an economic way of representing very large or very small numbers. A number in standard form is expressed as a number between 1 and 10 multiplied by a power of 10. For example:

$10.73 = 1.073 \times 10^1$
$252 = 2.52 \times 10^2$
$3485 = 3.485 \times 10^3$
$4.6 = 4.6 \times 10^0$
$0.67 = 6.7 \times 10^{-1}$

Introducing negative numbers

Negative numbers are very strange. You could have three cats, you could have 253 cats but who ever saw a minus cat? Mathematics is considered such a sensible, serious subject that children are sometimes expected to swallow it whole without protest or logical argument.

Negative numbers are an invention. They were invented because it was convenient. They fit in well with some existing ideas (such as adding and subtracting numbers) but they are not counting numbers. You cannot count negative three cats!

Negative numbers are useful when there is some zero or base point from which measurements are made. You have three pounds in the bank, you deposit five pounds, and then withdraw 10 pounds. You owe the bank two pounds. It seems sensible to label it with the number two and a sign to show that you owe two pounds: –2.

You describe a hill as 100 metres above sea level, so how would you describe a cave 10 metres under the sea? –10 m.

You put 5 into your calculator and take away 7. The calculator reads 2: oh no it does not, there is a small sign in front of the number: –2. You have some marbles in a bag, you are not sure how many:

- you put in three marbles and take out five;
- you have two fewer marbles in the bag than you started with: –2;
- you add three marbles. How many now? One more than you started with: +1.

This last activity works well as a whole-class activity. The children can follow up the ideas by creating their own marble problems. When asked to invent problems, children always seem to use much harder numbers than those found in exercises. If the teacher seems a little concerned about the difficulty, the children will happily produce even harder problems. This playful self-confidence can help the children to become enthusiastic about their mathematics.

Once you are using negative numbers it can seem appropriate to put a plus sign in front of the counting numbers to emphasise the difference. The positive numbers, zero and the negative numbers together are called the integers.

Glossary

This section is intended as a reference for teachers, to support subject knowledge and underpin planning, and not all of the terms need to be used directly with children.

Counting numbers: these are the whole numbers 1, 2, 3, 4 … Also called the natural numbers.
Integers: all the negative whole numbers, zero and the positive whole numbers …−4, −3, −2, −1, 0, +1, +2, +3, +4 …
Zero and the counting numbers are positive integers.
Ratio: a ratio is the comparison of two numbers. It can be written as 3:4 or as a fraction 3/4. If one person pays 80p towards a lottery ticket and another 20p, then it is only fair that their winnings should be divided in the ratio 80:20 or 4:1.
Rational numbers: the word rational has the same root as ratio. Rational numbers can be written as the ratio of one integer to another. So all the fractions are rational numbers, for example 3/4, 5/3, −4/5. Whole numbers are described as rational because they can all be written as the ratio of two integers. For example 2 can be written as 2/1. Decimal numbers of finite length (for example 0.725) are all rational because they can be written as fractions

(725/1000). Surprisingly, some infinite decimals (the ones with repeating sequences of digits) can also be written as fractions. For example:

0.333333333 … even though it goes on for ever can be written as 1/3
0.0909090909 … can be written as 1/11

Irrational numbers: It would be reasonable to assume that the rational numbers filled up the number line but it turns out that there are some numbers which cannot be written as one integer divided by another. The first irrational numbers usually encountered are √2 and π. We always use approximations for these numbers as the decimal expansions are infinite and never repeat. This is not a case of waiting for a bigger and better computer; it has been proved that these numbers will never end and never settle down to a repeating sequence!

Fractions, decimals and percentages, ratio and proportion

What experiences do we offer that are memorable in understanding the key ideas? Many of the activities advocated involving physical movement, large wall charts, discussion/arguments about misconceptions or extended projects with interactive wall displays are intended to provide mathematical signposts, significant events which children can recall and build upon. It is skilled teaching of a high order to provide interesting memories of fractions, decimals and percentages! So what do we want children to remember?

Fractions

Understanding the meaning of fractions is the first crucial stage. Studies of common errors and misconceptions have provided useful information about how difficulties might arise from the language and images used for fractions. Consider this scenario of a father having lunch with his children. There are three fish fingers left:

Child: '*Can I have some more?*'
Father: '*Okay then, you can have half.*'

Everyday use of language can be vague. In this situation would you expect the child to get half of a fish finger, or 'one and a half fish fingers', that is 'half of the three fish fingers that are left? Many of the mistakes that children make occur because they are not sure what they are finding a fraction of. One of the key ideas here is that of the 'whole'. Is the whole one or three fish fingers in this example?

Children whose main experience of fractions is shading in shapes which have already been divided up for them may develop a strong sense of 3/4 as one 'whole' divided into four parts with three parts shaded (see Figure 2.41). If they do not have to divide up the shapes themselves, they may never pay attention to the fact that all the component parts have to be the same size. Again, everyday language in which it is not uncommon to hear '*I'll have the big half*' is unhelpful and needs to be challenged. Children need to explore a variety of images to give them a robust understanding of fractions (see Figures 2.42 and 2.43).

Figure 2.44 shows an image for three divided by four, or three things shared between four people. This is just one way of dividing up the shapes; children can be encouraged to explore a variety of possible ways.

Figure 2.41 Three-quarters of square and circle: a familiar (perhaps over-familiar) image?

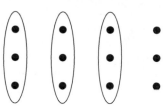

Figure 2.42 Three-quarters of 12 objects

Figure 2.43 An image of two and three-quarters on a number line

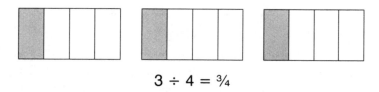

$$3 \div 4 = \tfrac{3}{4}$$

Figure 2.44 One way of dividing three things between four people

Just as children at Key Stage 1 work to explore whole numbers, at Key Stage 2 children need to explore and become very familiar with a few basic fractions. Fractions greater than one, such as two and a quarter, need to be familiar as well as fractions less than one.

Activities involving fractions

Measuring with paper strips one metre long, which the children fold themselves and mark as a quarter of a metre, half a metre and three quarters of a metre, can be helpful.

Favourite dice games can be adapted using dice marked 1/4, 1/2, 3/4, 1, 1¼, 1½.

Ordering fractions on a number line.

Counting rounds in fractions, for example count in intervals of 1/2 around the class.

Activities in which the children divide up and label shapes can give a feel for the relative sizes of simple fractions and prepare the ground for the addition of simple fractions (see Figure 2.45). It is important that children see, too, that parts do not have to be physically connected. For example, in the diagrams showing quarters in Figure 2.45 one half could be shown by sharing any two parts, not necessarily next to each other.

What is a half? Providing children with a set of objects to halve can be challenging – a piece of string, a packet of sweets, a bag of marbles, a litre bottle of water, a piece of plasticine, a paper triangle, a paper circle. This involves finding both a fraction of one whole, such as a whole piece of paper, and a fraction of a (whole) set of objects, such as a bag of marbles. (The set of objects needs to include both odd and even numbers to halve.)

Using paper strips folded in half and then again and again is a useful way of comparing fractions and discovering those which are equivalent. Children taking turns to shade fractions of the strip can soon make up a game by throwing a dice to determine what fraction to shade in and chasing each other to the end of the strip.

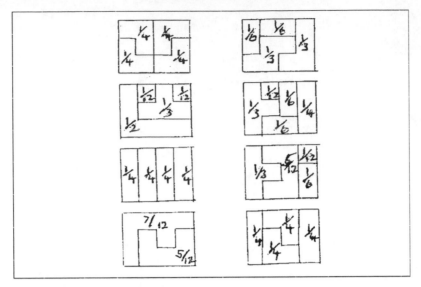

Figure 2.45 Fraction activity

Cuisenaire rods or colour factor can be used to explore fractions. The rod representing 10 units may be chosen to represent 'one whole' or the children may choose the rod which represents 8 units to be 'the whole'. Halves, quarters, eighths can be measured against each other, fractions can be added and subtracted and the results recorded, children can produce an impressive array of statements which they have generated by comparing the rods. In order to add one quarter and one eighth it can be seen that exchanging one quarter for two eighths it is possible to count up three eighths, using the idea of equivalent fractions and a common denominator. There is computer software that models equivalent fractions by producing fraction 'walls' like those that can be constructed using Cuisenaire rods (available at www.standards.dfes.gov.uk/primary/publications/mathematics/itps/).

Decimals

Decimals are a special type of fraction in which the whole is divided into 10 parts. Because our number system is based on 10, there is a simple way of writing decimals:

- for one tenth we write 0.1;
- for one hundredth we write 0.01.

Decimals can be seen as a natural extension of the place value system. In Section 2.3, a variety of representations were discussed, and these can be revisited and extended to explore decimals. The Gattegno chart can be used by pointing to a starting number such as 500 and asking the children to divide by 10 to get 50, then again to get 5, and then again to get 0.5:

0.1	0.2	0.3	0.4	0.5	0.6	0.7	0.8	0.9
1	2	3	4	5	6	7	8	9
10	20	30	40	50	60	70	80	90
100	200	300	400	500	600	700	800	900

Number lines can be reintroduced and divided into tenths and hundredths. Calculators can be used to explore what happens when numbers like 2000 are divided by 10 again and again. The principle of using physical movement to emphasise and make memorable the patterns in the numbers can be applied by using children to represent the digits in a calculation. For example, three chairs can be set out to represent hundreds, tens and ones with three children holding large cards with the digits 2 and 4 and 0 to make the number 240. The instruction from the teacher is 'divide by 10'. After some discussion amongst the children with the numbers, the child with the 0 moves away, the child with the 4 moves up and the child with the 2 moves up to show 24. To divide by 10 again will need some form of marker for the decimal point and another chair to represent the 'tenths'. This simple activity, requiring only a set of large cards marked with the digits 0 to 9, can be elaborated by the teacher and used to draw out any misconceptions. It emphasises that it is the digits which move to positions of different value. It then provides a useful 'shared memory' when the children are working with pencil and paper or calculator: 'Do you remember when we were dividing by 100 on the chairs?'

Misconceptions about decimals

In the section on mental mathematics misconceptions about the size of decimals were discussed (for example the longer the number, the bigger it is). A further misconception, which does not become obvious until children are involved in multiplying decimals – perhaps using a calculator to solve a practical problem – is the assumption that 'multiplication makes bigger'. This is true when multiplying by numbers larger than 1 but:

- $9 \times 0.1 = 0.9$ which is smaller than 9;
- a half times a half is a quarter.

Confronting the paradox is again effective in helping children to think through their ideas. The teacher may discuss with the children sequences involving multiplying by smaller and smaller numbers to get the children thinking and then provide activities in which the children have to use their understanding that multiplying does not always make bigger, such as the calculator activity described below.

Discussion activity

$12 \times 4 = 48$	$9 \times 9 = 81$
$12 \times 2 = 24$	$9 \times 3 = 27$
$12 \times 1 = 12$	$9 \times 1 = 9$
$12 \times 1/2 = 6$	$9 \times 1/3 = 3$
$12 \times 1/4 = 3$	$9 \times 1/9 = 1$

Children will usually agree that 12 lots of a half is 6, and be able to work out that 12 lots of a quarter is 3. The teacher's role is to emphasise that multiplying by 1/2 has given the answer of 6 which is smaller than 12.

Calculator activity

This activity involves choosing numbers which multiply to a given target. To emphasise that multiplication can result in an answer which is larger or smaller than the starting number, a mix of whole and decimal numbers is used.

Starting numbers are displayed for all the children to see:

5, 8, 0.2, 0.5, 10, 2

A target number is chosen from a set of cards prepared by the teacher to include products of the starting numbers:

5, 16, 1.6, 50, 40, 0.4, etc.

From the list of starting numbers the first player must choose two numbers which will multiply to hit the target.

The second player uses a calculator to see if the target has been hit. It is natural to discuss whether the numbers are too big or too small and this gives the teacher an opportunity to ask if there are any numbers the players can multiply by to make the answer smaller than the starting number. The vehemence with which some children will claim this to be impossible gives some indication of the power of this misconception.

Percentages

Yet another way of expressing parts of a whole is to use percentages, that is to divide the whole into hundredths. The essential idea of percentages can be gained by working with frequently occurring examples such as 10% or 50%. An understanding that 10% of one pound is ten pence provides the basis for a robust method of working out percentages when money is involved. Ways of working out 20%, 50% or 15% can be derived from this.

When expressing part of something, it is often possible to choose whether to use fractions, decimals or percentages. It is helpful to emphasise the connections between the different forms from an early stage.

A large number line on the wall marked in decimals, a set of cards and some string can form the basis for many activities linking fractions, decimals and percentages (see Figure 2.46). There are also a number of websites with number lines that can be used with interactive whiteboards (for example www.mathsonline.co.uk/freesite_tour/resource/whiteboard/decimals/dec_notes.html).

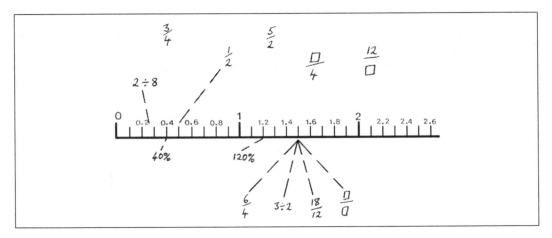

Figure 2.46 The links between fractions, decimals and percentages on a number line

Activities involving percentages

10% off

10% is a very useful 'benchmark' for estimating and understanding percentages. This activity enables children to get a sense of what 10% means.

There is a story of a disgruntled worker on a building site who cut 10 centimetres off all the metre rods used for measuring. The house was duly built using these false measures and then the problems emerged: you would hit your head on the door and have to stoop to use the sink. Imagine there was 10% off everything in your classroom. What would the effects be? How long would your pencil be?

Newspaper headlines

Percentages are sprinkled liberally around in newspaper articles and on the television news. They are often used to support arguments. Arguably, one of the most important reasons for understanding percentages is to support children's growth as citizens in understanding the world around them. Headlines such as '25% of water lost in leaky pipes' and 'School class size to rise by 5%' invite value judgements, but what do these figures mean and how can children be helped to understand and interpret them?

When children are making a newspaper using desktop publishing facilities as part of their activities in some other curriculum area, the following requirement can be included. The newspaper should include at least three statements involving percentages. In one of these statements the percentage given by the writer should be deliberately far too high, in one far too low and in the third statement the percentage should be quite reasonable. When the newspapers are displayed the children can discuss and identify the misleading percentages in the newspapers produced by other groups.

A simpler version of this activity is for the teacher to produce some headlines, real or invented, for the class to discuss.

Ratio and proportion

Ratio has already been referred to in relation to multiplication, related to ideas of scaling. The two ideas of ratio and proportion are linked also with ideas about fractions. Practical contexts involving recipes offer purposeful activities where, for example, discussions can be initiated from questions of scaling amounts of ingredients up or down for different numbers of people. Proportion of a quantity (say three black cars in a line of 12) is expressed using language such as 'one in every four of the cars is black'. This could also be seen as 'one quarter of the cars'. Ratio is the comparison of two or more quantities so that if in the line of cars there were four black cars and eight silver cars, the ratio would be 1:2 which can be expressed as 'two silver cars for every black car'. If there were 24 cars with the same ratio of 1:2 the two quantities would be doubled (eight black cars and 16 silver).

Properties of numbers

Odd, even, multiple, factor, square, prime, cube, square root

Part of becoming familiar with the numbers from 1 to 100 involves learning addition and multiplication facts and being able to invert the facts to subtract and divide. There are also numbers with special properties to be encountered and named. It is useful to have several activities for each property so that the children meeting the numbers in different contexts become familiar with them. '*Oh, it's square numbers again*' is the sort of response to be hoped for. This familiarity can be aided by the use of display. The class can also build up a database of numbers on a computer, recording for each number all the properties they can think of. The entry for 7 might read:

- a prime number;
- a factor of 42 and 49;
- the number of days in a week;
- the fourth odd number.

A guessing game can be developed with one group entering the properties and another group guessing the numbers.

Activity 1: Odd and even numbers

As children become used to working in an open way, they will respond confidently to very general questions, for example 'What can you find out about adding odd and even numbers?' The apparently vague question is actually carefully designed by the teacher to give the children room for interpretation. A more precisely phrased question would mean the teacher doing the work rather than the child (see key questions section in Section 1). The techniques used to encourage creative writing involving different responses from different children can be adapted to encourage creative mathematics. Figure 2.47 shows the work of a child who interpreted the question by adding not just two numbers but several!

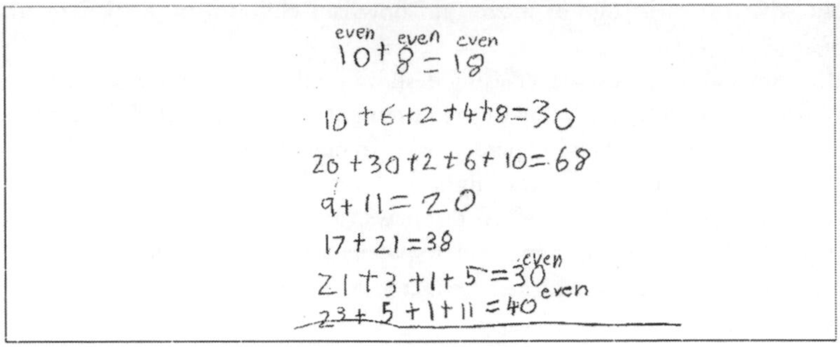

even   even   even
$10 + 8 = 18$

$10 + 6 + 2 + 4 + 8 = 30$
$20 + 30 + 2 + 6 + 10 = 68$
$9 + 11 = 20$
$17 + 21 = 38$
$21 + 3 + 1 + 5 = 30$ even
$23 + 5 + 1 + 11 = 40$ even

Figure 2.47 What can you find out about adding odd and even numbers?

Activity 2: Factor trees

This is a useful large group activity for bringing together lots of work on the properties of numbers. The children will need a good grasp of multiplication facts.

Draw a tree trunk and write the number 24 in the middle of the trunk (see Figure 2.48).

Draw in two branches and ask for two numbers that multiply to give 24.

Figure 2.48 Starting a 24 tree

There are several possible answers, 3 × 8 or 2 × 12 or 4 × 6 – any of these will do. Write the numbers on the branches.

Now move to one of the branches, draw in two more branches and ask for numbers that multiply to give 8.

Stop when you get to a number like 2 or 5 which cannot be broken down (see Figure 2.49).

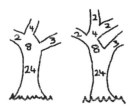

Figure 2.49 One way of continuing the tree

It is very easy to slip into adding, so the children can be warned to watch out for addition sums creeping in and to make sure that they have a 'multiplying tree'. With children choosing different starting numbers the group will soon have a forest of trees which can be sorted into different kinds (see Figure 2.50):

Trees with only two branches, both the same, for example 25 and 49. These are the squares of prime numbers.

Trees where all the branches end in 2, for example 32, 64 and 8. These are the powers of 2.

Tree-stumps with no branches at all, for example 2, 13 and 23. These are the prime numbers.

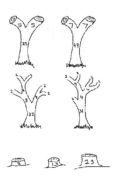

Figure 2.50 Looking for similar trees

When the idea of factor trees is well established a good activity to extend thinking is, for example 'I'd like a tree where all the branches end in 3'. The child then has to try various starting numbers to try and make such a tree. 'I'd like a tree with lots and lots of 'branches', is a challenging request.

Making these trees requires careful work. A useful check for the teacher and for the children is to multiply together all the numbers at the tips of the branches. This should give the starting number.

Glossary

This section is intended as a reference for teachers, to support subject knowledge and underpin planning, and not all of the terms need to be used directly with children.

Factor: 3 is a factor of 12 which means that 3 divides into 12 exactly.
Multiple: 12 is a multiple of 3 or 12 divides exactly by 3. So the factors of 12 are 1, 2, 3, 4, 6 and 12 and only these. The multiples of 12 go on for ever: 12, 24, 36, 48, 60 … 1,200 …
Prime numbers: have only two factors, themselves and 1. So 2, 3, 5, 7 and 11 are prime but 1, 9 and 15 are not. 1 is not prime as it only has one factor. The list of primes goes on and on. Indeed it has been shown that there is an infinite number of primes.
Square numbers are 1, 4, 9, 16 … They can be written as a number multiplied by itself, for example 1×1, 2×2, 3×3, 4×4 … or represented by a square array of dots (see Figure 2.51).

Figure 2.51 16 is a square number

Cube numbers: these are 1, 8, 27, 64 … They can be written as $1 \times 1 \times 1$, $2 \times 2 \times 2$ … etc. and could be represented by fitting together Multilink cubes to form larger cubes.

Square root: pressing 10 and the square root button on the calculator gives 3.142 … This is approximately the number which multiplied by itself will give 10. The name 'square root' is appropriate, since if a square has an area of 10 then the square root of 10 gives the length of the side of the square. Examples:

- the square root of 25 is 5;
- the square root of 100 is 10.

2.5 IDEAS LEADING TO ALGEBRA

Early generalisations: the search for pattern

Pattern is a very important element in mathematics because recognising a pattern or relationship leads to the possibility of predicting or generalising. Seeing a pattern involves focusing on what is the same in a situation and what is changing. By asking children to describe what they see as precisely as they can, early work on pattern encourages children to be observant and to develop their language skills.

Pattern can lead to work in shape and space as well as to number patterns. Looking at patterns in wallpaper, wrapping paper and materials can provide ideas for potato or string printing patterns. To provide instructions for printing the paper requires careful analysis. This might involve recording instructions to reproduce the pattern on paper once the printing block has been made. For example: print, rotate the block clockwise through 90 degrees, print, rotate the block 90 degrees anti-clockwise, print, rotate the block clockwise through 90 degrees, print and so on.

Looking at number squares can reveal patterns in the numbers. Large number squares, or number lines which can be unrolled on the floor for children to stand on, provide an opportunity for children to 'feel' patterns in their body. Counting in twos on a number square sends you jumping along the first line of the square, then back to the beginning of the second line. Counting on in nines moves you diagonally across the square. Making a pattern with Multilink cubes red: red, blue, red, red, blue … can be developed as a mathematical activity by asking questions such as: 'What colour will the twelfth one be? How do you know?'

Developing pattern and generalisation

The following case study describes some work with Year 6 children, which gave them opportunities to work with patterns in shapes and in numbers and to make generalisations. The practical activity of making the shapes and checking the number of cubes needed is the basis for the insight into the general rule.

Case study: Chris Hopkins

Growing shapes

A group of Year 6 children were shown a family of animals of carefully graded sizes as shown in Figure 2.52. These were made from Multilink cubes and, although hardly life-like, were accepted by the children as 'dogs'. I set up the dogs in line in the centre of the table and asked: 'Can you tell me what the next dog in the family would look like?' One child started to count the cubes in the largest dog, another moved the dogs closer together to compare the sizes. 'How many cubes would it need?', I prompted. I had expected partial answers, perhaps an observation on how many cubes there would be in the legs, but one pair of children who had been talking together said more or less simultaneously 'Fifteen'. 'Fifteen? How do you know that?' I asked in an admiring tone. 'One more on the legs and one more there' was the response – pointing to the body of the animal.

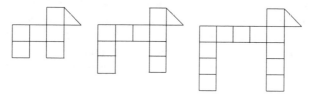

Figure 2.52 Family of dogs – in graded sizes

I asked for instructions on how to build the next animal in the family. I wanted to build it myself rather than ask the children to build it so that they would have to consider and verbalise the number of cubes used at each stage. Another pair of children was chosen to give the instructions. 'Four for the legs' came quickly. Finding the number for the 'body' needed more conferring, with different views as to whether four or six cubes would be needed. When I had made the animal, I placed it in the line. Again, one child rearranged the dogs side by side to judge 'by eye' whether the shapes were right. Small folded pieces of card were now distributed so that the children could make a label to stand by each animal giving the number of cubes (see Figure 2.53).

Figure 2.53 Making labels for the dogs to emphasise position and number of cubes

It was easy for the children to spot the 'going up in threes' pattern. (This was what the first child had spotted when she said 'One more on the legs and one more on the body'.) This 'going up in threes' pattern made it easy for the children to see that the next dog would need 15 cubes and the one after 18 cubes but the challenge I gave them now was to describe how to make the tenth animal. By jumping to the tenth animal and asking not for the total number of cubes but for instructions on how to build the legs and the body, I was shifting attention away from the 'going up in threes' pattern to the pattern that the third animal had three cubes in each leg and the fourth animal had four cubes in each leg so that the tenth animal would have 10 cubes in each leg.

After much counting and thinking, the children came up with two rival descriptions.

One pair claimed it was: '10 cubes for the legs, 12 across and the head making 33'. Another pair was convinced that it was '11 cubes for the legs and 10 across' (see Figure 2.54).

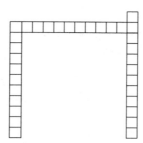

Figure 2.54 The tenth dog needs 33 cubes

After some argument/discussion it was agreed that both methods gave 33 cubes and that both were right. The animal (which was not very stable and did not look much like a dog!) was made and labelled.

The children, in pairs, then made their own animal families (see Figures 2.55 and 2.56). The gorillas (see Figure 2.56) were far more convincing as animals than the dogs. The children designing them lined them up and seemed to judge by eye rather than counting cubes. All the animal families the children made gave clear number patterns. Amazingly, as long as it is quite clear how to make the next one in the family, there will always be a number pattern.

Figure 2.55 A family of giraffes

Figure 2.56 A family of gorillas

Seeing the link with algebra

The tenth animal needed two lots of 10 cubes for the legs, 10 + 2 cubes for the body and one for the head:

2(10) + (10 + 2) + 1 = 33

So the nth animal would need two lots of n cubes for the legs, n + 2 cubes for the body and one for the head, as in Figure 2.57:

$$2n + (n + 2) + 1 = 3n + 3$$
$$\text{legs} \quad \text{body} \qquad \text{head}$$

Figure 2.57 Formula for making 'dogs'

With this particular group of children introducing the formal algebra did not seem appropriate; but having a sense of progression, knowing where the activity could lead, encouraged emphasis not on the 'going up in threes' pattern but on making the jump to predict how many cubes for the tenth or for the hundredth shape would be appropriate. It would also help to draw up a table showing the number of cubes for each dog. This would lead some children to abstract generalisation and their own first algebraic statements.

Further activities where patterns in numbers can be expressed as simple relationships in words or symbols can be found in Section 2.6.

Other activities leading to algebra

The equaliser

This apparatus is useful in dealing with ideas of equivalence; the equals sign shows this rather than 'makes' as young children seem to think. For example, put a weight of 5 on one side and balance it by placing two weights on the other side to model 5 = 2 + 3 or 2 + 3 = 5 (see Figure 2.58).

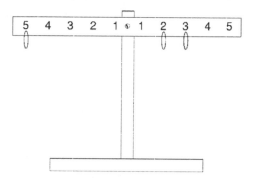

Figure 2.58 Equaliser showing 5 = 2 + 3

It can also be used to look at finding unknown numbers, for example put a weight of 5 of one side and a weight of 3 on the other side. Ask children to find out what other number you need to balance 5. For older children this could lead into challenges such as:

- find different ways to complete ■ + ▲ + ◆ = 4
- the How many ways? activity in Section 2.6 takes up the idea of finding different ways to make the same number.

Children can use it to find number bonds by choosing a number and putting a weight of that number on one side of the balance. They can then explore all the ways they can place two weights on the other side to balance the equaliser. Children can express statements orally or record in the form of equations:

3 + 2 = 5, 4 + 1 = 5, etc.

This also links with ideas for Activity 1 Function machines, in Section 2.6.

Think of a number

Activities of this sort can be set up to address unknowns, functions and inverses ('undoing' operations). For example, 'I'm thinking of a number. When I add 2 to my number I get 6. What is my number?' or, to set more of a challenge, use more steps and encourage 'undoing' – 'I'm thinking of a number. If

I double it, add 3 and multiply by 2, I get 22, what is my number?' Inverse operations will return to the starting number: $22 \div 2 = 11, 11 - 3 = 8, 8 \div 2 = 4$.

Graphs

Children in Key Stage 2 can draw graphs to show mathematical relationships; for example, graphs to show multiplication or conversion graphs such as Celsius to Fahrenheit (see 'Glossary' at end of Section 4 'Handling data'). By plotting different relationships (for example numbers 1 to 10 multiplied by 2, 3 and 4), children can compare the relationships and read off values. (There is much about graphing data collected in Section 4 of this book.)

2.6 SOLVING NUMERICAL PROBLEMS

Relating back to Section 1 'Using and applying mathematics', it is important to identify contexts in which problem solving aspects such as making decisions and applying knowledge and skills can be developed. This is in addition to the thinking that should be encouraged in mathematics teaching generally; for example, in asking children to explain and justify mental calculation methods. A very effective way of developing children's understanding of number is to select problems which encourage them to use and apply their knowledge. In this way children can be simultaneously working on a problem, using their creativity, developing logic and organisational skills and practising their number skills. The examples discussed here develop the need for a range of types of problem, not simply the kind of routine word problems discussed earlier.

Practical tasks

Practical tasks and real life problems are seen as separate categories so it is necessary to untangle the meaning behind the general phrases. The two sections that follow give examples of real life problems which can be thought of more formally as 'applied' mathematics, and problems within mathematics itself or 'pure' mathematics. Practical tasks need to be found in both applied and pure mathematics. Practical in the context of applied mathematics tends to mean realistic, everyday, such as tasks involving measuring and constructing, weighing or using money. Practical in a pure mathematics context means using apparatus such as cubes, geo-strips and geo-boards so that the children are working in a practical (in the sense of using their hands) rather than a theoretical way. Practical activities, in both senses, have been suggested throughout the book as a means of deepening children's involvement with their mathematics.

Real life problems

Real life problems should have some 'real' outcome, although they can vary in scale. Many classroom contexts involve the solving of mathematical problems such as displaying work in books or on walls. Children can be encouraged to estimate the amount of paper required to frame work, to measure (sometimes using a paper trimmer) borders for work and to cut card to size for book making or game card making.

Classroom statistics such as absences, numbers for dinners, sharing fruit and so on are real contexts for the application of numerical skills. Children can also be encouraged to think and talk about contexts in which they use money, such as saving coins in a money box or inserting coins in pay machines in the car park.

At the other end of the scale are more elaborate real life problems such as organising a class or school event such as a party, a class visit or a sports day. Reorganising the classroom or involvement in ordering stock from catalogues can provide insights, opportunities and practice in problem solving. The teacher needs to think carefully about the potential for mathematics, decide on how far the problem can be 'real' (will the children's solutions be put into practice?) and still allow for children to suggest ways to deal with the problem. A spin-off from this kind of work is the opportunity for assessing how children apply what they have learned in context. Do they use strategies in other contexts such as purer mathematics problems? Do they approach calculations as we would expect from our teaching? Are they independent in developing approaches to the problem?

To take planning a party as an example (other related contexts could be a picnic or a disco), a whole class will need to be organised to break the problem down and so there needs to be an initial sharing of ideas. The amount of autonomy given to the children will depend on their age and experience but groupings will allow you to look at aspects such as cooperation as well as mathematical understanding. There will be many possibilities for mathematical thinking. Surveys might be involved in planning food – what would most people like to drink? This would lead into work on value for money and capacity. How many bottles will we need? Is it cheaper to buy larger bottles? Are we likely to have fine weather to have the party out of doors? The teacher will be able to think of many more questions and can have ideas in mind to prompt if children are less forthcoming. Questions which help children to organise their thinking might include:

- What do I need to find out?
- Have I done anything like this before?
- What can I try?
- Would it help to model the problem?
- Does my solution work?

If the context is one with which children are familiar and there will be a party at the end, it is likely that motivation will be high. Often, too, these contexts reveal surprising insights into the understanding of individual children, which are not always apparent in more usual classroom mathematical tasks.

Problems within mathematics itself

This slightly strange phrase is a reminder that children find interest and involvement not only in practical, realistic problems but also in puzzles and problems presented as a challenge or in an imaginary, playful context. Two activities are described here which can be adapted to challenge and involve children from the age of five to eleven. The activities can profitably be used many times by the same children in a variety of increasingly demanding forms. Both activities give the children the opportunity to demonstrate many aspects of their numerical knowledge. They are therefore very useful when working with a group of children for the first time to give one a sense of the children's potential.

Activity 1: Function machines

The basic idea of a function machine is that numbers are fed into a machine, as illustrated in Figure 2.59. The machine performs the same action on each number (for example adds 4 or divides by 2), and a number is then fed out of the machine. This simple idea can be the basis of a wide range of activities with all ages of children.

At Key Stage 1, the activity can be set up with a cardboard box large enough for a child to sit inside. One child is chosen to sit inside the box and given in secret instructions as to what the 'machine' must do. The first secret instruction could be 'add 2 cubes'. A train of Multilink cubes is handed in, the child adds two cubes and passes out the train of cubes. An easel placed beside the box can be used to record with drawings or numbers the cubes going in and the cubes coming out. After a few turns the children outside the box are encouraged to predict what will happen to the cubes. When everyone in the group knows what the machine is doing a new 'secret instruction' can be used.

At Key Stage 2, a similar activity can be set up with a smaller box, using slips of paper to feed into the machine. The child acting as the machine each time performs the same operation, for example

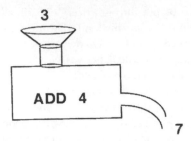

Figure 2.59 An 'ADD 4' function machine

Figure 2.60 Children represent a linked function machine: (a) $(5 + 3) \times 2 = 16$; (b) $(6 \times 2) \div 5 = ?$

multiplying each input number by 7. To extend this children themselves can represent the stages in a two step or linked machine (see Figure 2.60).

Function machines can be drawn on paper with children working in pairs to create machines and to guess what the machine does. This allows children to implement their own ideas.

A little more background information will help to make clear the potential of this apparently simple activity and indicate how the teacher can use it to help the children progress in their understanding of number. In working with Function machines, children are:

- noticing number patterns;
- guessing and predicting;
- practising number skills;
- using the idea of inverse operations.

The function machine can be used to emphasise the **operation**

5 – 3 = 8 is a common mistake

It has been suggested that even though children correctly copy out the subtraction sign and the equals sign, they do not attend to them and are using the well practised routine 'see two numbers and add them'. A child cannot just operate as a '3 machine' with no other instruction but needs to know whether she or he is, for example, an 'add 3' machine or a 'take away 3' machine.

The function machine can be used to emphasise **prediction**

If the operation is unknown, each new number fed in and fed out gives a clue as to what is happening inside the machine. Predicting what will happen to the next number fed in provides an opportunity to test the prediction.

The function machine can be used to emphasise the inverse operation

Using the function machine 'backwards' is particularly important. The function machine helps to make concrete the idea that even though the number fed in is unknown, if you know what happens to the number and what comes out at the end then you can work out the 'unknown number', thus:

? + 3 = 9

The activity can be extended by having linked function machines. For example, I put in a number, the first machine doubles the number, the next machine adds 5 and the answer is 13. What was the number? The idea of an 'unknown number' can then lead to algebraic ideas and the solution of equations such as:

? × 2 + 5 = 13

As children learn to count, they are provided with a range of practical experiences to help them make sense of the formal notation and signs, such as:

3 + 5 = 8

Using a function machine backwards is a practical experience which provides a useful basis for later algebraic work.

Once the children are used to working with the function machine, the teacher can encourage mathematical developments by use of the powerful question:

- What would happen if ...?
- What would happen if we put in complicated numbers like 2½?
- What would happen if we knew the numbers coming out of an 'Add 5' machine, but not the numbers going in?
- What would happen if two machines were linked together?

Computer software and websites can be used to produce a version of a function machine for interactive whiteboards.

Extension

A spreadsheet can be set up to act as a function machine. This could be related to the linked function machine using the same operations. For older children who have not yet used a spreadsheet, this is a good introductory activity which uses just two cells (see Figure 2.61).

	A	B	C
1		5	
2			
3			
4			16

Figure 2.61 A spreadsheet set up as a function machine

First set up the spreadsheet with a large cell size and clear numbers. The activity can then be introduced to a large group with the children later following up the work at the computer in pairs:

Step 1: move cursor to cell B1 and input the number 5.

Step 2: move cursor to cell C4, hide the screen from the children whilst you input the secret formula = B1 + 3 * 2 This means 'take the number in cell B1 add 3 to it and multiply by 2'. When you press return the number 16 will be entered in cell C4.

Step 3: before you let the children see the screen, move the cursor back to B1, this will hide the formula.

To enter numbers into this 'function machine' a number is entered to cell B1, cell C4 will immediately alter to give the output number. The children's task is to work out the formula. Numbers such as 10, 20 or 100 are very useful as they seem to make it easier to spot the formula. Some children will also realise that entering 0 can be helpful. Perhaps surprisingly, entering 1, 2, 3, 4, 5 ... systematically is often not helpful as it tends to focus attention on the gaps between the output numbers 8, 10, 12, 14, 16 ... The patterns are interesting but do not help to spot the formula.

When the children think that they have worked out the formula, move the cursor to any empty cell and enter the children's formula. Then move back to cell B1. If the children are right, their formula will give the right answer whatever number is placed in cell B1 – usually to celebratory cheers!

Later the children work in pairs with one child entering a formula for the other child to work out.

Activity 2: How many ways?

Rather than giving children a list of calculations and asking for the answers, it is possible to turn the activity on its head by giving the children the answer and asking them to invent the questions. 'How many different ways can you find ...?' is a key question. It encourages children to search for lots of different possibilities. In this next activity there is no limit to the answers the children can find.

Case study: Chris Hopkins

How many ways can you make ... 48?

A teacher worked with a Year 6 class in the carpeted area whilst the rest of the class worked on another number activity. She had an easel with a large sheet of paper, some coloured pens and a pack of cards labelled from 1 to 100. Circular sheets of paper, a large number line and some pieces of string were available.

One of the children was asked to choose a number from the pack and she chose 48. The teacher wrote a large 48 in the centre of the sheet of paper and asked: 'Can you tell me a calculation with the answer 48?' Hands went up and the first response was '24 + 24'. 'Is that right?' was the next question. There were murmurs of agreement and no protests, so she drew a line from the 48, and wrote 24 + 24. Several children now suggested examples '40 + 8, 6 × 8, 38 + 10 ...' and these were recorded. '7 × 7' was also suggested, but was greeted with 'No, it's not'. The teacher asked how they could change it to make the answer 48, and '7 × 7 – 1' was agreed and written up. After a while she pointed out that all the suggestions so far involved adding and multiplying and asked, 'What else could we have?'

Gradually the children's suggestions became more and more varied. When the large sheet of paper was satisfyingly full, each child was asked to choose a personal target number and to record on a circle of paper many different ways of making their target (see Figure 2.62).

The next day, a number line was fixed to a wall and the circles were attached by strings, like balloons, to the appropriate position on the number line (see Figure 2.63).

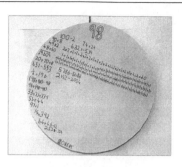

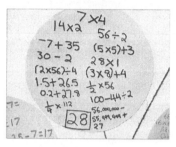

Figure 2.62 A simple question allows children to show their potential

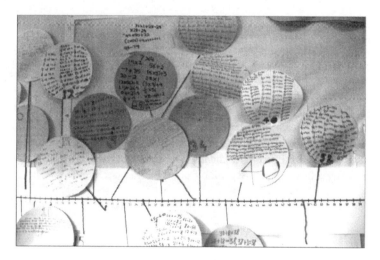

Figure 2.63 Attaching the ballooons to a number line

Assessment

This activity gives a lot of evidence of the level at which children spontaneously work with numbers and the level they can reach with encouragement from the teacher. In this class, a few children could confidently use fractions. Further work indicated that they could add fractions involving quarters, eighths and three quarters in their heads.

Children who are only confident with addition can generate strange looking sums such as the long string of 1 + 1 + 1 + 1 ... Next time children could be encouraged to use subtraction or division and look for patterns. The proud owner of this sum went on enthusiastically to search for more ideas.

Glossary

This section is intended as a reference for teachers to support subject knowledge which underpins planning, and not all of the terms need to be used directly with children.
Equivalence: different ways of expressing the same thing. Examples:

$24 = 20 + 4 = 12 + 12 = 25 - 1$
$1/2 = 2/4 = 4/8 = 0.5 = 50\%$

Function: in everyday language, a four-function calculator is one that will add, subtract, multiply and divide. More complex calculators have more 'function keys' such as square root, cube, sin and cos. The function is an operation, an action which is applied to numbers.
So examples of functions are:
Add 3 Divide by 4.
Inverse: in everyday language, the inverse is the opposite.
The inverse of 'walking three paces North' is 'walking three paces South'.
The inverse of 'putting on your coat' is 'taking off your coat'.
The idea of an inverse is one of the powerful ideas which keep cropping up in mathematics. It is well worth looking out for opportunities to do an action and then the opposite action, using the term 'inverse' in your conversation with the children:

- the inverse of 'add 3' is 'subtract 3';
- the inverse of 'multiply by 4' is 'divide by 4'.

Solving equations

Solving the problem $4 + \square = 7$ is an earlier form of $4 + x = 7$. Children are being asked to find an unknown. Where there are different solutions to an equation, for example ($\square + \square = 5$) there are two unknowns which are variable ($3 + 2, 4 + 1, 4.5 + 0.5$, etc.).

Where another relationship between the two unknowns is also given (for example $x + y = 5$ and $2x + y = 8$), there are two equations which can be solved at the same time (simultaneously, hence 'simultaneous equations'). In words, this can be expressed, 'I'm thinking of two numbers. If you add them you get 5. If you double the first and add the second to the result you get 8.' One way to solve this is to reduce the number of unknowns by subtracting one equation from the other (see Figure 2.64):

$$2x + y = 8$$
$$\underline{-x + y = 5}$$
$$x + 0 = 3$$

So $x = 3$

Figure 2.64 Solving simultaneous equations: step 1 subtractions

Put the x value back into one of the equations to find the other unknown (y) (see Figure 2.65):

$$2(3) + y = 8$$
$$6 + y = 8$$
$$y = 8 - 6 = 2$$

Figure 2.65 Solving simultaneous equations: step 2 substitution

Shape, space and measure

3.1 SHAPE AND SPACE: INTRODUCTION

There is currently a strong tendency to over-emphasise arithmetic as if this were the only mathematics children need to learn. Of course working with numbers is important, but a full mathematics curriculum will also develop children's spatial and problem-solving skills. In 20 years' time, when these children are adults, computer technology – a very visual medium – will be all-pervasive. Thinking visually is an important and often neglected dimension of intellectual activity. Some children instinctively form images to help them to solve problems; they see how to find a solution. Far more children can be helped to develop the skills of thinking about a problem by forming and manipulating an image in their heads or visualising. The ability to visualise can be practised and developed. As the spatial aspect of mental mathematics, it is increasingly being seen as of central importance to children's learning. Valuing the space and shape curriculum is an important start to developing children's spatial mathematical ability.

Work on shape and space can sometimes lack a sense of purpose and progression, degenerating into just the learning of names of shapes and transformations. (Of course, there are technical terms to be learned, and there are definitions in the Glossary at the end of Section 3.2 for reference.) Coherence can be given to shape and space work, by ensuring that children are making and monitoring decisions to solve spatial problems, developing the ability to communicate mathematically verbally and visually, and above all reasoning and generalising about spatial properties in increasingly sophisticated ways.

The activities in this section are therefore of an exploratory or problem-solving nature and emphasise:

- reasoning;
- communicating; and
- visualising.

Since the reasoning, communicating and visualising in these activities are about the properties of shapes and transformations, children will necessarily also develop their understanding of how shapes are classified and their technical vocabulary.

It is important to present children with a variety of examples for a technical word, otherwise they may get a limited idea of what the word refers to (see Figure 3.1). Many children think that a 'tilted' square is not a square, because they have only learned to match one image to the word rather than being encouraged to identify the key properties and to confront tricky examples. Similarly some children think that only equilateral triangles can be triangles, refusing to recognise irregular triangles or even 'upside down' ones, because they have only learned to attach the name to one kind, and that always with a 'horizontal' base. Other children may include, in a set of triangles, shapes which are nearly triangles, but with four sides, because they are 'triangular looking'.

In Recent Research in Mathematics Education 5–16 (Ofsted 1995) it is stated that:

> Careful choice of examples improves children's concept formation. The ideal examples to use in teaching are those that are 'only just' examples, and the ideal non-examples are those which are very nearly examples.

Figure 3.1 A range of triangles

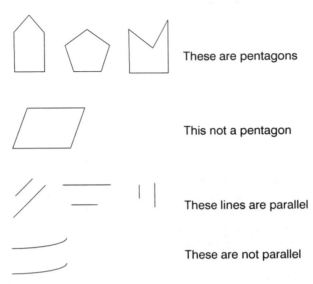

Figure 3.2 Shape dictionary

It can be useful for children to make a shape dictionary in which they illustrate terms with diagrams and explanations. Children's dictionaries could include explanations in their own words of examples of a concept as well as examples that do not fit the concept, see Figure 3.2 for an example.

Teaching points

One important principle here is that children are given the opportunity to discuss the properties of shapes as well as to learn the names, in order to understand the definitions. The term 'properties' usually refers to features or attributes of shapes, such as straight or curved sides, flat or curved faces, numbers of angles and sides, equality of angles and sides, parallelness and symmetry. Another important principle is that this discussion is associated with actively manipulating, constructing and distorting shapes, either practically or mentally. Children may investigate what happens when alterations are made, looking at what changes and what stays the same. If children discuss trying to make circles with string and chalk, with their bodies, or by programming with robots or Logo, they will have a clearer idea of what is and what is not a circle and develop an internalised understanding of the definition. They will then be doing more thinking than if they are just asked to say the word 'circle' in response to a few images of the shape.

Case study: *Geraldine Wood*

Visualising: an initial assessment activity

Figure 3.3 Lee and Angie's shapes

Asking children to visualise can be quite revealing as an assessment activity (see Figure 3.3). At the beginning of a topic on shape, I asked some Year 4 children to close their eyes and:

Imagine a square. Cut off one corner, take the corner away.
Can you describe what you have left? What does the shape look like now?

Angie: 'It has three corners.'
Me: 'Count the corners.'
Angie: 'It has five corners. It has four sides.'

Angie initially focuses on just three corners, perhaps the right-angled ones. The question prompts her to include all five corners. Her response of four sides is puzzling – perhaps Angie thinks that the cut side in some way 'does not count' as a side.

I asked the children to secretly draw their image in order to help them 'fix' it and then to look at it.

Natalie: 'It's like a square. It has five corners. Three sides are the same, one is different. Three have L-shaped corners.'

Natalie counts the corners, but, like Angie, seems to count only four sides. She recognises right angles but does not use the term.

Bilal: 'There are two bits sticking out. One facing left, one facing down. The corners don't join up. The top two bits have two corners and there is a corner at the bottom left.'

I am not quite sure what Bilal is describing! He seems confident about corners, but his description, presumably of sides as 'bits facing left and down', would benefit from some more standard vocabulary to make his meaning clearer.

These responses are beginning to make me think we will need to do a lot of work, exploring not only the effects of chopping off corners, but indeed exploring shapes in general, using paper and scissors, and also geoboards and elastic bands, and making shapes out of dough, plasticine, geostrips and straws.

Next, I asked the children to describe their shape to me, so that I could draw it:

Bilal: 'Draw two corners just at the top. Join the corners together. You know the left corner, if you just go down and draw another corner. From the bottom left corner, draw a line across. From the right top corner, draw a line down to nothing, not too far, to make a square' (see Figure 3.4).

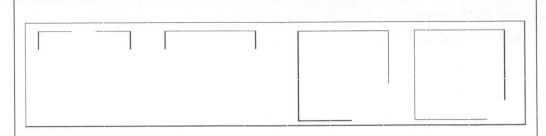

Figure 3.4 Trying to follow Bilal's instructions

This exercise is clearly making Bilal try to give clear instructions and to imagine himself in the place of his listener. It is very good for communication skills – I will try this with the class working in pairs to describe shapes to each other when we have talked about the terminology more. Bilal's skilful description would be much easier to understand if he used standard vocabulary, for instance 'right angle', vertical' and 'horizontal'. I had great difficulty in understanding what to draw, much to the children's amusement, until I realised that Bilal's shape was an outline – so his corner cut off would create a space, not more corners! This was the surprise element of the activity – but perhaps not so surprising really; there is usually someone in the group who visualises in a way that has never occurred to you before.

Visualising activities

An interesting aspect of visualising activities is that the children are put in the powerful position of knowing what their shape looks like. The teacher or partner can listen and ask for clearer instructions, but the child who is doing the describing is the authority on the shape. Examples of activities are:

• Imagine that you pick up four straws and arrange them, touching, on the table. What do your four straws look like?
• Imagine that you are inside a cube. You touch a corner of the cube, and then another corner – how many corners can you touch?
• You are sitting in the corner of a square – what can you see? The square starts to grow bigger and bigger and bigger – what can you see now?
• Imagine walking through a Smartie tube or Toblerone box – what would you see?
• There is a spider in the top corner of the room. What would the tabletop look like to the spider? What about other objects, and different vantage points?

Once the children are used to the idea of visualising in this way, it can become part of regular discussion activities. A few minutes spent visualising can be used by the teacher to teach shape and space in a way that develops mathematical thinking and reasoning, as well as to remind the children of shapes and vocabulary that they have recently met, and to assess the children's understanding of the properties of shapes.

3.2 SHAPE AND SPACE ACTIVITIES

Activities in this section have been selected because they represent some key approaches to the shape and space curriculum, and require children to be actively engaged in thinking. They also use various kinds of apparatus and give the children opportunities to work practically in different contexts.

Any approach can usually be used at a variety of levels; for instance, you can engage three year olds or adults in predicting what shape a folded and cut piece of paper will reveal when it is unfolded (see Activity 2). The mental challenge rapidly increases with more folds or changes of angle; but the requirement to justify the prediction turns this activity into a logical problem, demanding mathematical communication skills as well as reasoning. Open questions like 'Why?' and 'How do you know that?' can intensify the intellectual demands of a practical activity like folding and cutting.

Through these activities, various aspects of properties of shapes and properties of position and movement are addressed. For instance, properties of shape are the main concern of the classifying activities, while the concept of angle can be introduced through body maths and IT activities. Some activities deal with several aspects at once: Logo, for instance, will involve children in ideas of movement and position, especially angle, as well as properties of shapes. The main coverage of the different aspects is shown in Table 3.1:

Table 3.1 Activities and the ideas they address

Activity	Aspects of shape and space addressed
1. Hide and describe	Visualising and describing shapes, positions and movements
2. Folding and cutting	Visualising and describing shapes, positions and movements
3. Making boxes	Making 3-D shapes and recognising properties; using and understanding measures
4. How many different?	Classification of shapes and solving problems, understanding congruence and recognising symmetries
5. What is my rule? Making patterns	Transformations by translation, reflection and rotation; making and describing patterns
6. Using IT	Constructing 2-D shapes; transformations by translation, reflection and rotation; visualising; angle as a measure of turn
7. Body maths	Angle as a measure of turn: right angles, quarter and half turns; degrees and appropriate terms (for example 'acute', 'obtuse')

Activity 1: Hide and describe

Visualising and describing shapes, positions and movements

This activity can be used to develop children's language in precisely describing properties of shape. It also involves more general communication skills such as putting yourself in the place of someone who cannot see what you are describing, or listening with attention to detail.

- With a partner, each take five Multilink cubes (all the same colour), sit back to back and fix the cubes together so that your partner cannot see what you are doing.
- Then, still keeping your model hidden, describe it so that your partner can make it with his or her five Multilink.

This will involve the children in using positional language like: on top of, underneath, next to, left, right, middle, opposite (appropriate to the age group).

Variations

An easier version uses cubes of different colours. It might seem obvious, but individualising the cubes in this way makes instructions less challenging to follow since each cube can be identified separately by colour.

Drawing different viewpoints on squared paper involves children in relating 2-D representations to 3-D models. Combining several views requires skill in visualising from the partner who tries to build the model from the drawing (see Figure 3.5).

Drawing models on isometric paper is a more challenging task for older children (see Figure 3.6)

Describing a geometrical drawing for a friend to draw can involve shapes and properties of varying degrees of difficulty. Language may relate to:

- fractions – halfway up, a third of the way along;
- angles – right angle, very pointed; or
- other properties – diagonal, parallel.

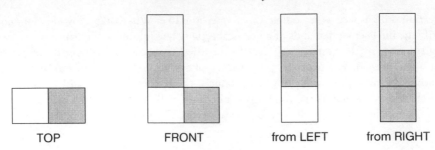

Figure 3.5 Different viewpoints

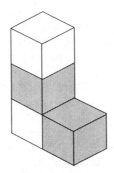

Figure 3.6 Drawing the 3-D shape on isometric paper

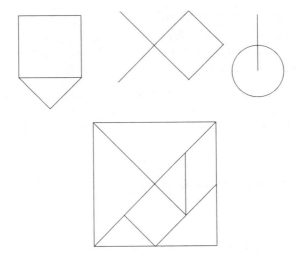

Figure 3.7 Shapes to describe

Or children can describe a simple pattern to each other, in which case they can use language of position and movement, such as reflection and rotation (see Activity 5 and Figure 3.7).

This activity is more challenging and enjoyable if the describer does not look at what their partner is drawing until they have finished. It is sometimes best to organise this as a whole class activity, so that no one is disturbed in trying to do quiet work while it is going on. Identifying children as A and B in pairs, each with a different 'secret 'sheet, as well as sheets with boxes for them to draw in, will help children who are not used to this kind of activity. Young children can offer positive criticism to partners, and can be heard saying things like, 'Well that's quite good, you've nearly got it right, but the triangle should be in between the squares', whereas older children enjoy deliberately exploiting lack of preciseness by drawing the unexpected, and the describers can then be more self critical: 'Oh, I should have said the lines were straight!'

The teacher can playfully demonstrate alternative interpretations by drawing on the board according to the children's instructions (for instance by drawing curved lines if straight ones are not specified, or obtuse angles when a child says 'corner' but means 'right angle'). However, beware rising frustration levels!

Feely bag activities

These usually involve a bag or box with objects. One person puts their hand in, and selects one object to describe without looking at it. If you provide a set of objects identical to those in the bag, the listening group can try to pick out the one matching the description.

To focus children's attention on particular properties, provide items which are similar except in one respect: for instance, a collection of quadrilaterals of different shapes and sizes will encourage children to talk about angles and relative length of sides. Instead of providing a matching set of objects, children can be invited to draw the object from the description and then compare results.

Activity 2: Folding and cutting

Visualising and describing shapes, positions and movements

This activity involves prediction and visualising, and can easily be adapted to provide varying degrees of challenge (see Figure 3.8).

* Fold a piece of paper in half, then in half again. Can you make one cut so that you get a square when you unfold it?
* Can you explain how you know where to make the cut so that you are sure of getting a square?

Children usually judge by eye, but asking them to instruct someone else where to make the cut will often produce some idea that the cut has to be made between two points which are equidistant from the central corner or that the angles at the new corners must be the same. Can you explain why this works (see Figure 3.9)?

This question challenges more experienced children to reason that the angles of the corners they are cutting must be half a right angle in order to form the corners of the square. Alternatively, the sides of the triangle they cut out form the bisected diagonals of the square and so must be the same length. This requires children to articulate their visualising and to think logically about the relationships between properties. You are unlikely to get answers in quite these sophisticated terms, but the underlying reasoning can be expressed by children in their own language.

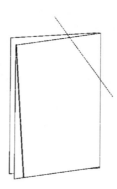

Figure 3.8 Will this cut give a square?

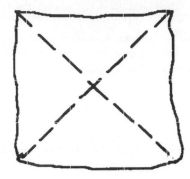

Figure 3.9 Unfolding to see if the shape is a square

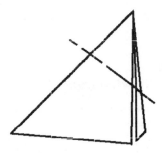

Figure 3.10 How do you cut to get an octagon?

Variations

Can you make an octagon with one cut? Can you make your shape regular (all angles and sides the same (see Figure 3.10)?

This involves children in thinking how many congruent triangles make up an octagon. A hexagon can be made by folding a piece of paper in half, then folding into thirds from a central point and cutting to get six triangles folded on top of each other. (This requires a bit of adjusting to get the thirds equal, matching the sections overlaying each other, before creasing the folds definitely.)

For younger children, fold a square cloth or large sheet of paper in half and half again.

• Can you cut a folded piece of paper to make a person, a tree or a dog?

Cutting from a folded piece of paper to produce symmetrical shapes encourages children to think in terms of a fraction of a shape. Depending on scissor skills, more complicated designs can be made with people holding hands, doilies or snowflakes (using hexagons as a basis). In many cases these activities are creative. To make them explicitly mathematical, children need to be required to think about the changes and shapes involved. Children can investigate the relationship between the number of folds, the resulting number of shapes and their symmetry. Setting children specific challenges, giving instructions to partners and asking them to predict before unfolding, all help to encourage thinking about the properties and relationships between them.

Activity 3: Making boxes

Making 3-D shapes and recognising properties; using and understanding measures

- Can you make a box for something tricky?

Provide children with a collection of irregularly shaped items, such as toys, dolls, teapots or watering-cans, a ball, a pyramid … and some interlocking plastic shapes such as Polydron or Clixi. This activity will involve the children estimating or measuring the dimensions of their chosen object, and thinking about the plane shapes needed to make the net of the 3-D shape they select for the box. As a design activity, children will benefit from making their initial construction and then thinking about improvements in terms of the elegance of the design and the practicalities of making a snug fit.

- Can you make the net for your box out of card?

To make the net children will need to think about the arrangement of the shapes and their dimensions in 2-D, and then transform this to 3-D mentally and practically. Again, children will benefit from having several attempts, and refining rough drafts in sugar paper before a final version in card.

Other constraints can be introduced, such as:

- Which design uses the least amount of paper? Children need to consider how to measure the area of different nets: squared paper will help here. Relationships between surface area and volume can be systematically explored as a follow up.
- Which box holds the most? This is particularly useful for assessing children's understanding of finding the volume and (possibly) their strategies for multiplication.
- Can you make a miniature version of your box which is half the size? How many little boxes will fit into your big one (see Figure 3.11)?

Children usually halve all the dimensions of their box, which they expect will produce a box with half the volume. They are surprised when, for instance, a cube with all three dimensions half of another cube, fits more than twice into the larger one. Explaining why this happens is the challenge to reason mathematically in this activity. A variety of commercial packaging can be a useful stimulus. Chocolates are often packed in interesting ways, with different arrangements for fitting smaller versions inside larger ones, for instance with chocolate triangular prisms inside boxes shaped as trapezoidal or hexagonal prisms.

- Can you go into mass production and make several nets which tessellate from one piece of card?

Environmentally and economically, this is encouraging children to consider cost of materials and wastage, but also to visualise and investigate different arrangements (see also Activity 5 'What is my rule? Making patterns').

- Can you make designs on the faces of your net so that they are the right way up when it is assembled?

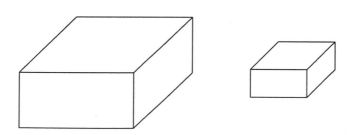

Figure 3.11 Halving all the lengths makes a surprisingly small box

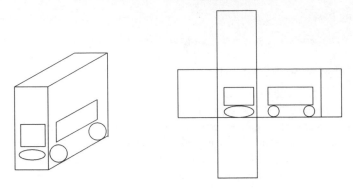

Figure 3.12 Designs on a net

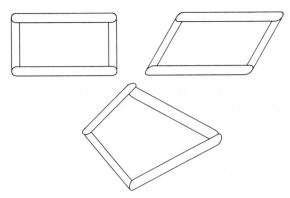

Figure 3.13 Geostrip shapes – how can they be changed?

Essentially this is a creative activity, which involves relating the 2-D image to the 3-D by visualising where the faces will be in relation to each other when the net is made up (see Figure 3.12).

Activity 4: How many different …?

Classifying shapes and solving problems, understanding congruence and recognising symmetries

This activity can be structured to focus attention on different properties of shapes, according to the resources used. Here the focus is on properties of symmetry and parallelism. If the children work as a group, with the requirement that they must reach agreement through discussion, then they can clarify meanings and give reasons for arguments. This provides the teacher with valuable insights into their understanding.

- Take four geostrips and make sure you have different lengths among them. (It does not matter how many of each length you have, so long as you have four strips altogether; you can have two of each length, or three the same and one different or all different.)
- How many different four sided shapes can you make?
- Everybody make one shape.
- Compare yours with other people's shapes. Are any the same?

The advantage of geostrips is that you can easily change the angles, while keeping the same arrangement of side lengths. Two children with the same geostrips can make different shapes, turning a rectangle into another parallelogram that is not a rectangle, for instance. (In some cases this is trickier: 'Can you change a kite into something else, for instance?') (see Figure 3.13.)

Children should now be encouraged to discuss what 'the same' means. Children may debate whether differently sized versions of the same shape are allowed, or whether the same shape in different orientations is really the same or not. This involves them in ideas of similarity and congruence. Shapes are similar if they are identical in all but size (for example, all squares are similar, all spheres are similar). Congruence is a special case of similarity in that both the size and shape are identical.

• Keep one example of each shape and then make some different ones.

There will probably be discussions about some non-examples: open shapes with four sides, for example. Definitions and rules about allowing or not allowing variations will have to be agreed.

• What counts as a quadrilateral?'

The justifications put forward in this kind of discussion are very valuable and may be quite sophisticated, involving issues of what a side or a shape means (see Figure 3.14).

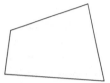

Figure 3.14 These shapes are made from four geostrips. Are they quadrilaterals?

In the case of the kite (see Figure 3.15), is an arrowhead a different shape, or just a special kind of kite? Does a kite have to be something you can fly, or is the mathematical meaning different? The important issue for the children's learning is the reasoning involved about the relationship between properties and the appreciation of the need for a consistent definition. With the arrowhead, the discussion will focus on acute and obtuse angles and whether having obtuse angles stops a shape from being a kite. Kites are usually considered to be shapes with two pairs of adjacent equal sides giving one axis of symmetry, so an arrowhead can be considered a special kind of kite.

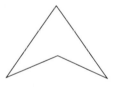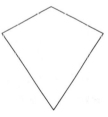

Figure 3.15 A kite is a quadrilateral with two adjacent pairs of sides equal in length

• Check these are different. Now are there any more possibilities?

This requires children to imagine examples and calls on skills of visualising and logical thinking about what might be possible.

• Can you find a way of checking that you have them all?

Developing a system for checking requires more logical thinking; children may vary the angles within one shape at a time. This means keeping one property fixed (the relationship between the length of the sides) and systematically varying another (the angles). This is an important way of thinking mathematically.

• Decide on a way of making groups of shapes that go together, and label your collection.

Depending on their experience, children may classify shapes according to a range of properties – shapes which:

- remind you of shapes in the environment, for example house shapes;
- have one or more axes of symmetry;
- have right angles;
- have angles larger or smaller than right angles – obtuse or acute angles;
- have pairs of parallel sides;
- have pairs of equal sides.

Older children can be asked to make some rules for other groups to identify as true or false, along the lines of:

- All quadrilaterals with an axis of symmetry …
- You cannot make a shape with parallel sides with …

If children are challenged to explain why statements are true then they are encouraged to reason mathematically and to provide arguments which may verge on proof. This kind of investigation can result in the children discovering some important geometrical relationships. In working with shapes made out of geostrips children can observe what changes and what stays the same. For example, 'However I change the angles of my parallelogram, opposite angles remain the same! However I change the angles of my kite, the long diagonal cuts the short diagonal in half.'

To ensure that children focus on relationships involving one particular property, the activity must be structured more tightly: '*How many different four-sided shapes with at least one axis of symmetry can you make?*' (see Figure 3.16). The children can be invited to classify the shapes by being provided with large sheets of paper and some labels for one axis of symmetry, two axes of symmetry, no axes of symmetry (see Figure 3.17). Or the children may record their shapes by drawing, cutting them out of paper, or making them with straws.

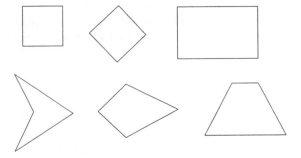

Figure 3.16 Shapes with at least one axis of symmetry

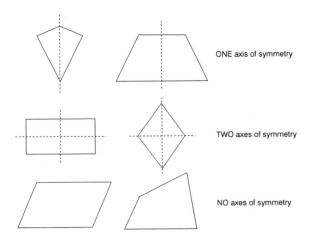

Figure 3.17 Classifying shapes

Children can make squares, rhombuses, rectangles, kites, arrowheads and trapezia, discovering which ones can be made from each other by changing the angles.

Does changing the angles of a shape affect the number of lines of symmetry? It is intriguing that, no matter how hard you try, it is impossible to turn the kite into an asymmetrical shape by altering the angles, whereas a rectangle surprisingly turns into a parallelogram without any axis of symmetry. Structuring the activity in this way will make it more likely that children will discuss relationships between properties like symmetry and pairs of equal sides. There is likely to be discussion about whether any parallelogram has an axis of symmetry, and it is useful to have some mirrors available. Children might go on to investigate shapes with rotational symmetry. Other questions are:

- How many different quadrilaterals can you make with at least:
  - One pair of sides parallel?
  - One pair of equal sides?

Other variations

Similar activities can be carried out with other apparatus. In all these examples, the way the activity is started and maintained will be the same, and similar issues will arise.

Take a three by three nailboard or geoboard.

- How many different triangles can you make?

The same activity could be done by drawing on dotty paper. Resulting triangles may be:

- ones that are the same but different sizes – similar shapes;
- ones that are identical but in different positions – congruent shapes;
- shapes which are reflections of each other – congruent shapes;
- shapes which are rotations of each other – congruent shapes.

With pentominoes (five squares joined edge to edge, see Figure 3.18) issues will arise about:

- shapes which are reflections of each other;
- shapes which are rotations of each other;

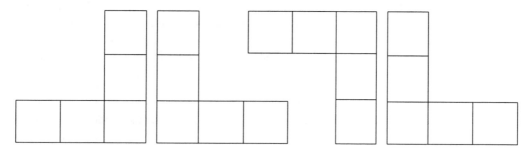

Figure 3.18 Children need to discuss whether they will consider these shapes, made with five squares, to be 'the same'

- systematic checking by fixing four squares then moving one square.

- How many different shapes can you make with two identical shapes? (for example, two squares, two equilateral triangles).

Or children could be invited to make 3-D shapes out of:

- five Multilink;
- six Polydron or Clixi pieces of various shapes;
- a number of straws.

The teacher needs to be aware of the mathematical relationships which children might discover from the activity and also the issues about definitions of shapes; some conventions are more universal than others, and definitions vary. It is generally agreed that a square is a kind of rectangle and both are kinds of parallelogram. The Glossary at the end of Section 3.2 will help.

Guess my rule

When children have had experience of making and classifying 2-D or 3-D shapes, they can play a guessing game using labels they have written for sets of shapes. For a collection of 3-D shapes, such labels might be:

- six faces;
- some triangular faces;
- one plane of symmetry;
- parallel faces;
- all right angles;
- all acute angles.

One person has a set ring and secretly selects a label for the set. Other people take it in turns to choose a shape, and the first person must say whether it goes in the set or out. Gradually there emerges a group of shapes in the set, and a group outside the set, which children can examine for similarities and use to guide their choice of the next shape to offer. When it is their turn to offer a shape, they can then guess what is on the label for the set. When children have played this game a few times, they may want to write other labels and make up their own rules for the sets. The issue that emerges is the need for precision in doing this. For instance does 'square faces' mean all faces, or more than one face, or at least one face square?

Activity 5: What is my rule? Making patterns

Transformations by translation, reflection and rotation; making and describing patterns

Patterns can be observed in the natural or built environment, and in the creations of many cultures, so this kind of activity can be linked to many areas of the curriculum. A pattern in mathematical terms is not just an arrangement of shapes and lines, but must have some rule governing it so that it can continue indefinitely. If children are asked to analyse patterns, then an absorbing aesthetic and creative activity becomes also a logical and mathematical one, involving articulating mathematical rules and identifying shapes, positions and transformations.

To copy patterns, and continue them as in Figure 3.19, children must analyse the rule that governs the pattern's construction, even if they do this intuitively. The simplest kind of pattern is one that repeats in a linear fashion, by adding on in one direction only. This is sometimes called an AB pattern, with two elements A and B, making up the basic element AB which is repeated (ABABAB …). This can be made more complex by having more elements, as in an ABC or an ABCD pattern, or elements may be repeated within the unit: ABB, ABB, ABB. They become more complex again if the unit is not just repeated, but increased in some way, perhaps by adding on one element each time or doubling:

AB, ABC, ABCD, ABCDE
AB, AABB, AAABBB, AAAABBBB
AB, AABB, AAAABBBB, AAAAAAAABBBBBBBB

Patterns become more complex if they are not just linear, but grow in different directions at once. The simplest way of doing this is to just surround an arrangement, but a variety of rules may be created by children.

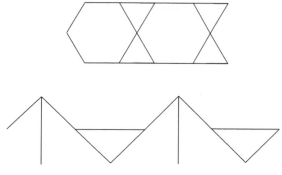

Figure 3.19 Copy and continue these patterns

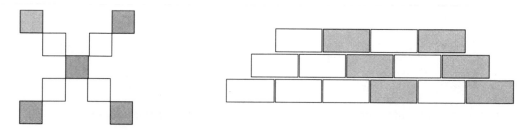

Figure 3.20 Growing patterns according to rules

- Make an arrangement with a few squares. Now grow your pattern, by adding on a few more squares.
- How did you know where to put them?
- Can you add some more to make your shape grow, keeping to the same rule for adding on each time.
- See if you can write down your rule (see Figure 3.20).

- Can your friend continue your pattern?
- Can they say what your rule is?

They may say something like:

- Your rule is that you join onto the outer corners each time; or
- You add one onto each row on the right each time.

Using different colours for each stage is a useful way of identifying these. Children may discover alternative rules for the same pattern. Obviously this can be done with a variety of shapes, and in 3-D as well as 2-D.

Interesting number patterns can be discovered (see Section 2.5, growing shapes case study).

Transformations

One kind of rule that is often used to create a pattern involves moving a figure in a regular way, by reflecting, rotating or translating (sliding). These kinds of movements or transformations can be found in various combinations in patterns from many cultures. Young children will often intuitively use reflections when arranging shapes, so the resulting patterns have one or more axes of reflective symmetry. Rotations and translations are easily created by printing.

- Stick some string onto pieces of card in the shape of some letters.
- Can you make a pattern for some wrapping paper, so that the pattern could continue indefinitely? (see Figure 3.21).

More about transformations can be found at the end of Section 3.2.

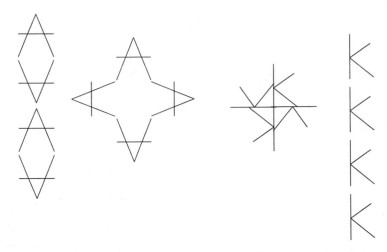

Figure 3.21 Patterns made by reflecting, rotating or translating a simple basic shape

Tiling patterns

Fitting shapes together, so that they will cover a surface indefinitely with the same pattern, will form a tiling.

- Make some different tiling patterns with rectangles. Describe the rules for the different patterns (see Figure 3.22).
- Try making other tiling patterns just using one polygon, regular or irregular. Or you can use two polygons (see Figure 3.23).

- Again, children can continue each others' patterns. The placing of the shapes should follow a regular pattern so that it is clear that the tiling could be extended indefinitely. Older children can investigate what is going on with the angles at the meeting point or vertex of the tiling.

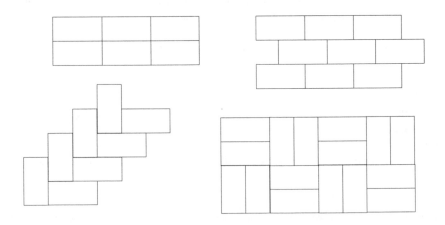

Figure 3.22 Could you describe, over the telephone, how to fit the shapes together?

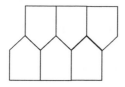
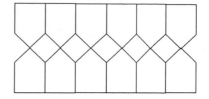

Figure 3.23 Tiling of irregular pentagons and of irregular pentagons with squares

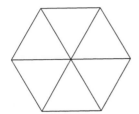
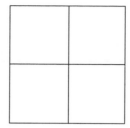

Figure 3.24 Focusing on the points at which shapes meet

Why do some polygons fit together round a point? Why do some polygons not fit together (see Figure 3.24).

- This can lead to discussions about angles. If children know that the angles round a point make 360° (or that four 90° angles fit together) they can work out the size of the angles of other shapes, from the number of them meeting at a vertex in a tiling. They may notice combinations of angles which together make straight lines, so the angles add up to 180°. They can also reason that in order for identical regular polygons to make an edge to edge tiling on their own, their angles must be factors of 360 (such tiling patterns are known as regular tessellations) and they can go on to test this generalisation.
- Children can also make patterns using computer software now widely available on the internet (such as Shodor Interactive: look for 'Tessellate!').

Activity 6: Using ICT

Constructing 2-D shapes; transformations by translation, reflection and rotation; visualising; angle as a measure of turn

Logo is a computer program based on a cursor in the shape of a turtle, moving around the screen. The children enter instructions to turn the turtle and move the turtle forward drawing a line. There is a natural progression in the precision and complexity of the instructions needed from:

- the children playing at being robots using their own bodies to move around in response to instructions;
- using robotic toys which move around on the floor or table;
- working with the computer program.

In all three activities the children need to reason to work out what instructions will give the desired effect and to give sufficiently precise instructions. Working in small groups with IT encourages them to articulate their reasoning to convince each other of what to do.

Playing robots

This activity works well in the hall or playground. One child acts as the 'robot' and a second child gives instructions.

• The robot comes from the factory able to understand simple instructions like turn left, turn right, forward five, back three steps.
• Can you give instructions to the robot to walk round a skittle to a bench?

The instructions will have to be more precise if the robot is sufficiently trusting to shut their eyes!

Robotic toys

There are several robotic toys available which can be programmed to move around in response to instructions.

These include Roamer (Valiant Technology) and BeeBot (TTS Group). Children, working in small groups, can program the Roamer or BeeBot to move around obstacles or to trace out shapes on the floor. There is immediate feedback; if the children's estimates of distance and angle are not accurate, the robot will not do what they expect. An example using Roamer might be:

• Can you program the Roamer to follow a roadway?

Children can make roadways or mazes for the Roamer with chalk or masking tape. They can then challenge other groups to program the Roamer to follow their route. This is best done if the children decide on the set of instructions for their route, then map out the roadway to follow the actual path of the Roamer. This is because the Roamer will only move in whole units, and the roadway needs to use these too. If the roadway is quite wide this allows some leeway for estimating angles. Inexperienced children will need to put in one or two instructions at a time, then adjust the next accordingly, but later they can be challenged to write all the instructions in one go.

Using Logo on the computer

The transition to typing instruction to the computer follows naturally from the work with robots (see Figure 3.25):

• FD 200 – forward 200 units;
• RT 90 – turn right through 90 degrees;
• FD 200 RT 90 FD 50 RT 90 FD 50 … will begin to draw a castle.

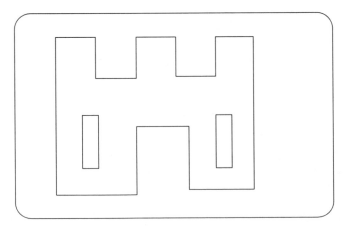

Figure 3.25 Using Logo

Logo is widely available in schools, and free versions are available on the internet. A great deal of useful mathematical activity can be based on a small set of instructions. As well as direct instructions such as the FD, BK, and RT mentioned above, there is a repeat instruction. REPEAT 3 [FD 40 RT 120] will repeat three times the instructions in the square brackets, to draw an equilateral triangle.

It is possible for the children to teach the computer a new word. So if the children would like the computer to draw a castle whenever they type in the word CASTLE, they can do this by entering the full set of instructions for a castle.

If children have decided what to draw for themselves, they will be more committed in trying to solve problems they come across. Once children have created a program for a simple shape, they can draw it in different positions on the screen, or rotate the shape and so create patterns (see Figure 3.26).

Children will gain much in terms of discussion from working in twos or threes, but the teacher needs to monitor interaction. A chair labelled HOT SEAT and a convention that only the child in this seat can type in instructions can be a useful organisational device.

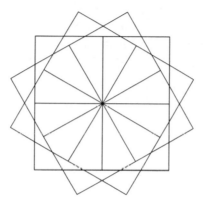

Figure 3.26 Different patterns

Activity 7: Body maths

Angle as a measure of turn: right angles, quarter and half turns; degrees and appropriate terms (for example, 'acute', 'obtuse')

There is something very powerful and memorable about using your own body to act out a mathematical situation. Possibilities arise when working on many different aspects of mathematics. Some examples are given here but many more activities involving position and movement can be acted out in a similar way. For instance, young children can walk in circles or triangles in different ways, then later relate this to the idea of rotating through 360° in conjunction with work on Logo, as discussed previously.

Reflection

When the children are working in the hall, a line is marked out on the floor as a mirror. One child stands a pace in front of the 'mirror' and slowly moves an arm or a leg. Another child acts as the mirror image and follows the movement. The teacher can ask the child in front of the mirror:

- Move back one step.
- Move to the left two steps.
- What must the image do?

Once the ideas have been explored the children can work in pairs to develop a slow dance type movement.

Rotation

Using a compass the children can find which direction is North in their classroom. With all the children standing up facing north, the teacher can give a series of instructions.

- Turn 90 degrees clockwise.
- Turn 90 degrees clockwise again.
- What compass direction are you facing in now?

If a swivel chair is available, the fundamental idea of angle as an amount of turn can be explored by having a child sitting in the chair with an arm outstretched. The rest of the class can imagine looking down from the ceiling and decide what angle has been moved through from north, or a fixed point. This can help to link the familiar idea of turning with the abstract drawing of two lines which is used to represent angle in books.

In tests of spatial understanding, many children said that the first angle in Figure 3.27 was larger than the second. This misconception seems to be based on paying attention to the length of the lines rather than the amount of the turn. Activities which emphasise the physical turning through an angle, with the lines used to show the starting direction and the final direction, can help to avoid this misconception and will also be helpful at a later stage when children are learning to use a protractor.

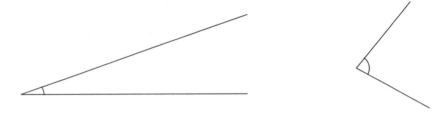

Figure 3.27 Which angle is larger?

Glossary

This section is intended as a reference for teachers, to support subject knowledge and underpin planning, and not all the terms need to be used directly with children.

Polygon: poly (many) gon (angle) is a plane (flat) shape formed by straight lines. Some of these have been given special names, but it is possible to describe them all by the number of their sides: TRIangle, QUADrilateral, PENTagon, HEXagon, HEPTagon (or septagon), OCTagon, NONagon, DECagon, HENDEcagon (or undecagon), DODECagon ...

Polygons which have all sides and all angles equal are called *regular* polygons (see Figure 3.28). Polygons which have all sides equal but different angles are not regular, nor are polygons with all angles equal but different length sides. It is important that children do meet irregular shapes.

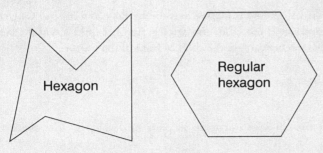

Figure 3.28 Irregular and regular hexagon

Triangles may be classified by means of equality of sides:

- equilateral – all sides equal;
- isosceles – two sides equal;
- scalene – no sides equal;

or by the size of the largest angle:

- right angled – 90°;
- acute angled – less than 90°;
- obtuse angled – more than 90°.

Quadrilaterals are four sided shapes: they may be classified by means of parallel or equal sides and right angles:

- *square* – a regular quadrilateral;
- *rectangle* – a quadrilateral whose interior angles are right angles;
- *oblong* – a rectangle with one pair of sides longer than the other;
- *rhombus* – a quadrilateral with four equal sides;
- *trapezium* – a quadrilateral with a pair of parallel sides (isosceles trapezium if the other two sides are of equal length);
- *parallelogram* – a quadrilateral with two pairs of parallel sides;
- *kite* – a quadrilateral with two pairs of adjacent equal sides;

Notice that the definitions *include* special cases: a square has four equal sides and so a square is a rhombus; a square has two pairs of opposite sides parallel and so a square *is* a parallelogram.

Congruence: is the idea of shapes being identical, despite being in different orientations. They are the same shape and size, so that one will fit exactly on top of the other.

Similarity: refers to shapes which are the same, i.e. have the same angles and whose corresponding sides are in the same ratio to each other, although the shapes may be of different sizes, for example, a 16 cm by 10 cm rectangle and an 8 cm by 5 cm rectangle are similar (see Figure 3.29).

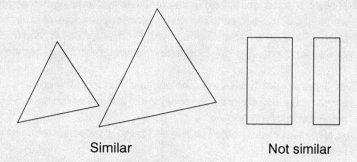

Similar   Not similar

Figure 3.29 Similar shapes have sides in the same ratio

Polyiamond: is used to describe flat shapes that are made by joining a certain number of equilateral triangles edge to edge. A diamond is formed from two equilateral triangles (this is a rhombus with angles of 60 and 120). A tetriamond is made of four equilateral triangles joined edge to edge. Some tetriamonds are the nets of a regular tetrahedron.

Polyomino: is used to describe flat shapes that are made by joining a certain number of squares edge to edge. A domino is an oblong with sides in the ratio 2:1, there are 12 different pentominoes (5 squares), the nets for a cube are hexominoes.

Polyhedron: poly (many) hedron (face) *(plural:* polyhedra). A polyhedron is a solid or three dimensional shape with plane (flat) faces, each of which is a polygon. Faces meet at an edge, and edges meet at a vertex *(plural:* vertices). A common error is to use names for plane shapes to describe solids (for example, calling a cube, a square).

- *Cuboid* – a solid whose plane faces are all rectangles. A **cube** is a special cuboid with square faces.
- *Prism* – a polyhedron whose cross section parallel to its end faces is the same as (that is, congruent to) both end faces. Toblerone packets are useful examples of triangular prisms. Cuboids are rectangular prisms. Prisms are good for making sandwiches because their slices are all the same size.
- *Pyramid* – a polyhedron with triangular side faces meeting at a point. Cross sections parallel to the base are the same shape as the base but of diminishing size (i.e. similar). The base can be any polygon.
- A *regular polyhedron* is one whose faces are regular polygons and whose vertices are all identical. There are five regular polyhedra, known as the **Platonic** solids: regular tetrahedron (4 equilateral triangles), regular octahedron (8 equilateral triangles), regular icosahedron (20 equilateral triangles), cube (6 squares), and regular dodecahedron (12 regular pentagons).

Coordinates: coordinates are used to specify locations. A common use is in map references, as in a street finder, where a page is divided into squares which are numbered vertically and given letters horizontally, resulting in references like BQ37. Children can be introduced to these ideas by placing pictures of coloured objects on a two-way grid, so that objects match in rows and colours match in columns. Later children may play games of find the treasure' with invented maps of treasure islands. Such work will link strongly with geography, leading to the use of maps such as those produced by the Ordnance Survey, which have numbered scales along two axes, so that numbers refer to lines, not squares. This allows for the intervals between lines to be subdivided into ten, in effect dividing each square into a hundred small squares so that more precise locations can be identified with a six figure reference.

There is a variety of computer software which practises the use of coordinates, such as the Primary National Strategy's Interactive Teaching Program, Coordinates available from the PNS website www.standards.dfes.gov.uk/primary/teachingresources/mathematics/nns_itps/coordinates/.

Children can also use coordinates to name points which form the corners of 2-D shapes.

Coordinates can be used to describe the positions of shapes which have been transformed; for instance, by reflection or rotation.

Children can also meet coordinates in advanced Logo work when required to set x and set y to make sprites.

Coordinates are used in four quadrants when scales are extended to include negative numbers on both axes.

Transformations: are different kinds of movement applied to a plane figure.

- *Translation* is movement without turning. Children make translation patterns for themselves when they do potato prints or stencil patterns. They can find these repeating patterns in fabrics, wallpaper or wrapping paper.
- *Reflection* is movement by reflecting as in a mirror. A shape is said to have reflective symmetry if it can be folded along a line of symmetry. When folded one half is seen to fit

exactly on the other half. Viewed in the mirror, the reflected half looks exactly the same as the half obscured by the mirror, so the picture looks complete. Some shapes have more than one line of symmetry.

- *Rotation* is turning about a fixed point. All shapes can be rotated through an angle of 360° to fit upon themselves. A shape is said to have rotational symmetry if it fits upon itself when rotated through a smaller angle. A half turn of 180° will fit the letter S upon itself. A square fits on itself four times as it is rotated, so it has rotational symmetry of order 4.
- *Enlargement:* translations, reflections and rotations all leave the size of the shape unaltered. Enlargement is the term used to describe a change in the size but not in the shape, in other words, enlargement always results in a similar shape. A photocopier can be used to make enlargements of any picture or shape. An enlargement, scale factor 2 is made by doubling all the lengths of a shape.
- *Tessellation/tiling:* the pattern created when shapes are used to cover the plane without leaving any gaps. A regular *tessellation* is formed when a single regular polygon is used edge to edge to cover the plane; there are just three regular tessellations (equilateral triangle, square and regular hexagon). A *semi-regular* tessellation is formed when more than one regular polygon can be used in such a way that the arrangement of polygons about each vertex (or meeting point) of the tiling pattern is identical (for example, octagons and squares).

3.3 MEASUREMENT: GENERAL PRINCIPLES

Introduction

Measurement is an aspect of the mathematics curriculum which can easily be seen to be 'useful' in everyday life. Packaged food is labelled by cost per pound or kilogramme. Measurement is used to work out how much paper and paint will be needed to decorate a room, and working days, journeys and so on, are organised around the measurement of time. Sometimes measurements are gauged roughly based on estimation, as in knowing that a cupboard which fits in one space will definitely fit another because it is obvious, by eye, that the second space is bigger. Sometimes it is not quite so clear, and so appropriate approximation using a piece of string held up against the cupboard and the new space, in turn, will show whether there will be a fit. Where a snug fit is required, it might be necessary to use a standard measuring tool which gives a clear numerical comparison and has small enough subdivisions to make fine distinctions easier. There is a range of approaches to comparison, on which it is helpful to draw in suiting the purpose. All depend on a feeling for measure.

In our society both metric and Imperial systems of measure operate, and this is something to be borne in mind in teaching children. Adults may feel more comfortable in expressing body measures (weight, height, etc.) in Imperial measures while getting used to buying petrol in litres, and shops are required to mark food packaging in metric measures. There will need to be recognition of these two systems in work with children but, generally, the metric system is the main focus for work in the classroom. Imperial measures are discussed where they arise naturally from children's experience, for example in comparing height in the two systems.

Developing in children a 'feel for measure', an understanding of the use of standard measures and experience in interpreting different systems of measure is what this section addresses. The case study offers a view of a measures in a problem-solving situation.

At the Foundation Stage and Key Stage 1 the main aspects to be taught are comparison, the use of common non-standard and standard units of measure (for example, length, mass, capacity), choice of appropriate measuring equipment and reading of scales. In addition children need to be taught the relevant vocabulary for measure.

At Key Stage 2 children should understand the need for standard units of measure. Progression is addressed by a greater emphasis on the choice and use of standard units of measure, sensible estimating in contexts, deeper understanding of relationships and conversions between units, and some knowledge of approximate metric/Imperial measures. They should be able to choose and use instruments and read scales to an appropriate level of accuracy. Understanding of number is important in supporting the interpretation of numerical readings and in aspects such as rounding to the nearest unit. In addition children at this stage will work on perimeter and areas, including the use of formulae developed from counting squares in rectangles.

Standard and non-standard measures

Comparison and ordering

In most texts for teachers, a progression of children's learning in measurement is outlined. It is suggested that children develop from direct comparison (such as standing back to back to see who is taller) to indirect comparison using non-standard units (Foundation Stage and Key Stage 1) (such as finding out how many hand spans tall child A and B are and comparing through counting the hand spans) and then on to the use of standard units of measure (Key Stage 2), also indirect, but this time heights are compared through metres and centimetres or feet and inches. It might appear that more formal methods of measure are more advanced and therefore more correct but sometimes direct comparisons and non-standard units are actually more appropriate. For example, in cooking at home, the size of small cakes is compared by eye, while in a factory an exact weight of cake mixture is measured out.

The key point here is that different degrees of formality are used according to context, and children need to build up confidence in making decisions about the best approach in a given situation. In setting up a task children can be offered a range of materials, including standard measures, and, by observation of how they are used, the teacher can assess what children know already and what should be taught next. In this way children are using and applying their developing mathematical knowledge and skills in context and developing understanding that appropriate choices need to be made and justified in solving problems.

To help children understand that units need to be equal to make comparison fair, tasks can be set up where children are offered a variety of units (for example, pencils of different length for measuring length compared with uniform length felt tip pens) and two groups can be asked to measure the same object, both with pencils and with pens. As they record results they should be able to see that the pens give groups the same result but the pencils are less likely to. The teacher will need to structure questions carefully to encourage reasoning:

- Why did you get 15 pencils and eight pens for the length?
- Why did this group get 10 pencils and you got 12 pencils?
- Which is better to measure with and why?

Through children's responses the teacher will be able to judge understanding and plan appropriate work to extend it. Do they need more of this kind of experience to build generalised views, or do they seem to understand that the uniform unit is more helpful in communication with others?

It would be reasonable to expect that many children at the Foundation Stage and Key Stage 1 will tend to use comparison to tackle measurement tasks. For example, in response to the question 'How can we find out who is the tallest?', they are likely to suggest standing next to one another. However, they will also have had the experience of being weighed and will be aware of tools such as tape measures. In allowing them to try to use such standard measures and interpret information from them, the teacher can look out for understanding. With the tape measure, for example, a child might hold it up against the object to be measured but not know about the meaning of the numbers or where to start counting from. The intervention here might be to set up tasks involving making rulers with

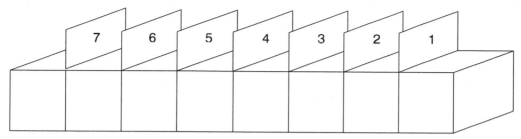

Figure 3.30 Unifix with markers

Unifix cubes and labelling with numbers to help understanding of the tape or rules as a strip of units stuck together (see Figure 3.30).

Calibration

At Key Stage 2 children can develop their understanding of calibration by making calibrated containers to measure capacity. A transparent cup can be marked at each successive addition of an eggcupful of

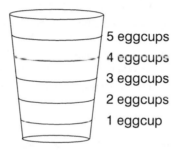

5 eggcups
4 eggcups
3 eggcups
2 eggcups
1 eggcup

Figure 3.31 Calibrated cup

water for example, and then used to measure the capacity of other containers (see Figure 3.31). This can then be compared with a standard measure such as a 500 millilitre container, and understanding can be helped by discussing how many 1 millilitre containers would be needed to fill it.

Relationships between standard units can be explored by such activities as pouring 1 millilitre containerfuls into a 10 millilitre container and so on up the scale, getting children to predict how many they think they will use. Similarly, children can place centimetre length strips along a decimetre, and

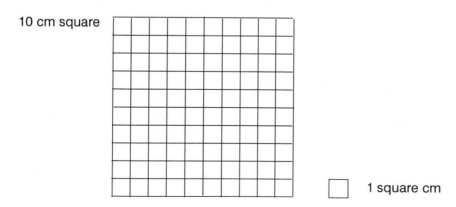

10 cm square

1 square cm

Figure 3.32 Matching smaller units to larger

decimetres along a metre, to see that 10 cm = 1 dm and 10 dm = 1m. For area, children can compare 1 square centimetre of paper with a 10 centimetre square (see Figure 3.32) and a 10 centimetre square with a metre square. With volume, a metre cube (skeletal) can be made with lengths of dowelling, and children can be challenged to work out how many centimetre cubes would fit along one side, across one face and in the whole cube.

The names of the units can be analysed for meaning in helping to see the relationships. There is usually a base unit (metre, litre) on which subdivisions and multiples are based. Latin words are used to denote the subdivisions and Greek words the multiples. So for capacity, litre is the base unit, millilitres (thousandth of a litre) are the usual subdivisions. There are also centilitre (hundredth) and decilitre (tenth). For measure of distance this is also the kilometre (a thousand metres).

With grammes, there are multiples: hectogramme (one hundred grammes) and kilogramme (one thousand grammes). There are also subdivisions: centigramme (one hundredth of a gramme) and milligramme (one thousandth of a gramme). The usual prefixes and their values are as follows:

- milli – one thousandth;
- centi – one hundredth;
- deci – one tenth;
- deca – ten;
- hecto – one hundred;
- kilo – one thousand.

Children can be encouraged to make their own posters or dictionaries giving examples and explanations, and these can be used as classroom references. There are also published mathematical dictionaries for the same purpose. The metric system is underpinned by the place value (base 10) system, and as such, provides a valuable context to reinforce number understanding. Making links between different areas of mathematics can help children's mathematical development. The history of measures is a rich source of investigation; for example, finding out where measures such as feet and inches came from.

Choosing appropriate standard measures

At Key Stage 1, children should begin to be taught to both use and estimate with standard units. In general the base unit such as the metre or litre are given as starting points, and children are asked to find things which measure 'about the same as', 'more' or 'less' than it. Subsequently, the unit is halved (half metre or half litre) and similar exercises are suggested. In both steps children can be encouraged to make collections for a display of objects which can be thus sorted. With weighing, use of the gramme presents problems because it is difficult to find simple balances which can accurately differentiate with such small amounts, and so the first standard weight might be a 100 gramme weight and, using the appropriate prefix for 100, named a hectogramme or hecto. Similarly in other measures it is often suggested that interim measures, not commonly used in 'real life' can be introduced to help children deal with subdivisions (for fractional parts) in steps matching number size more accessible to them. For example, in tackling length, children can move from body measures to the metre, then the half metre (by folding in half) and the quarter metre, and then on to the decimetre (ten in one metre), allowing a smaller subdivision but still dealing with numbers accessible to most Key Stage 1 children. Finally, the centimetre can be introduced as a smaller part of the decimetre, followed by the millimetre.

The last two (centimetre and millimetre) have usually been introduced in Key Stage 2 but there will be overlap where children are able to deal with the numbers involved, have experience of measuring and see the need for them. Children might for example become interested in the relationship between centimetres and millimetres from looking at rulers in the classroom. At each stage, objects in the environment can be compared with the measure so children develop a feel for the measure in relation to familiar objects. As children need to use measure and finer comparisons are required, say in science activities, the subdivisions are seen to be necessary.

Use and interpretation of measuring tools

There is a wide variety of tools for measurement, the use of which require understanding and skills. The examples which follow illustrate common difficulties which might arise.

A ruler can be used to measure length and children need to understand the nature of what they are measuring (length), how to line up the ruler and how to interpret the number read from the scale. A child might be helped by making their own ruler based on units used to measure, for example, a ruler based on footprints (see Figure 3.33).

Figure 3.33 Foot ruler

Using this to measure in the classroom and discussing the results could then lead into discussion of other rulers and how to measure in centimetres. Centimetre squares could be offered singly to be built up into a strip, if necessary, and then the strip compared with a school ruler.

Another problem with reading linear scales is in reading measures between marked points. This is an area which children will need to discuss in the context of practical tasks, such as reading the temperature from a thermometer in science lessons. Reading values between marked points also links with fractions and decimals.

Weighing scales present this difficulty, too. They can also cause difficulty because they show weight (unseen) as a point on a scale. Spring balances, where children can see the object being pulled down and a marker on a scale moving at the same time, can help.

Another measuring tool commonly used in primary schools which needs careful introduction and monitoring is the trundle wheel. To demonstrate that one turn of the wheel measures one metre, paint can be applied (if the wheel is made of suitable material) and a line printed on paper, which can then be compared to a metre stick. Alternatively, string can be cut to the length of the wheel's circumference (a bit fiddly!) and again compared. Then the wheel can be moved and stopped at each click, asking children, '*How many metres have we gone now?*'

With all these potentially tricky areas, the key is not to avoid or attempt all instruction prior to use of the tools but to set up tasks which require their use and involve the children in making sense of the results they obtain. Children should be encouraged to estimate measurements, and to give measurements to an appropriate degree of accuracy. A sense of measurement using both Imperial and metric units can be fostered by encouraging children to use both systems in a range of contexts. In addition digital displays can be introduced so that different readings can be compared, for example with digital and analogue clocks or for comparing a reading of 250g with how that would look on a linear scale.

Estimating

In measuring, judgements are made about closeness, according to purpose. '*Does this shirt fit?*' '*Am I going to be able to get this armchair through the door?*' Estimation often appears in teacher resource books as a natural part of measurement work and children are routinely asked to estimate, or to make a good guess at the result, before actually measuring to check. Children may not be clear about the point of estimation in this situation and are often reluctant to make estimates which are immediately shown to be inaccurate. If we are clear that estimation is about developing a feel and sense about measures, similar to a feel for number, then the point of estimation will be clearer to children. Estimation, in practice, is likely to relate to rough calculations prior to more careful planning and measuring such as costing a carpet roughly on rounded measures before carpet fitters measure more accurately to cut and fit the carpet. Estimation and a feel for measure also play a part in rule of thumb conversions between different systems, for example, a bag of sugar is about 1 kilogramme or 2 pounds if you want a base for comparison.

To help children develop estimations based on experience, the teacher could ask children to predict whether an object will take more or less (handspans, conkers, cupfuls …) based on a task they have just completed. Then later they can be asked, 'How many more (or less) do you think it will be?' With standard units, games can be devised to develop estimating skills. A set of objects can be made for weighing (for example, 50 g up to 100 g). Two players each select an object and estimate the weight. Write estimates down. Weigh the objects and take counters to represent each 10 g you were out by. Count up the counters when all objects are weighed, and the winner is the one with the least counters. Similar games can be set up for other aspects such as length (varying lengths of ribbon are good for this). To extend to larger fixed objects such as 'height of the door', children can have cards illustrating the objects to select but measure the objects in situ (see Figure 3.34).

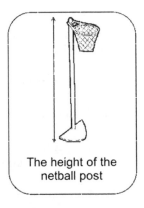 is about the same length as

The height of the netball post

The width of our classroom window

Figure 3.34 Estimation games. The children select from a set of cards showing objects around their school

Assessing for starting points

To make an assessment of children's understanding of a particular measure on beginning a new topic, there are tasks which can be presented to children with a choice of possible ways to solve them. The methods children use can give the teacher evidence of understanding and allow planning for extension of learning. It is also important to bear in mind possible misconceptions that may need to be addressed, for example:

- the bigger an object, the heavier it is;
- the taller a container, the greater its capacity (regardless of the width).

The teacher can prepare a set of objects to be compared. For length, these might be objects (curved as well as straight) such as ribbons, sticks, pencils and scissors. For weighing, a set of parcels could be made, different sizes and masses, some 'tricky', for example, large but light or small but heavy. For capacity, a set of containers can be collected. Depending on the age and confidence of the children the number of objects could be from three to six.

The teacher asks the children to say which one they think is longest (holds the most, is heaviest, etc.) and why they think that. They should then be asked how they could check, and offered a variety of material to choose from, including non-standard and standard methods. For example, for length, rulers, tape measures, or string could be offered. Some children might choose to make a direct comparison with pairs of objects and order the objects, from different pairings. If children are stuck the teacher could make suggestions, 'Could you use this to help?' The approaches used by children can be observed in gathering evidence for assessment to inform planning of the next step. Similarly, for weight and capacity, standard and non-standard units and tools can be available and the teacher can analyse what children select and how they use it.

3.4 ASPECTS OF MEASUREMENT

For each of these aspects of measurement key concepts and potential misconceptions will be identified together with sample activities for the Foundation Stage, and Key Stages 1 and 2.

Length

'Length is the distance between the ends of an object, along it' (ILEA 1976: Checkpoints Cards, Length Card 1). The concept of length can be difficult if the object is flexible, and children might feel a ribbon is a different length extended than it would be rolled up.

From Piaget's work comes observation of children's perception that the length of an object can be altered by a change in its position (see Figure 3.35).

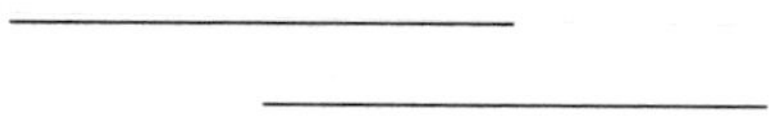

Figure 3.35 Are these lines the same length?

It would appear that children look at the ends of the lines rather than at the lines as a whole. Concentrating on the ends of the lines also encourages some children to say that the lines in Figure 3.36 are the same length.

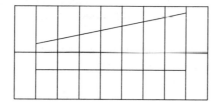

Figure 3.36 (from Dickson, Brown and Gibson, 1984)

The idea of the distance (between two points) can also be difficult because instead of an object to compare there is a space to be filled. Children need experience of measuring both lengths of objects (curved as well as straight) and distances.

At the Foundation Stage and Key Stage 1 children can compare directly (placing the bear on a bed to see if it is the right size) or use body measures such as feet or hands, material such as sticks, straws or interlocking cubes and will need to line up or fill space with repeated units before being encouraged to see that one unit can be used repeatedly by moving it along. Watching how children use units will reveal whether they understand that units must not overlap or have gaps in between. Metre length sticks or paper strips can be introduced and, again, getting children to place several end to end can show them clearly how many metres long something is before they develop the idea of repeated use of one unit. Half metres and quarters can be obtained from folding paper strips as children become more concerned about 'the bit left over' (this can also be done with hand and feet measures). This allows a practical context for developing the concept of fractions and, with older children, decimals.

The teacher needs to look out for children using fractional terms, or phrases such as 'and a little bit more' or 'not quite', in deciding when it might be helpful to introduce ways to deal with fractions of measures. Decimetre strips (10 centimetres) can be introduced before centimetres and millimetres as children need to make smaller distinctions in measure.

Use of these last two units is most likely to be developed at Key Stage 2 as children will need to be familiar with larger numbers to be able to read and interpret results. This, however, is not to say that no children at Key Stage 1 can use or understand them but that the teacher needs to assess appropriate intervention for children at both stages.

Problems occur with rulers where children are not sure how to line up with the object being measured. Children often read from 1 rather than from 0 or the end of the ruler beyond the calibration. Matching centi-cubes to the spaces on the ruler can help because the child can see that one cube fills the space between two centimetre marks. To match up with the 1 centimetre mark, the cube must be lined up with 0 at the other end. Children can have a selection of strips of 1 centimetre squares or centicubes and be asked to count the squares (cubes) in each case. Then they can be asked to line them up against the ruler to the number they have counted. The teacher can ask them where the end of the strip of squares (cubes) matches the ruler.

The measuring of length will be needed in many technology activities and in science. For example, if children are testing the distance a toy car will reach after rolling from the end of a ramp, they need to find a way of comparing the distances of each after rolling. They may choose to walk out the distance ('It's 80 footsteps'), stretch out lengths of string or use a metre rule. The teacher can observe and discuss the task as they work and make assessments of knowledge and understanding. Older children might be comparing distances of places away from the school. The teacher can discuss with the children how they will approach the task. What will they do if they need to follow curved routes rather than 'as the crow flies'? How will they read the subdivisions on the ruler?

Capacity and volume

Capacity can be thought of as the amount a container holds. It is sometimes referred to as 'internal volume'. A practical example to distinguish between volume and capacity is a drink container in a child's lunch box. Its capacity (internal volume) is how much drink it holds, while its volume (external) is how much space it takes up in the lunch box. In some cases, a Thermos flask for example, the container has thick walls and the capacity is much less than the total volume occupied by the flask. Another way of looking at it is that the drink itself has volume (but needs to be contained to be measured) while the container has capacity.

It is difficult for children to know what volume is, especially in the case of liquids. With sand or plasticine, they can put their hands around it and feel. Looking at the volume of cubes the child has to visualise the building up from smaller cubes and needs also to understand length.

In the Foundation Stage and Key Stage 1, work with capacity (or internal volume) will include practical experience with a variety of containers and a variety of materials to put in the containers, solid and liquid, and also discrete objects such as beans, cubes, conkers. This might be set up in sand or water trays or as story or play contexts, for example, 'How many drinks can you get from this bottle at the teddies' tea party?' Looking at volume (external) can be introduced practically through children's manipulation of material such as plasticine or play dough. Do they realise that they have the same amount even if they change the shape (if none is removed or added)? These discussions can be included as part of the manipulative experience set up for children.

Children can also be encouraged to look at what happens to water levels when objects are immersed. They can be asked to predict which object will make the water 'go up' more. For experience with sand and water, at times the teacher will provide a set of containers to challenge thinking – flat, wide and tall, thin – and see whether children think they have more or less water as they pour from one to the other. Questions about the level of the water, for example, 'Why is the water higher now?' can lead into looking at children's ideas of what is happening.

Harrison (1987) raised an interesting observation with young children when he saw that they seemed to be focusing on fullness rather than capacity. He gave an example of a girl (aged 4) who thought that a cup 'held more' than a teapot. Harrison suggests that she was focusing on the fact that she had just filled the cup. The teacher needs to look out for such phenomena and consider also the language we use. Harrison suggests that since there is not an equivalent to longer, when dealing with the comparison of lengths (for example, 'is capaciouser than'), it is helpful to use phrases such as 'larger/smaller than' or 'can hold more than' in the context of capacity. Children can be asked to take a particular measure (a cup, a litre container or a bottle, for example) and pour it into a set of different containers. They can be asked to look at how far up the water comes and discuss why they think that is. Real life contexts such as the school parties can be used to apply children's estimations and calculations. 'How many bottles of coke will we need? How can we find out? About how many drinks will each person have?'

At Key Stage 2, the range of units should be extended into millilitres and the understanding of the relationship between the units developed through physical experience – 'Find out by pouring how many times you need to empty the centilitre container into the litre to fill it'. The most likely contexts for using these measures will be in other curriculum areas such as science.

To measure the volume of solid shapes, a basic unit is required. The most frequently used unit is the cube with sides of 1 centimetre (1 cm^3): note that a volume of 1 cm^3 has a capacity of 1 millilitre; larger volumes can be measured in cubic metres (1 m^3). The move towards an understanding of the volume of cuboids can be made through building models with cubes. Calculating the volume can be developed through systematic counting of the cubes (one layer has four cubes, there are two layers, and so the volume is eight cubes), leading to repeated addition and multiplication. Children could explore the patterns obtained in the numbers of unit cubes used to make different sized cubes. They could be asked to solve a problem of wrapping 12 gift boxes to be sent through the post, using the smallest amount of paper. The different shapes made from the same number of cubes could be explored, to help develop the concept of conservation of volume. If the volume stays the same what does distinguish one shape from another?

Area

Although this aspect is introduced formally in Key Stage 2, early ideas of area are encountered in covering surfaces; for example, predicting how many sheets of newspaper will be needed to cover the table. Other contexts relevant here are estimating how much wallpaper or carpet is needed in the home corner or in a dolls' house. The language to be developed will involve the amount of material needed for covering and wrapping. Activities could include wrapping parcels, making tablecloths for the home corner or covers for the Three Bears' beds. Conservation of area appears to be grasped later than in learning to measure length and so experiences of cutting up and rearranging shapes could be encouraged well before Key Stage 2 (Gifford 2005).

In this section there is a strong emphasis on practical contexts. However, there are many valuable practical activities in the form of puzzles and problems using mathematical apparatus (for example, geoboards, squared paper, acetate sheets) that are not concerned with practical in the sense of 'everyday'. It is important that children have a strong foundation in number and in geometry, and that they have a secure understanding of mathematical concepts and ideas.

How accurately do we need to know the area of a garden or a wall? There are problems which can be posed, such as calculating the amount of grass seed required to make a lawn, or the number of pots of paint required to decorate the hall, but these are contrived and hypothetical, rather than realistic and practical.

However, the concept of area is not only important in its own right, but also fundamental to a full understanding of:

- multiplication – the idea of a two-dimensional array is a valuable model of multiplication;
- fractions and ratio;
- geometric transformations and operations such as dissection, enlargement, and tessellation;
- higher mathematical ideas such as calculus;
- scientific ideas such as surface tension, pressure, photosynthesis, evaporation.

So area is an important building block in mathematical and scientific development. Whilst accepting that it should be taught meaningfully, it is not always necessary to take a lot of time and trouble concocting practical situations which pretend to contain area. Materials such as transparent grids and geoboards are useful for posing problems involving area. On geoboards ask children to make shapes with a particular area, for example, eight squares. Ask, 'Look at the shapes. Will the perimeter remain the same?' (Geoboards have nails at the points of a square grid, elastic bands are stretched between the nails to make shapes.)

A common misconception is to overgeneralise the correct result that the area of a rectangle is obtained by multiplying the length by the breadth by applying this to all areas regardless of the shape in question. This can be avoided by ensuring that children find the area of many different kinds of shape, including irregular shapes such as leaves, and also insisting that children are precise in their use of mathematical statements, for example, 'The area of a rectangle is length × breadth'.

Perimeter

Perimeter, an aspect of measuring length, is often confused with area. Dickson et al. (1984) suggest that this might be due to early formalisation through the introduction of formulae before children have had sufficient experience of exploring the shapes practically. They suggest activities to show that area can be varied while perimeter stays constant, and vice versa. If a shape has all its sides doubled but retains the same angles, its area will be quadrupled.

Using squared paper or a geoboard the teacher can ask: 'How many shapes can you make from 12 squares?' '*What are the perimeters of those shapes?*' 'How many shapes can you make with a perimeter of 12?' 'Find the area of each of the shapes. Is it always the same?'

The perimeter of a circle is called the circumference. When using trundle wheels, children can be asked to measure the diameter of the wheel and compare this with the circumference. 'Do all trundle wheels have the same diameter?' 'Can you find a cylinder that will roll through 30 centimetres?' 'What is the diameter for a 30 centimetre roll?' By experiment, children can find that the circumference is roughly three times the diameter. The actual ratio is not a rational number (see the Glossary in Section 2.4). The decimal expansion has been shown to go on and on: 3.141592 … The ratio Circumference of circle/Diameter is called π; when measuring, simple approximations such as 3, 3.1 or 3.14 are used according to the degree of accuracy required.

Weight and mass

So far in this section weight has been referred to and a comment for the teacher is needed on its relationship to mass. Weight is a force – the gravitational pull exerted on an object – whereas mass is the amount of matter in an object. The weight, or downward force on an object, can change depending on where the measurement is made. The mass of an object, in contrast, remains the same no matter where the measurement is made. With young children there might seem to be little point in differentiating between the two and there may be more familiarity with the term 'weight'. They will also be engaged in the practical activity of 'weighing'. As work in science develops the distinction can be made in the context of weightlessness in outer space. Here 'weighing' will be used for comparing objects against 'masses of' for example, 100 g, 1 kg.

The difficulty with weight is that it is not visible in the same way that length is. From holding objects, children can feel the pull downwards, and they can see the downward movement of see-saws, bar balances and spring balances. Early ideas about the weight of objects can be influenced by other attributes such as length or shape. In the main, young children will predict that a large box will be heavier than a small one. If children are asked to hold objects they can be encouraged to talk about how they 'feel', but the size of an object can influence how heavy something feels to hold. For example a small, dense object like an iron key might feel heavier than an object which weighs more but spreads more widely over the hand. The pressure on the hand is not evenly spread. This problem can be overcome to some extent by placing objects in bags, held with arms relaxed these can give a clearer sense of the downward pull and make comparing clearer. As previously mentioned, spring balances linked to a linear scale also show this pull. A simpler version of a spring balance can be set up, using a container (for example, large yogurt pot) with an elasticated loop to hold (see Figure 3.37). Objects can be placed in the container and, if it is held up against paper attached to the wall, starting and end points can be marked and children can see the results of the extending elastic. They can then be encouraged to predict: 'If the scissors made the pot go down to here, where will it go with the stapler inside? Which do you think is heavier?'

knotted rubber bands

large yogurt pot with rim

Figure 3.37 A simple spring balance

At the Foundation Stage and Key Stage 1, weighing will involve direct comparison. For example, in cooking, recipes can be based on comparisons such as using the amount of flour which balances two eggs. A variety of balances, including bucket-sized containers, can be provided together with sand or water to give experience with a tool for weighing. Stamps can be added to the parcels in a post office according to mass, using standard or non-standard units. For example, if a parcel balances three large bricks, it will have a stamp of value three; but a parcel balancing five bricks will 'cost' five. Children can make parcels and stamps for their post office. Other 'play' shops can also contain scales as part of the experience provided.

At the early stages of using balancing scales, teachers need to look out for instances where children are having to adjust the amount of material against which they are balancing their object. Often the children will realise an adjustment needs to be made when the scales are not balanced, but they may add more when removing would have been appropriate (or vice versa). These situations are rich in possibilities for discussion and thinking. The teacher will learn more about what it is the child does and does not currently understand by engaging in dialogue rather than simply correcting the child, and the subsequent planning then becomes more informed. First, the child can be asked to describe what is happening. Does he or she talk about the link between 'going down' and heavier? Does he or she have an image of what the scales will look like when balance is close? Careful, supportive questioning is important here, for example, 'Can you tell me ...?' 'What can you see?' 'What do you think will happen if ...(we put more cubes in/take some cubes out)?'

At Key Stage 2, labels collected and read can yield examples of common quantities such as family-sized cans, cereal packets and loose-purchased fruit and vegetables. In cooking, children can adjust recipes to feed different numbers of people from those given on the recipe. Questions such as 'Should all ingredients be doubled?' will lead to discussion of ratio and proportions. A context where comparison between metric and Imperial quantities arises is in looking at wartime rations and recipes, and children can explore rough equivalences by comparing ounces and pounds and grams with the scales. In using scales they would be expected to develop their understanding of readings between various subdivisions.

Measuring time

The main distinction involved in work on time is that between telling the time and a concept of time.

The first involves the reading of a dial which has units like any other measure but is presented in quite a complex display on an analogue clock, where the numerals have different meanings depending on the unit. For example, the 3 can refer to hours (as in 3 o'clock) or a quarter past or 15 minutes. With the greater prevalence of digital clocks nowadays, it has been suggested that children are growing up with quite a different model of time, not circular but linear (see 'Resources' section, BEAM 1994, Starting from Scratch – Measures). In the classroom it will be necessary to have examples of both analogue and digital clocks and, if the two run side by side, children can see how particular times significant to them (for example, 'School starts at' 'Blue Peter is on at') are shown. It might be the case that, rather than one type replacing the other, the two types have their different uses. For example, to estimate the 'chunk' of time left in a lesson, the teacher can gain a quick impression from a glance at the shape between the current time and the end time. However, if the teacher is catching a train home from school, a digital clock will allow quicker calculation of how many minutes he or she has to reach the station. Perhaps, people brought up mainly with experience of digital displays will find it easier to relate to them, and the analogue 'supporters' are holding on to an image which they themselves were brought up with. Analogue watches and clocks continue to be produced and so children should be given experience in dealing with them. The reading of dials requires that children have other knowledge such as reading numerals, counting in fives and knowing fractions, such as 'half' and 'quarter'. The reading of the dial may not connect with understanding of times of the day. A child might be able to read 'nine o'clock' when shown the hands in place or 'nine fifteen' when looking at a display. While this builds confidence and is a useful skill, the child may not relate the times to when events occur. It is probably best to integrate time telling and estimating into the everyday life of the classroom, beginning with looking at what the clock shows at significant times of the day.

There are children's books, based on stories and games, such as 'What's the Time, Mr Wolf?', which can be used as a starting point to make class books. One group of Year 2 children, who needed reinforcement on reading hours on the clock, made a book entitled 'What's the Time 3C?' By good fortune, times were often 'o'clocks', so each child illustrated a page. Raymond's was 'What's the time, Raymond?' '9 o'clock – Time for Miss to open the door'. He illustrated the page, and all the children made clock faces with movable hands to stick onto their page. The children in the class could move the hands to the time described.

This activity was started by getting children to imagine a clock they knew and then draw it. The teacher was trying an activity which was described in an article by Helen Pengelly (1985). Figure 3.38 shows some of the clocks they drew. The drawings showed the teacher some of the things the children already knew about clocks and telling the time, and allowed her to think about what might be appropriate next. For example, Amy knows there are numbers around the clock face and where 12

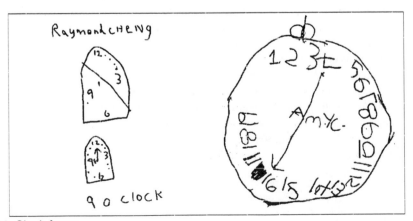

Figure 3.38 Clock faces

is, but she continues writing numbers beyond 12. She would benefit perhaps from looking at clocks, drawing them and fitting numerals onto clocks.

For the book, the teacher gave the children paper circles, and asked the children to fold the circles into halves and then into quarters. They were then asked to put in 12, 6, 3 and 9, after looking at a clock face, and then fill in the remaining numerals. Raymond, who drew a clock face with only the 12, 3, 9 and 6 and was very confident in reading and drawing times, could be given experience in calculating time intervals, problems from contexts familiar to him, and so on.

The second aspect of time, the *concept* of time, is about ideas of time passing and the measurement of intervals. For example, 'How long does it take you to walk to school?' One Reception child said to his teacher, while experimenting with a set of sand timers, 'I'm going away until the last one's finished', showing he has some idea that time will have passed when the sand has run out. The teacher was surprised to find that his estimation was quite good, and he returned within a few seconds of the sand running out! Making a variety of timers, for example, water and sand with holes in paper cups, and setting up activities to do alongside can help with these ideas. The children can be asked, 'How many times can you hop before the sand runs out?' or 'How many times can you write your name before this clockwork toy stops running?' Sand timers measuring 1 minute, 3 minutes and 5 minutes are useful. Children often respond to tasks such, 'Who can get changed for PE before the sand runs through?' (This might require more than one turn, depending on the age and speed of children!)

At Key Stage 2 children need to be able to calculate times, including reading and interpreting timetables to help solve problems. Further development of time includes ratio and proportion, compound measures (such as speed) and consideration of time zones around the world.

Case study: *Richard Harrison and Geraldine Wood*

Food technology

The case study is from a Year 5 class. The children were asked to design packaging for a selection of goods to be sold. They were working with two teachers, Richard and Geraldine. They introduced the activity by saying, *'We are going to sell these things in our delicatessen and we need to design some packaging'*. This was creating a context for learning rather than saying, *'We are going to learn about mass and volume. First of all I want you to weigh these objects and then tomorrow we will find their volume'*. This is not, however, to say that the task was not supported by aims for learning; for example, one aim was for children to make sensible approximations and this is evidenced in the account. For a mathematics focused problem, the children would need to be brought together at the end of each session to review the task and for the teacher to draw out the key learning involved, on measure and on strategies used in solving the problem.

A table was prepared with bowls containing six different food masses, which Richard and Geraldine had selected because of their differing densities, so they had to work these out themselves first! The sugar had the greatest density, and the pasta was the lightest for its size. It was important for the children to feel and compare the materials, so the bowls were wide (see Figure 3.39). Scoops were provided so that the children could fill boxes easily later on.

Richard showed the children the materials and set the problem, which was to:

- select a standard mass for the packaging;
- estimate the size of the box;
- make a prototype;
- find out 'how far out' the box was (and to be prepared to be wrong!) and work from there to improve the dimensions of the box.

Figure 3.39 Bowls of rice, pine nuts, pasta, popping corn, cous cous and sugar

Geraldine identified the different roles which children should take in their groups, and made arrangements for children to keep a diary which recorded the ideas and decisions that were made, before, during, and after each session (see Figure 3.40).

There were a number of masses available. Children had to select an appropriate one to be the 'standard' for their delicatessen (see Figure 3.41). They were encouraged to take any of the masses (not only the one they had chosen as their standard) to the bowls of substances in order to make further comparisons (see Figure 3.42).

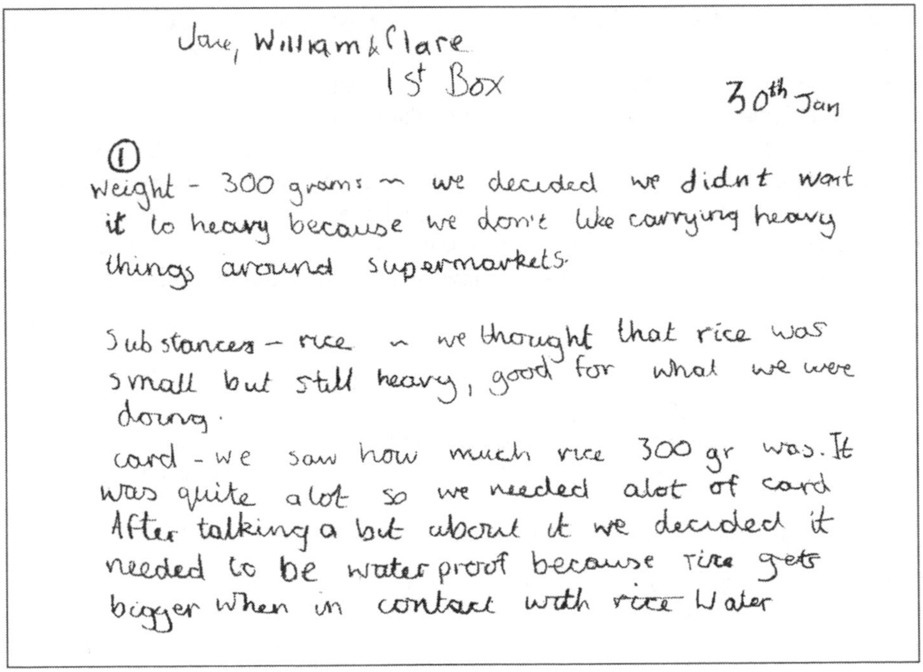

Jane, William & Clare
1st Box
30th Jan

① Weight - 300 grams ~ we decided we didn't want it to heavy because we don't like carrying heavy things around supermarkets.

Substances - rice ~ we thought that rice was small but still heavy, good for what we were doing.

card - we saw how much rice 300 gr was. It was quite alot so we needed alot of card After talking a bit about it we decided it needed to be waterproof because rice gets bigger when in contact with rice Water

Figure 3.40 Children's record of their decisions about mass and substance

Figure 3.41 Choosing a standard mass

Figure 3.42 Estimating mass

The children were given access to commercial packaging to analyse the design, and were encouraged to make nets of their boxes (see Figures 3.43 and 3.44). They had to remember to keep records of the dimensions of the box. The nets were then made into boxes. The children were able to establish the 'nearness' of their estimate. The boxes were either too big or too small. They were encouraged to think about how to refine the prototype (see Figures 3.45 and 3.46).

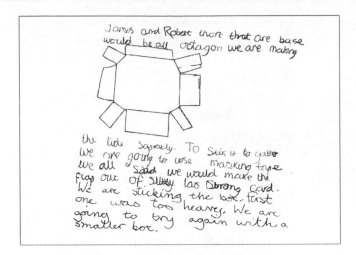

Figure 3.43 Design for a box with an octagonal base

Figure 3.44 Drawing the net

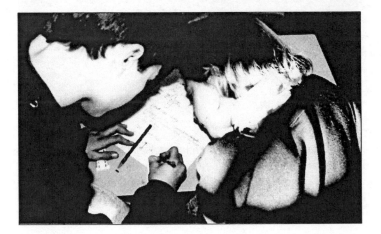

Figure 3.45 Refining the prototype

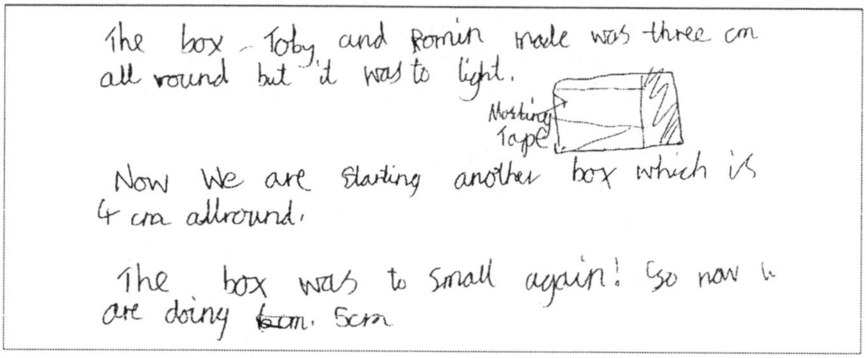

The box Toby and Romin made was three cm all round but it was to light.
Masking Tape
Now We are starting another box which is 4 cm allround.
The box was to small again! So now we are doing ~~6cm.~~ 5cm

Figure 3.46 Adjusting the size of the box

DRIED
PEAS

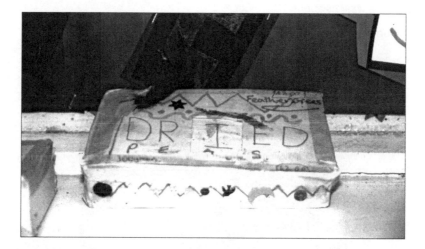

Figure 3.47 Packaging for 300 grammes of dried peas

Front view
DRIED
PEAS.
Side view

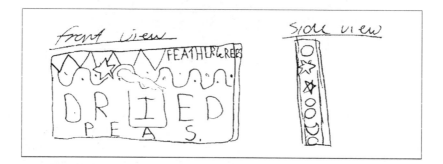

Figure 3.48 Front and side view of the packaging

Having reached a satisfactorily-sized box which would contain their standard mass, the design and technology aspect emerged, and the children used a variety of materials to decorate their boxes (see Figures 3.47 and 3.48).

Although the teachers intended that the box should contain only metric masses, some old Imperial examples had survived. In the second lesson they discovered one child, Rheem, trying to balance metric against Imperial mass. Because she could not maintain a balance easily, she investigated systematically, balancing a 1 ounce mass against grammes, then a 2 ounce mass, and so on. She concluded that the best approximation was '*180 grams is equivalent to three ounces*'. The teachers were pleased with this because it was a child-initiated investigation and one of their main aims, that of sensible approximation, was being served. Rheem had to make many judgments about how closely the metric and imperial masses should match and the kind of numbers she wanted in her conclusion.

One of the groups had carefully measured the dimensions of their prototype and found it was too big. The pupils said to the teachers, '*We don't know what to do with the numbers.*' Here is a flow sequence of what the teacher tried to do:

'*Tell me what you've done so far.*'
'*What do you think would happen if you made the numbers smaller?*'
'*How much smaller?*'
'*OK, try it and see what happens.*'

The questioning was not instructive, but it was 'opening out', or enabling.

Figure 3.49 Weighing on balance scales

Zoe and Charlotte's box was far too big. Before they proceeded to cut it down (a common strategy used to solve this particular problem), Richard suggested that they fill it and weigh it to see what the mass of the box would have been when full. It weighed the same as 1730 grammes (see Figure 3.49). This was an opportunity to explore alternative expressions. They had used 1 kilogramme mass, 7 hundred-gramme masses and 3 ten-gramme masses, and the following table was compiled:

kilogrammes	hundred-grammes	ten-grammes	grammes
1	7	3	0

This could then be read out in several different ways, for example:

'One kilogram, seven hundred and thirty grams.'
'One thousand seven hundred and thirty grams.'
'One point seven three zero kilograms.'

Thus the teacher was able to introduce the decimal point as a marker or unit point (to show which one was being used as a unit). A structured set of measuring units offered a meaningful approach to decimal notation.

The groups quickly discovered they needed to know how heavy the box was and subtract this from the full mass. So it was not necessary for the teachers to teach this (that is, 'gross' and 'net' mass). But they had been prepared to!

Alex, Chantelle and Kaya were one group to demonstrate the success of approximation (should it be 'successive approximation'?). This can be shown best like a strip cartoon (see Figure 3.50).

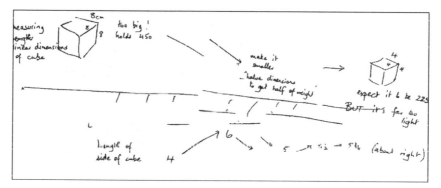

Figure 3.50 Teacher's record of children's thinking

So, having observed these children using and applying their skills of approximation, some thoughts occurred to the teachers (with implications for differentiation in future sessions):

What do they know now?
Do they know how volume 'behaves' now?
What work would be suitable next for this group?
Could they make a bowl half the size of this one, but still the same shape?

(Not so easy as it seems – halving all the sides does not give half the volume!)

It was a great joy to the teacher when, in the third or fourth session, Kaya explained that '*a raisin is about five times as heavy as a lentil but a whole lot bigger*' (and of course she had not found the mass of a single raisin). Many of the children used phrases like '*heavy for their size*'.

The children were encouraged to record all their hypothesising, ideas, thoughts, plans, decision making, differences of opinion, discoveries and disappointments as they worked through the investigation (see Figure 3.51). In the initial discussion with the children, the teacher talked about the value of each child having a role to play within the group, one of these roles being the scribe. The children discussed who would take on this responsibility, and it was understood that the job could be rotated around the group. This aspect of the investigation had to be monitored closely as the children quickly became absorbed in the action and neglected to record events as and when they occurred. With two adults taking the group, this being an ideal situation, it was possible for them to circulate among the children, monitoring the situation closely and questioning the children, reminding them of the importance of keeping a written account (see Figure 3.52).

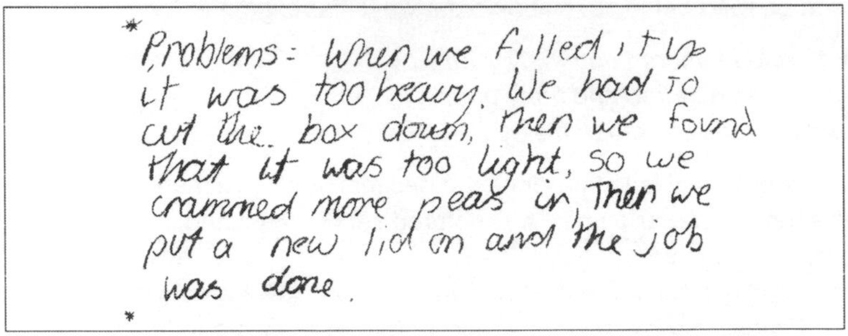

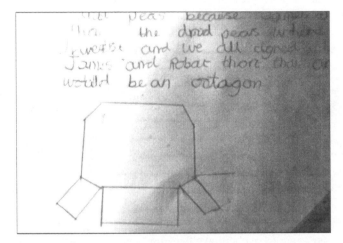

> *Problems: When we filled it up it was too heavy. We had to cut the box down, then we found that it was too light, so we crammed more peas in, Then we put a new lid on and the job was done.*

Figure 3.51 Children recording problem solving

Figure 3.52 Record of children's decisions

In hindsight it was realised that there was a need to reinforce the question, '*What do we need to record?*' This could have been built into the beginning of the second session so that the children could establish for themselves the important aspects of their path through the investigation. Useful questions as a result of this discussion, written on a card and centrally placed so that the children could refer to them, would have helped keep the recording relevant to the investigation. Some children became very involved in the aesthetic value of the box, and this detracted from the mathematics of the task. However, the recording enabled the children to maintain interest, understanding and continuity, so that the activity could be picked up at any time and continued over the course of a week (see Figure 3.53 overleaf).

It was also important to make records of the children's work in order to be aware of necessary teaching points, questions to raise the children's awareness of their discoveries and to enable us to make assessments of the children's learning. Notes were also made on the effects of the organisation on the investigation, which would help when a similar investigation is introduced in the future.

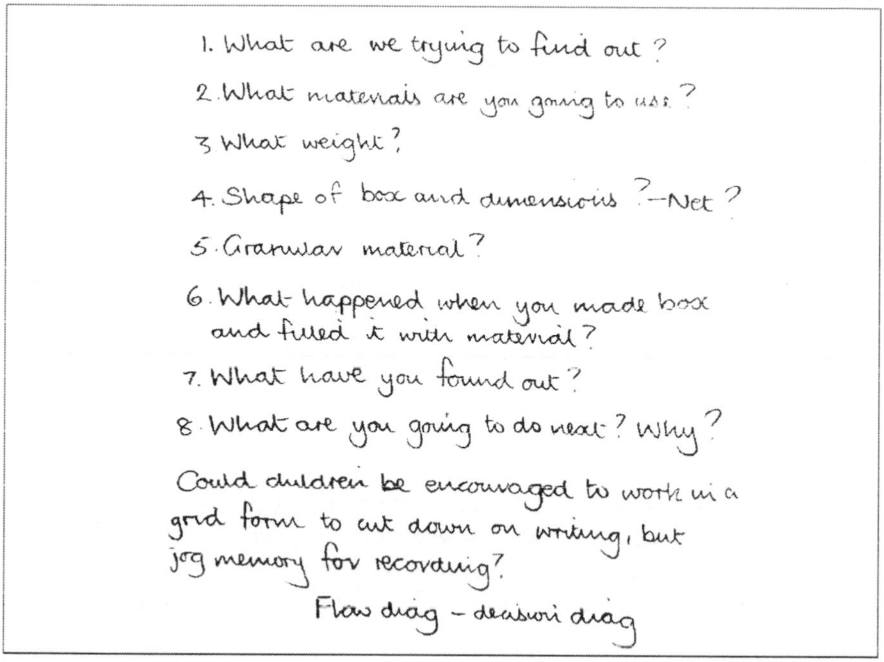

1. What are we trying to find out?

2. What materials are you going to use?

3. What weight?

4. Shape of box and dimensions? —Net?

5. Granular material?

6. What happened when you made box and filled it with material?

7. What have you found out?

8. What are you going to do next? Why?

Could children be encouraged to work in a grid form to cut down on writing, but jog memory for recording?

Flow diag – decision diag

Figure 3.53 Teacher's notes

Organising the classroom and children appropriately

Organisation is important in any lesson. But measurement is a particular case in point because it requires access to materials, tools, and a variety of apparatus. In the case study, the teachers even had to rearrange the furniture so that children had unrestricted access to the six bowls (of raisins, oats, sugar, peas, lentils and rice), to the consumables with which to construct boxes, and to different kinds of balances, masses, etc. They also had very definite rules about how to fill the containers they had made (over the bowls), when and where they were allowed to use the balances (they could not, for example, take a balance to the granular substances in order to weigh out as much as they needed). The key point here is that the organisation of the classroom and of the children determined the level of problem solving, and, therefore, the mathematical learning. That was why it had to be set up so carefully, and why the teachers continually had to monitor the effectiveness of the rule system.

Solving problems involving measure

To extend the ideas encountered in the case study into other areas and age groups, it will be useful to reflect on ways in which problems involving measure can be planned.

1. In order to apply skills of measuring, as was noted earlier there needs to be purpose in the task. Why is it important to know how long, heavy or full something is?
2. Opportunities for measurement occur in different contexts in school: in play, in other curriculum areas and arising from story or fantasy contexts, for example.
3. Early in the Foundation Stage and Key Stage 1, children's play involves much comparison – choosing particular length bricks to fit a structure, using different sized containers in sand and water, fitting clothes to dolls and dolls to beds. The teacher's role is crucial in developing thinking by

talking with children about what they are doing, helping them to predict which brick, container or bed will suit their needs, and developing the language of comparison. At times the teacher will intervene judiciously to challenge thinking; for example, the teacher might place a set of containers in the water, which will puzzle children because the shapes appear to hold more or less than they do.

4. Story contexts can lead into fantasy measuring tasks such as making artefacts for the Three Bears, glasses for the giant, or judging which of our possessions would be useful to the Borrowers. Reading Alice in Wonderland can lead into many speculations about scale and proportion.

5. Many science and technology tasks require measurement, for example designing packaging for a particular object, or finding ways to compare the effects on flight of adding paper clips to paper aeroplanes. In the latter example, measure is required in setting up differently weighted aeroplanes and in comparing distances flown. Both contexts could use standard or non-standard measures according to the children's understanding.

Glossary

This section is intended as a reference for teachers, to support subject knowledge and underpin planning, and not all of the terms need be used directly with children.

Approximate: an approximate measure is a known measure given to a lesser degree of accuracy. For example an object weighing 1.545 kg is approximately one and a half kilogrammes.

Estimate: an estimate is an informed guess, or a value calculated using approximate values. For example: the door is about 2 metres high, or the area of a field measuring 220 metres by 312 metres is about 60,000m^2.

Standard units of measure:

	Metric	*Imperial*
Length	cm, m, km	inches, feet, yards, mile
Area	cm2, m2, hectares	sq.in., sq.ft., sq.yd., acres
Volume	cm3, m3	cubic in., cubic ft.
Capacity	ml, cl, l	fluid ounces (fl. oz.), pint, gallon
Weight	g, kg, tonnes	oz, pounds (lb), stones hundredweight (cwt), ton

Everyday equivalences (note that these are approximations):

	Metric	*Imperial*
Length	2.5 cm	1 inch
	30 cm	1 foot (12 inches)
	1 m	39 inches (3 feet 3 inches)
	8 km	5 miles
Area	6 cm2	1 sq. in.
	1 m2	11 sq. ft. (just over 1 sq. yd.)
Volume	16 cm3	1 cubic in.
	1 m3	37 cubic feet (nearly 1.4 cu. yd.)
Capacity	570 ml	1 pint (20 fl. oz.)
	1 l	1.75 pints
	5 l	1 gallon (8 pints)
Weight	25 g	1 oz
	1 kg	2.2 lb (16 oz. in 1lb)
	50 kg	8 stones (14 lb in 1 stone) or 1 cwt
	1 tonne (1 000kg)	1 ton (20 cwt)

Handling data

4.1 INTRODUCTION

Handling data is a statutory part of the content of the National Curriculum but it is much more than that. It is a life skill.

We are bombarded by data in the media: what a healthy diet should be, our chances of winning in the National Lottery, who is ahead in the opinion polls and so on. If children are to be educated to become adults able to make informed and sensible decisions, they will need to develop understanding of the ways in which data can be used to inform, persuade or even coerce. They will need to question the accuracy of the information, know something about how data was collected, be able to read tables and graphs and be aware of plausible interpretations, explanations and conclusions. Children should be helped to develop a critical, questioning approach, for example through being able to examine claims made by advertisers and interest groups.

Discussions about the likelihood or probability of events can emerge from the collection of data to answer particular questions, and data will sometimes need to be collected to address questions of probability. Explorations of games, or investigation into the frequency of events relevant to children, can build towards an understanding of the chances of winning (or not winning!) in competitions and towards informed decision making; for example, in making choices about insurance or risky enterprises.

If children are to understand the issues involved in all stages of the data handling process, they need to have the opportunity to address questions of relevance to them, arising from their own experiences and interests.

Handling data in the classroom

Data handling is experienced in many different ways in the classroom and the National Curriculum. Here are some examples:

- Classroom organisation: through contexts such as tidying (identifying common attributes in objects which are stored together). For example, children can be involved in addressing 'What is the best way to arrange the books in the Book Corner?' (arising from a real need to find a particular book or type of story).
- Issues affecting children out of school, for example 'Is my bedtime reasonable compared with that of other children in my class?' (from work on time or from ordinary discussions children have in the course of a day).
- Science: children can investigate preferred living conditions for minibeasts and will need to make decisions about what data will need to be collected and how they can represent their data to make interpretation easier and so on.
- History: children might look for differences and similarities between toys past and present. To do this they could display and discuss old photographs of toys and set up questionnaires to investigate the toy preferences for people of different ages to see if choices have changed between generations. This would involve the children in evaluating how the way in which they phrase the questions can affect the answers obtained.

- In school life: there are issues that can be investigated with the support of data collected by children, for example, is it true that the playground is dominated by one type of play? How can data be used to argue for a particular viewpoint?
- Story/fantasy contexts: in the Key Stage 1 case study described later in this Section, children investigate like or dislike of carrots. This arose from the Three Billy Goats Gruff story. If work were extended into preferred diet, story or fantasy characters could become an interest as subjects in a database as well as real people. For example, does the Very Hungry Caterpillar have a balanced diet?

All of the above examples involve a question or enquiry of potential interest to the children, a set of relevant data to handle, the need to represent findings in a clear way, interpretation of results and making deductions from results.

The data handling process

This is often presented as a circular process, as in Figure 4.1:

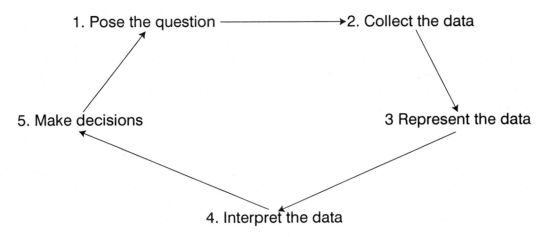

Figure 4.1 Data handling cycle (Adapted from Graham 1990: 15)

The cycle has various points which mark stages in the process. The first of these is a starting question. This needs to be of relevance and interest to the children. It may need to be framed so that it is clear what data it is appropriate to collect, although this is not always obvious. For example, what data could be collected to investigate who is the healthiest person? Secondly, decisions will need to be made about how to collect the data. Next, the data must be processed and presented. Finally, interpretations can be made and deductions offered. At this point the cycle is completed, but there might be a return to the original question as further questions will emerge which require another turn around the cycle. These questions will arise from new lines of enquiry emerging as work progresses, or because there was a problem with the design of some aspect of the work. The questions asked may not elicit appropriate data, for example. The cycle can appear very neat but the reality is not always as tidy as this!

The following is an example of the data handling cycle in practice. The teacher spots an argument between children about which story she will read next to the class and she decides to use the context to introduce the idea of making decisions by voting. She asks the children which stories they want and lists them on a large piece of paper or on the board. She then asks them to indicate preference by putting hands up while she counts and records choices by tallying or noting names. Then children can help to count so that a result can be obtained. There was a question (Which story?), a method of collecting data (hands up to be counted and the teacher might have discussed with the children how to do this), a representation (lists of names or marks against titles) and interpretation (Which story did most people want? How do we know?). In this case, the question arose spontaneously and was dealt with on the spot in a fairly informal way. This work can be approached with differing degrees of formality depending on the context and the data handling process can also be entered at different points. For example, a question can arise from the collection of data stage. Counting how many children have school lunch might give rise to comment *'When we were in Class 1 nearly everyone had packed lunch'*, and the teacher might take the opportunity to follow up with some kind of investigation such as comparing different classes. This question is also a good example of how what appears clear initially can throw up difficulties in practice. For example, how will we deal with children who vary their lunch, having school dinners sometimes but packed lunch on other days?

The staged model of the data handling process is a useful framework in planning and evaluating the experiences offered to children, but it is a model which is not reproduced in exactly the same way in all such contexts. Elements of the data handling cycle may be condensed. For example a Reception class investigated the most popular fruit by choosing an apple, an orange or a banana and placing the chosen fruits on a labeled plate. Collection and representation were thus combined. In the lunch example interest was sparked at Stage 2 as data was collected for school administration purposes. Similarly, a question could arise at Stage 4 as, for instance, in the interpretation stage of data handling in the media. One of the sparks for the Key Stage 2 case study, to be described later in this Section, was the reading of statistics about asthma and increased levels of pollution reported in the press.

What is important to stress here is that the whole cycle is applicable at all Key Stages but there will be differences in emphases on the stages and degrees of sophistication and their independence in designing questions and methods of collecting data. Also, in interpretation of results, the teacher will encourage children to give reasoned judgements but the degree to which this is done and the complexity of the hypotheses and variables involved will vary dramatically. To illustrate progression Table 4.1 demonstrates a typical class topic, toys, and shows how it might be developed at the Foundation Stage, Key Stage 1, early Key Stage 2 and later Key Stage 2, addressing the stages in the data handling cycle above.

The teacher's role in the process

It is important that children have opportunities to explore their own questions and ideas. What, then, is the role of the teacher at different stages in the cycle?

1. Posing the question

If data handling is to be purposeful the teacher needs to be aware of opportunities which might lead to purposeful data handling.

In relation to the toys, this work will probably be part of a whole class theme or topic (for example, play, childhood or toys) and the context for investigation here is related to a history strand.

Children will need help to identify the actual question to be investigated. The teacher first needs to initiate discussion about toys, so children are encouraged to bring in and/or talk about their toys. There would be a whole-class discussion where emerging issues with potential for investigation are picked up by the teacher. For example, a child might say *'My mum had a teddy'* and children will make other points about parents and their toys. The teacher's role here is to support these ideas and to make suggestions, for example 'How could we find out about the toys our parents (older siblings, grandparents, etc.) played with?' Actual toys, photographs, books and talking to individuals are all possible sources of information which can be used in sorting and classifying a set of objects by one or more criteria. Toys, and pictures or photographs of them, might be classified by owner (for example, boy, girl, parent, grandparent), type (for example, car, doll, board game) or ordered according to age to reinforce the idea of a time line.

Table 4.1 Progression in data handling

	Foundation Stage/ Key Stage 1	Early Key Stage 2	Later Key Stage 2
Posing the question	What is my favourite toy?	What sort of toys did children play with when … (mum, gran, Mr W) were children?	How have toys changed through the ages?
	Questions will tend to be personal, related to child's experience	Questions slightly more abstract, looking more at children in general	Questions reflect a broader historical view
	Questions will emerge from discussion	Questions more topic centred	Questions will be more carefully refined
Collecting the data	Toys, photos Talk to adults	Photos, non-fiction books Interviewing people	Range of source material books, paintings, photos, writing, etc., Museum visits
Representing the data	Toys displayed in sets, tally or tick charts, drawings, pictograms. Use of ICT to display data related to concrete objects	Tables or drawing and producing different graphs (e.g. pictograms, bar charts or diagrams (, e.g. Venn or Carroll), using ICT where appropriate	Choose/select from different ways to represent data. Use ICT to select appropriate ways to represent the data
	Arrangements of pictures/objects can lead to pictorial representations They will mainly be counts.	Children will begin to learn about axes, meanings of different charts/graphs and consider scale	Children will be more selective about appropriate representation and can use ICT to present specific features
		Using computers to represent data allows for more variety	They will begin to learn about how varying aspects such as scale can give different messages.
Interpreting the data	Reading results – 20 children have teddies	22 parents played with dolls	In all our books about toys there were no computer games
		15 of our class played with dolls	In our class 15 children play computer games.
	Deductions – most children in our class like teddies	More people of our parent's age played with dolls than we did	Some toys that children played with in the past are still used now. There are new toys which were not used in the past because they needed microchips.
	Interpretation very close to the data read and still personal	Inference made from comparing data for 2 two groups known to the children	More generalised statements made from a wider sample.
			Discussion can take place about the representativeness of the data.

At all stages children will initially be reading the results of their data and then being encouraged to look for patterns and make deductions. Interpretation involves reading the explicit information and then using this information to make general statements.

The teacher's role so far has been to identify possible starting points and incorporate them into planning. She will need to consider the sort of questions which will provide rich starting points for children's learning. Such questions will not always be neat and well focused. Because of this, children's attempts at data collection will not always enable them to answer the original question. We sometimes want children to learn from mistakes or trial and to see that the way you frame questions influences the kind of data you can collect. With the toys, the question might be 'What is your favourite toy?' This will possibly result in each child in the class responding with a different toy. It might be fruitful either to go on to narrow the choice or give the question a sharper focus (for example 'Do girls and boys like different toys?'). Sometimes the teacher will decide to resolve these difficulties at the start. Sometimes she might decide that these discussions will take thinking forward. She will make judgements about the learning she wishes to promote in particular contexts.

To maintain an environment which encourages positive attitudes, decision making and some risk taking, all suggestions should be accepted as genuine questions with the potential for exploration. The children could be asked to brainstorm and pool ideas from which a selection can be made. The teacher can then judge whether the child would benefit from exploring a particular line of enquiry, or whether further discussion might lead to amendment or withdrawal of the line of enquiry.

Progression in helping children to frame questions can be seen as moving children from a close personal view into a broader perspective. So children in the Foundation Stage and Key Stage 1 will pose questions which are personal and immediate ('*my toy*'). Later children will be able to ask questions about groups to which they can relate ('*brothers and sisters*', their '*friends*', then '*children of my age*'). By the end of Key Stage 2 children should generally be encouraged to develop questions about groups more distanced in time and place from themselves ('*toys my parents played with*', '*my grandparents*', then '*toys through the ages*', '*Is this class typical of the school? What would happen if we asked younger/older children … children in another town or country?*')

2. Collecting the data

Children should be given the opportunity to suggest and then to try out ways of collecting data.

The data which they will collect might be obvious in some cases, as in an enquiry centred on the question '*What is your favourite toy?*', but less so in others. For example, if children want to investigate ways to improve the lost property system in school, what will they need to find out? What kinds of information will help? In each case discussion will be necessary, to help children to come up with ideas for themselves in the first instance. Of course, these initial attempts at data collection might result in data which does not answer their question. For example, suppose the question was '*Do you play with roller skates?*'. Left to their own devices children might merely list the names of children in the class as they are asked whether they play with roller skates or not. They might not, without help, see that what is also needed is a system for coding responses such as ticks/crosses or 'yes/no' labels. Just as children need help with the framing of questions, they will need help at this stage in the process. The teacher's role here will be to engage children in discussion about why their method has not worked and about how else they might do it. ('*Have* you asked everyone?' 'How do you know?' 'Can you see who plays with roller skates and who doesn't?').

Another issue to be aware of is whether data would be better grouped or presented discretely. For example, if prices of toys were a factor in the investigation, the data might be better grouped in ranges (0–99p, £1.00–£1.99, £2.00–£2.99, etc.) to produce a more useful result (representation).

During the discussions about possible methods of collecting data, the teacher's role will be to decide whether the children's proposed strategy will be a fruitful learning experience. Will they simply become disheartened and waste time collecting data which is not very useful, or not recorded in a way which will facilitate interpretation, or can the learning from this experience be built upon in deepening their understanding? It is the teacher's professional judgement which will determine the appropriate point at which to make a suggestion to the children, building on their ideas but also introducing new ones. Among the various ways of collecting data that the teacher could suggest are questionnaires (progressing from one question with a yes or no answer to a schedule of questions around a theme), looking up information in books and taking and tabulating measures of various kinds and making and recording observations.

Progression: in the Early Stages, Foundation Stage and Key Stage 1, children will be generally focusing on straightforward questions requiring limited discrete data, so that the data collection system is concrete (for example, collecting favourite toys, pictorial (for example, each child drawing a picture of how they came to school) moving on to simple tally charts or lists (for example, writing names or ticking them off on a list) and finding responses to single questions.

At Key Stage 2 the range of approaches should be widened as children progress into thinking about how different questions and ways of framing them might influence the kinds or response obtained. For example, if they want to find out about preferences for toys according to gender, would it be better to offer a list for respondents to select from or should the question be left quite open? They will also be able to consider in more depth the possible variables involved, for example if they hypothesise that the age of a child influences their choice of toy, then age must be incorporated into a questionnaire.

3. Representing the data

'A picture is worth a thousand words.' Chinese proverb.

Data is presented in tables, graphs and charts to provide information clearly at a glance and to highlight patterns, relationships and trends. Pictorial and graphical representation is a means of mathematical communication and children will need to explore the various forms in which the information they collect can be expressed visually. The terms used to describe the different types of graphs and charts that children are likely to meet in Key Stages 1 and 2, as well as examples of the graphs themselves, can be found in the glossary at the end of this Section.

The data handling computer packages that children can use present information in tabular form or graphically at the touch of a button, but we would argue that children might miss the opportunity to learn the conventions of organising and presenting data if they do not have the opportunity to construct their own graphs as well. Not that these skills are an end in themselves, nor should children spend a disproportionate amount of time colouring or decorating their graphs; but actually having to label axes, devise keys, and decide on scale might be instrumental in helping children to develop an understanding about and confidence in using and interpreting graphs, charts and diagrams. Being able to interpret the diagrams is most important.

The illustration of statistical data is progressive and the teacher's role will be to help move the child from reality to its representation in abstract form. In the early stages graphs should be made from real objects; later, pictures of objects might be used in place of the real things; and finally, symbols can be used to stand for the real objects. The children will need to meet both counting/bar charts and graphs showing relationships such as scatter diagrams.

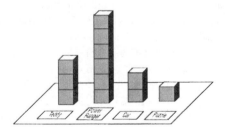

Figure 4.2 Table top display

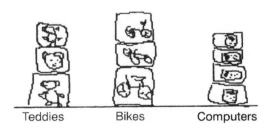

Teddies   Bikes   Computers

Figure 4.3 Misleading graph with different sizes of paper

COUNTING/BAR CHARTS

Foundation Stage/Key Stage 1: the earliest graphs may arise from sorting, and/or matching. Toys might be sorted and classified using criteria related to their properties, for example size, material, power, and displayed in set hoops. 'People graphs' can be made with children themselves, standing in lines (for block graphs) or sitting in hoops (for sets), for example.

Since the above graphs are not necessarily count graphs, they can be attempted with children as pre-counting activities. When graphs based on counting are introduced the teacher will need to introduce the idea of a base line. Initially children should be helped to make a graph with three-dimensional material, such as counting cubes, bricks, or even matchboxes, using the table top as a base, as shown in Figure 4.2.

Bus			*1 bus represents 10 children*
Car			*1 car represents 10 children*
Walk				*1 pair of feet represents 10 children*

Figure 4.4 Pictogram

Progression to the stage of making picture graphs will require the teacher to reinforce the idea of the base line, and help the children realise the need for identical units and the need for those units to be placed edge to edge. The teacher can prompt discussion of the need for this uniformity if different children are given different sized paper on which to draw their favourite toy. The papers can be placed in position to allow discussion. Questions about the numbers of toys represented and whether it is fair if one toy is on a smaller piece of paper than another will help to elicit children's ideas of the need for the conventions to meet the need of accurate communication, as illustrated in Figure 4.3

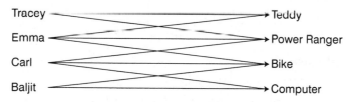

Figure 4.5 Graph showing a relationship between two different sets of data

In the early stages there is no need for the vertical axis to be drawn or labelled since the pictures or 'units' can be counted where numerical comparison is appropriate. However, as the size of the count increases so will the need to label the vertical axis; and, although it might be acceptable initially to label the spaces, the teacher at Key Stage 2 will need to ensure that children label the lines.

Key Stage 2: progression in the representation of count graphs is achieved by using a continuous strip or bar to represent the total count or frequency, and by the use of scale in drawing the graph.

One method of introducing children to scale is to build a three-dimensional graph from matchboxes where the matchboxes each contain, for example, ten counters. Children then get the idea that one unit on a scale (the matchbox) can represent several counts. Similarly children can be encouraged to draw pictures where one drawing representing multiple objects can be made (see pictogram, Figure 4.4). If the symbol represents multiples of 10, children will need to discuss how to represent numbers like 87 or 23.

A parallel development is the representation of data which involves measuring rather than counting. Children might draw around the outline of their feet, cut these out and lay them against a base line to make comparisons of length. Further degrees of abstraction are achieved by representing the length of their feet by a paper strip. Scale can then be introduced by halving or quartering the length of the strip.

As children's understanding of the measuring units and their interrelationship develops so can the idea that the vertical axis be apportioned to represent these different units. For example, a distance of 2.5 m might be represented by a 25 cm long bar on a graph. A series of such bars would show the distances travelled by a selection of toy cars rolling down a slope.

Early in Key Stage 1 relationships can be seen by linking data with arrows. Thus, in Figure 4.5, the arrows stand for the relationship 'has'. Alternatively, such relationships could be represented on a two-way table (see Table 4.2).

Table 4.2 A two-way table

	Teddy	Power Ranger	Bike	Computer Game
Tracey	✓	✓		
Emma	✓	✓	✓	
Carl		✓	✓	✓
Baljit			✓	✓

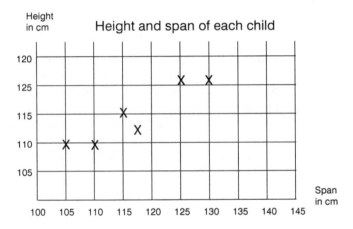

Figure 4.6 Scatter diagram

Later in Key Stage 2, children can mark points on a grid representing two sets of numerical data (for example, arm span and height) to see whether there is a relationship between the two. On a floor grid or on paper each child could be represented by a named sticky dot or labelled arrows leading to the points, depending on the size of the graph. This is the beginning of work with scatter diagrams, as shown in Figure 4.6.

In investigating the relationship between reach and height, which is supposed to be close, a scatter diagram would show how many people have greater reach than height, how many have greater height than reach and how many have equal measurements. Body shapes can be classified into 'squares' (arm and reach the same) or 'rectangles' (arm and reach significantly different) according to the results! A correlation between the sets of data is shown by the arrangement of the points.

Both count and relationship graphs in the later stages require the children to identify and plot points on a square grid based on two number lines intersecting at right angles. This means that the teacher will need to introduce the children to the use of ordered pairs, or coordinates. The teacher will need to emphasise the convention that points are located by first finding the distance from the vertical line (that is, along the horizontal axis) and then the distance from the horizontal line (that is, up the vertical axis) and give the children opportunities to familiarise themselves with this notation. Of course this work links with the development of map work skills; and, for further reinforcement, 'Treasure Island' maps can be drawn and directions given using coordinates.

Further extensions to children's graphing skills will occur when data needs to be grouped in order to show any relationship. This will require the teacher to introduce the children to the convention of describing class intervals. For example, the cost of toys could be grouped in intervals £0–£4.99, £5–£9.99.

Although children will meet pie charts in their everyday lives and in data handling packages, displaying information in this diagrammatic form is difficult. Since their construction is based on sectors of a circle which are fractions of 360°, making pie charts is likely to be too demanding for most children in Key Stages 1 and 2. However, they are able, by using computer packages (for example, graphing packages, spreadsheets, databases to produce this type of representation and focus on the interpretation of the results).

A pie chart could also be made practically. Put children into groups according to some attribute, such as hair colour. Ask them to form a circle which will show a larger part of the circumference will be taken up by the larger group, for example if there were 16 children with brown hair in a class of 30, they would see that slightly more than half the circle would be 'brown hair'. To draw the pie chart, use objects such as counters to match the groups (one colour for each hair colour). Arrange them in a circle (as was done with the children) and, again, it will be seen that just over half of the circle is taken up by the brown hair category. Measure the greatest width across the circle (the diameter) with a ruler; set a pair of compasses to half the diameter (the radius) and use that measurement to draw a circle. Arrange the counters around the edge of the circle, mark off sections depending on the numbers of the different groups and draw lines to the centre of the circle to show the sectors.

The key aspects of the pie chart is that it is useful in showing proportion and that the pie must make sense as a whole. In the example (see Figure 4.7) the pie is a nonsense because the children in this class feature more than once and the pie shows more than 100% of the class. The bar chart (see Figure 4.8) is more helpful in showing the frequency of ownership of the individual toys and children will need help in deciding which type of graphic display to use for their particular purposes. Notice that the bars do not touch each other.

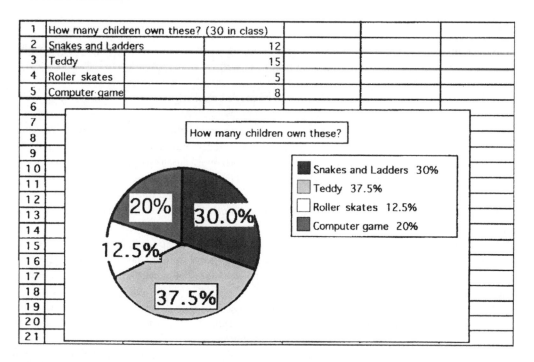

Figure 4.7 A pie chart that makes no sense

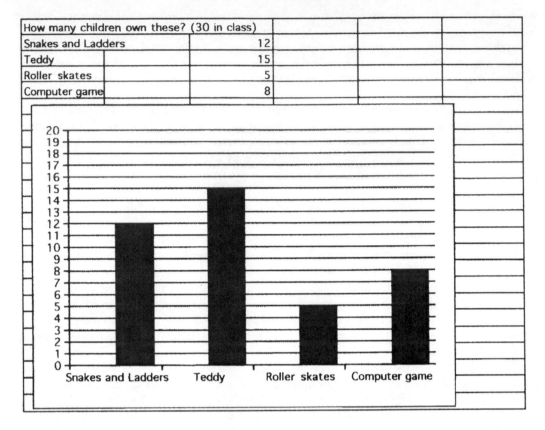

How many children own these? (30 in class)					
Snakes and Ladders		12			
Teddy		15			
Roller skates		5			
Computer game		8			

Figure 4.8 A bar chart showing the same data

4. Interpreting data

It is important that the end result of much data handling work is not just the display of a graph in the classroom but that children have opportunities to interpret the graph and see how it answers the question. However, the question of interpretation is not always fully addressed, so the teacher will need to include, in planning, time for children to be able to read and interpret other graphs as well as their own.

Well drawn graphs can help us to interpret data, but they can also be used to misrepresent them, so it is important that children learn to interpret the data represented. They must be encouraged to 'read' a graph for the explicit information it presents if they are not to be duped by representation devices which exaggerate trends. Reading graphs can be encouraged by asking closed questions. 'How many children chose teddy as their favourite toy?' 'How many more children chose roller skates as their favourite toy than chose computer games?' Children can also be asked to frame questions to ask each other.

When 'reading' graphs with children, the teacher may find that the language structure becomes complex; but it is important for children to hear it and to respond to it so that they develop their skills in identifying and communicating mathematical relationships. For example, *'How many more ...?'* *'What is the most common ...?'*

At a deeper level children will also need to be encouraged to seek patterns and relationships which the graph might reveal, remembering, of course, that the lack of a pattern or relationship may in itself be a significant finding. Again the teacher will probably need to lead the questioning. In doing so she will not only be helping the children to find relationships, but will also be providing a model for children to use in future situations. Comments such as, *'The metal cars went fastest down the ramp'* are beginning to lead children into looking for pattern in their findings which can then be followed up with further investigation.

A yet deeper level is achieved when children are encouraged to make deductions from the data they have collected. Deductions can be prompted by open questions from the teacher. For example, 'Why do you think the teddy bear has been a popular toy for such a long time?' might prompt the children to make the interpretation that children like to cuddle toys.

Since the interpretation of visual representation of data is more important than the actual drawing, the teacher will need to ensure that any display of graphs is accompanied by questions which encourage children to analyse the information.

It is highly likely that in interpreting the data and making deductions more questions will be posed. This might indicate that a new problem has been posed which will require a further run through the data handling cycle, or it might be that the question raises issues about the design of the project itself. Was enough information collected? Was it the right information? Should we have found out …? In effect, the teacher is encouraging the children to evaluate their research design, a skill which will not only eventually permeate all areas of the curriculum but will help children to develop a healthy scepticism with which to interpret the vast amount of information they will receive during their lifetimes.

4.2 CASE STUDIES

In this section we will examine two case studies and show how aspects of the data handling process apply in each case. The Foundation Stage case study is from a Reception class and the Key Stage 2 case study is from a Year 5 class. The intention is that the reality of the model in action will clarify aspects of the teaching role and show what sort of evidence might support assessment of data handling experience.

Case study at the Foundation Stage: *Suzanne Cowan and Kathy Goodman*

As part of the 'broad-based' topic of 'stories' in the Reception class, the children's work had been planned around the story of the Three Billy Goats Gruff. The teacher had used the story to develop the following concepts: three, first, second, third, last, under, over. They had constructed the infamous bridge from a variety of boxes which was tall enough for the children to walk under, even if it was not strong enough for the children to walk over! Here is what subsequently happened.

At carpet time there was some discussion about what goats might eat. The teacher asked 'I wonder if we eat the same?' 'Well, we don't eat grass', volunteered Natalie. 'Carrots!' contributed Ade eagerly. 'Yes, I think you are right,' replied the teacher encouragingly, only to be challenged by those children who thought that carrots were 'Yuk!' or a similarly disparaging adjective. The vocal straw poll that followed suggested that more boys than girls liked carrots. Regaining the children's attention she *posed the question* 'Do you think that more boys than girls like carrots?' The children were discouraged from calling out their replies and instead were asked to think about how they might find out. Skilfully, the teacher helped the children to formulate a question and then prompted them to think about how they might collect the information to help them find an answer. Her aim was to engage the children in designing a data capture sheet.

She targeted some individuals *(collecting the data):* 'Dean, how do you think we could find out?' 'We could ask our friends.' 'Yes, and how would you remember how many liked or didn't like carrots?' 'We can write it', replied Natalie. 'Show me how on this sheet of paper', responded the teacher inviting the child to come up to the easel. 'You can write their names and yes and no', volunteered Petra. The teacher accepted this response but still prompted the children to consider further. 'You could do that but it would take a long time. What if I put a line down my paper like this and put a mark here (in the left hand column) for every one who doesn't like carrots, and a mark here (right hand column) for everyone who does. Let's see if it works.' The teacher offered the symbols of a smiley and sad face to head the columns and began to *collect information* from the children marking the appropriate column with a tally *(and representing data)* (see Figure 4.9).

The children then counted the tally marks. Four children did not like carrots and 13 did *(interpreting the data)*. There was a feeling that the task had been successfully completed and indeed some children were ready to move off the carpet when the teacher intervened to prompt them to think further. *'But does this tell us whether more boys than girls like carrots?'* she quizzed*, posing another question.*

The children decided that they only needed to find out whether a person was a boy or girl if they liked carrots. *'How can we show this on the data capture sheet?'* asked the teacher. Petra was invited to the easel and given the felt tip. She adjusted the sheet (see Figure 4.10):

'I think that will work very well', responded the teacher. *'Let's give it a try.'* She reassured the children that they would all have a turn asking their friends whether they liked carrots, but that it would be much too confusing if they all did it at once, so some of the children would be carrying on with their work and others would come around to ask them whether they liked or disliked carrots. She 'dispatched' from the carpet area those children who were obviously at their limit of concentration. Some were directed to the sand tray, others to the role play area and another group to a construction activity. The remaining group of six children were told to get paper, to make their data capture sheet and then to collect their data. The teacher appealed to children's sense of playing at being market researchers by providing them with clipboards. She then called a group of children to work with her on a language activity whilst the 'data collectors' delighted in asking their peers whether they liked carrots and were even amused at asking whether they were a boy or a girl.

Figure 4.9 Tally chart

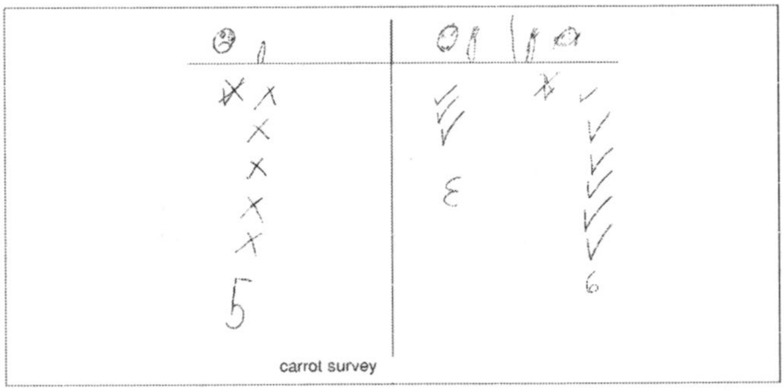

carrot survey

Figure 4.10 Adjusted tally here

At the start of the afternoon session, after the register had been taken, the children were asked to share their findings. They brought their clipboards to the front of the group to 'show' what they had found out. The teacher had anticipated that this would give the opportunity for the children to talk to their peers for the purpose of describing their findings; but because there was little consensus among the researchers with respect to the number of children who liked or disliked carrots, the carpet session produced much rich discussion among the children as to why the results should be so different. *'Did anyone change their mind about liking carrots?'* asked the teacher. *'Do you think Wesley asked everyone in the class?'* As might be anticipated with such young children it transpired that some children had not been consistent in their answers and not only had Wesley not asked some children about whether they liked or disliked carrots, he had asked some twice!

Through well constructed questioning the teacher prompted the children to think about how such difficulties might be avoided in future but resisted the temptation to 'sanitise' the children's data. The following day, she told them, they would make a graph.

The teacher chose to help the children make a pictorial representation of their findings by introducing a chart for the children to complete. They were told that in the top row they would put a picture for each child who did not like carrots. In the next they would put a picture for each boy who liked carrots, and the bottom row a picture for each girl who liked carrots. The children continued with representing like and dislike of carrots by expression and said that they would use a picture of a carrot for children who liked carrots. They then began to translate their information into pictorial form producing graphs like the one shown in Figure 4.11. Once the teacher could see that the children had understood the task she moved her attention to another group of children who had been working on a 'maintenance' activity (working independently of the teacher).

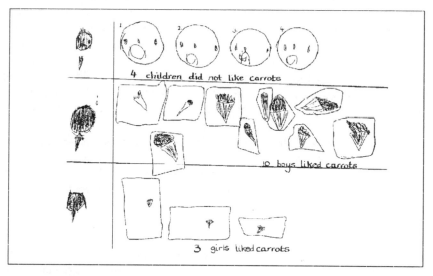

Figure 4.11 Carrot graph

When the graphs were completed the children counted their symbols to find out what their data showed, and the teacher scribed their oral contributions. All agreed that more boys than girls like carrots. 'In *this* class', cautioned the teacher, giving the children the opportunity to suggest that it might be different in another class – but none of the children suggested testing their findings on a wider population. The teacher had earlier seized the moment and she decided not to follow up further at this point.

Case study at Key Stage 2: *Kathy Goodman*

During the spring term, a Year 5 class had followed the topic of looking after themselves as part of their work in science and their personal and social education curriculum. The plan was for the children to study the Victorians in the summer term.

A spell of warm weather had sparked off debate in the media about the incidence of asthma. Since the debate focused on the issue of pollution, the teacher chose to use this to make links between the two topics.

The children watched recorded clips from regional news and were given newspaper cuttings. Without prompting they began to volunteer their own experiences with asthma. There were graphic tales from children who had asthma and those who had had asthma in the past and clearly some felt left out because they did not have to go to the office at lunchtimes to use their inhalers!

When the discussion got to the point of sounding like the conversations overheard in the doctor's surgery, the teacher steered its focus to that of the causes of asthma. She then sat with a group to record their ideas.

Fully anticipating that the question was posed and that the children would be happy to collect data on the causes of asthma, she was surprised to find the children becoming much more interested in the question of whether asthma could be cured. Clearly, given the sample of the school population from which the data was to be collected, this investigation would not be likely to result in rich data handling experience for the children. The teacher did, however, pick up on another part of the discussion where the children were quite animated in their views about whether children can grow out of asthma. This then became the 'big' question.

Having posed the question the children needed no prompting to discuss how they would collect information. *'We can ask everyone in the school!' 'We can do a survey.' 'Can we do a questionnaire like when people stop you in the street?' 'We can print out some graphs on the computer.'* The children's suggestions were received enthusiastically by the teacher and they were excited by the idea of writing a questionnaire on the computer and 'doing some graphs'.

The children had jumped straight to the stages of collecting and representing data. They needed help from the teacher to think more deeply about whom they would ask and the specific questions they would need to ask to find the answer to their main question. Suggestions from the teacher referred back to some of the earlier discussion, for example is there a link between what causes your asthma and whether or not you grow out of it?

Interestingly enough, several children already had some ideas about this. Jasmin thought that *'You might have asthma from car fumes when you are small because you are near the car fumes.'* Joel took this idea further drawing on some sophisticated thinking. He thought that *'You might grow out of asthma because the amount of pollution in the body is less to the size of body as you get bigger.'*

The children then settled in two groups, by choice one of girls and one of boys, to draft their questionnaires. It can be seen from their questions that the children were keen to follow their own lines of enquiry (see Figure 4.12). The questionnaire was then transferred to Junior Pinpoint, a data handling program which constructs a database from the questions posed in the questionnaire (see Figure 4.13). The children were very excited by the sophistication of their published document and could not wait to pilot it on the other members of the class.

Initially, the boys had planned only to survey junior children, but during the pilot Ralph offered the hypothesis *'If you do grow out of asthma there would be less children in Year 6 with asthma than in Red Class (Reception)'*; and so that group decided to include Infant children in their survey. They then evaluated their original questions with particular reference to whether they thought the younger children would be able to understand them. Similarly, the evaluation of the girls' pilot focused on whether or not the questions made sense.

o.Name: _____ Do People Grow out of asthma?
_____

1. Do you have asthma?
Ex.2.Did you ever have asthma?
3.If so then how old were you?
5. Does asthma run in your family?
How long have you had asthma?
6. What do you think brings on your asthma?
Has your asthma got better as you've got older?
7. Have you ever had an asthma attack?

Figure 4.12 Questionnaire in children's writing

What is your name?		
Are you a boy or a girl?	☐ boy	☐ girl
Do you have asthma?	☐ Yes	☐ No
How long have you had asthma?	――――――years	
Did you ever have asthma?	☐ Yes	☐ No
If so how old were you when it started?	――――――	
How old were you when it stopped?	――――――	
Does asthma run in your family?	☐ Yes	☐ No
What do you think brings on your asthma?	――――――	
Have you ever had an asthma attack?	☐ Yes	☐ No
If so how old were you when you had it?	――――――	
Has your asthma got better as you have grown older?	☐ Yes	☐ No

Figure 4.13 Questionnaire produced in Junior Pinpoint

Adjustments to the original questionnaire were made and the children then organised themselves to visit the classrooms to collect their data. Anna could collect information from Years 3 and 4, by administering the questionnaire to the class as a group, whilst Jasmin and Rosie collected information from the reception children who would have to be interviewed.

Hayley would begin work on entering the data as soon as she had a class set of completed sheets.

The children's enthusiasm and the pressure of time led to the omission of a vital stage which was regretted by all later in the project. The information from the pilot survey was not entered into the database for interrogation. In other words, the questionnaire was not evaluated with reference to the scope and limitations of the data handling program. For example, Rosie's insistence on just leaving spaces for people to fill in the causes of their asthma because *'it gives them a chance to answer for themselves' rather than use the multiple choice opti*on in the questionnaire design meant that this data was not easily processed by the computer.

As the children returned to the computer stations with their completed questionnaires so they began to make their entries. Since the whole school had been surveyed there was a large number of entries to be made. Although the educational value of working with real data is evident, that of typing in so many entries can be demotivating. A compromise was reached. Each child made ten entries at convenient times during the day, and the rest were made by the teacher and an assistant. This meant that a system had to be devised so that the children could keep track of the entries. They decided that they would need to keep a note on the hard copy of the number of the corresponding record in the database, and, since there were times when the children needed to refer back to the original documents, this proved to be a very useful precaution.

Excitement levels rose again when the data entries had been completed. The children wanted to play with the program's graphing facility. They were not so interested in the variables as the visual images they could produce! 3-D pie charts were the favourite. They clearly challenged the capabilities of the program and tested its boundaries of graphical representation by asking for a pie chart of all the names of the children in the survey, but for the teacher this was an opportunity to encourage the children to be critical of the graphs they produced (see Figure 4.14).

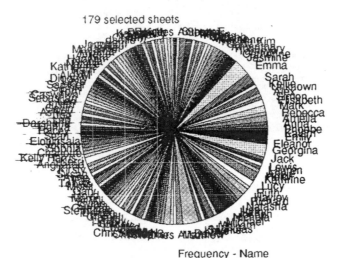

179 selected sheets

Frequency - Name

Figure 4.14 The software will produce this pie chart – but what use is it?

Having given the children the opportunity to explore the program, the teacher refocused the class on the question they were trying to answer. Which graphs would help to show whether children grow out of asthma?

Martin said he wanted to look at a graph of the children in school who had asthma. He produced a pie chart and found that not all children had answered this question. He then went back into the database to find those records, located the hard copy and amended the entries as appropriate. This time he produced a bar chart. With the two types of graph to hand (see Figure 4.15), the teacher asked which of the graphs was more useful. Martin thought that the bar chart was more useful because it gave him the numbers of children with or without asthma. He was challenged by David who thought that the pie chart showed that about an eighth of the children in school have asthma. When the teacher asked whether he thought the actual numbers of people would help find the answer to the question he was adamant that it was the 'amount' not the number. The mathematical term was not readily to hand for David, but clearly he was moving towards grasping the concept of proportion.

'*But does this graph show whether children grow out of asthma?*' prompted the teacher. 'No', replied Ralph, who was keen to test his hypothesis that if children did grow out of asthma there would be more children in Reception with asthma than in Year 6.

The children now needed to interrogate the data further. Using only the records of children with asthma, the computer was asked to draw a graph of comparative ages. The graph in Figure 4.16 was drawn and gave rise to discussion about the information it gave. The children tended not to read the graph for information, but moved straight to interpretation. '*What does this graph tell me?*' the teacher asked. Martin ventured '*Six is the best age for asthma.*' '*The best age Martin? What do you mean "the best age"?*' '*I mean that because there are more children aged six with asthma than aged five, so six is the best start off age for asthma.*' There was some good logic behind Martin's thinking but all that he could tell from the graph was that more children *in the group he surveyed* had started to have asthma at age 6.

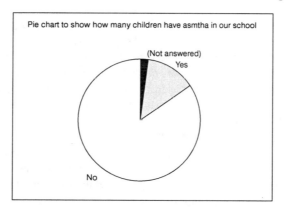

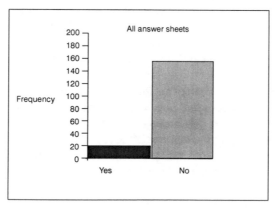

Figure 4.15 Pie and bar charts

Note that the bars of the bar chart should not be touching – see Discrete data in the Glossary

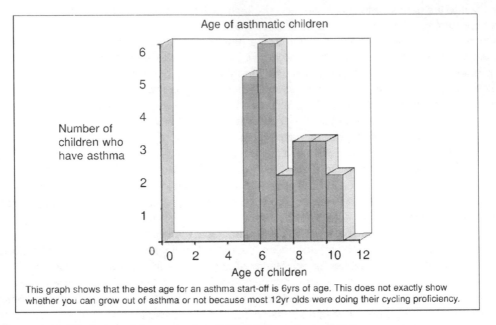

Age of asthmatic children

Number of children who have asthma

Age of children

This graph shows that the best age for an asthma start-off is 6yrs of age. This does not exactly show whether you can grow out of asthma or not because most 12yr olds were doing their cycling proficiency.

Figure 4.16 What does this graph show? (Child's own text added)

In retrospect, maybe slightly more closed questioning might have prompted the children to read more of the information presented by the graph for example 'How many five-year-olds have asthma?' Further areas discussed were the lack of columns for ages 0 to 4. 'That's because everyone we asked was over five', came the confident reply from David. 'So are we able to say that this graph shows that children grow out of asthma?' asked the teacher. 'Oh no!' cried Ralph, his head clasped in his hands, 'We didn't survey all the Year 6 children. They were doing their cycling proficiency!'

Discussion of the graphs generated further lines of enquiry. The girls were interested to know whether the incidence of asthma in a family affected the chances of having and/or growing out of it. The boys were interested to discover whether there was any difference between the number of girls growing out of asthma and the number of boys.

In order to produce the appropriate graphs the girls had to select the records of those children who were asthma free to discover whether they had incidence of asthma in their families. They were very interested to discover that all the 'asthma-free' children came from 'asthma-free' families. From this, they deduced that asthma must run in families. 'It might be different in another school', suggested Jasmin, appreciating the danger of generalising from a sample.

First, the boys produced a pie chart of the total number of boys and girls in the survey. They then looked at the number of boys and girls who have asthma. Reading the graph posed no problem; clearly more boys than girls had asthma. 'OK', encouraged the teacher, 'but let's look back to the graph showing the number of boys in the school.' 'What conclusions can we draw if we look at the two graphs together?' The children were being prompted to deal with some complex thinking, using their knowledge of ratio and proportion. It was clear that they had understood the significance of comparing the two graphs and that they were able to make the appropriate deduction. Their difficulty was in finding the appropriate words to express their findings. 'Look', said Joel, 'this, [Figure 4.17a] shows that there are more girls, than boys and this [Figure 4.17b] shows that more boys than girls have asthma so that means more boys than girls have asthma.' 'But do we need the two graphs to show us that more boys than girls have asthma?' There were sighs of frustration. 'If you are a boy you are more likely to have asthma', offered David. Rosie had become interested in the boys' problem at this point. 'Putting it all together', she ventured, 'it means that the fraction of boys surveyed who had asthma was larger than the fraction of girls that had asthma. So, in our survey, it seems as though boys have more chance of getting asthma.' Ralph then found the word he was looking for: 'If you are a boy, you are more vulnerable to asthma' he concluded with an air of satisfaction.

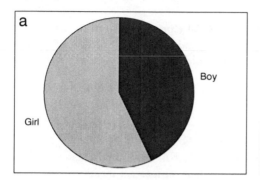
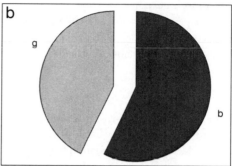

Figure 4.17 What conclusions can be drawn from these graphs?

The children had deviated somewhat from their original question '*Do you grow out of asthma?*', and yet the questions that were arising in discussion were all legitimately part of the overarching question. When sharing their findings, they were critical of the validity of their method of data collection. '*Really*', said Martin, '*I would, personally, question children who have asthma now and those who have had it. I would need to find out whether they had had medicines or special diets, for example.*' '*Well, to make it a fair test*' suggested Rosie, '*you would need to find some young children and ask them about their asthma over several years.*' Both suggestions would clearly help the children to find the answer to their problem but would be impractical in a school.

4.3 MATHEMATICAL THINKING AND DATA HANDLING

Solving problems

In the Foundation Stage case study, the children were asked to think about how they would go about collecting the data and how they would keep track of the information they were gathering. The children decided that they needed a data capture sheet which showed whether the children surveyed liked or disliked carrots and whether they were a boy or a girl.

When they had asked some children they realised that they could not tell how many ticks were boys and how many were girls. They had therefore not identified the key factors they needed to answer their question (monitoring decisions). The teacher talked about this with the children and they adjusted their data capture sheet so that they could find out what they wanted. Because the teacher allowed the children to use that data sheet they were able to discover the limitations of their initial decision.

In the Key Stage 2 case study the children were encouraged to plan so that they would collect data systematically. They were able to decide at the outset how they would obtain information related to the sex of respondent, for example. They were expected to more readily identify the key factors. This does not mean that everything ran smoothly, and, indeed, there was still a great deal of revision, through monitoring, as they proceeded.

Mathematical communication

In the Foundation Stage case study the teacher gave children the opportunity to explain to their peers what they had found out and for others to ask questions. The presentation of results was a pictorial representation, with a written caption (scribed by the teacher in this case).

Giving children the opportunity to explain why they chose a particular way of collecting and representing their data and sharing their findings will help develop their mathematical language and skills of communication.

In the Key Stage 2 case study children used a wider range of representations of their findings and were expected to make decisions about presenting information and results in the most appropriate way. They were being taught how to articulate reasons for their choices.

Reasoning mathematically

At both Key Stages mathematical reasoning was developed by asking children to interpret their results to search for pattern and relationships and to make related predictions.

Some children in the Foundation Stage case study interpreted their results in the statement 'Lots of boys like carrots'. The teacher helped them to refine the implicit comparison by asking, 'So, do more boys than girls like carrots?' Children might be prompted to develop predictions through interest in what other classes might feel about eating carrots, for example 'I wonder whether lots of boys like carrots in Miss A's Class?' This can then be the starting point for the next turn around the data handling cycle.

At Key Stage 2 the children were expected to be more critical and less egocentric in their interpretation of results of data collection. They were expected to be more sophisticated in their analysis and to be able to make deductions beyond the immediately obvious. The key to this is in presenting a rich and relevant context in which we know that children will need to learn about and use mathematical knowledge, skills and understanding. There will be possibilities to respond in different ways according to their confidence and competence, and there will be challenge built in to take their thinking further. As teachers we need to consider the type of questions we ask to stimulate thinking or to find out what sense children are making of the task.

We consider next some points in relation to the role of computer databases in children's data handling.

The use of computer databases

ICT can be used in a variety of ways to support data handling in both Key Stages 1 and 2. In the Key Stage 2 case study, the database played an important part. It should be noted that the Key Stage 1 work could also have incorporated the use of a database, but did not in this instance.

Computer software allows children to handle data efficiently and to have opportunities to interpret a wider range of representations than they could produce themselves. For example, at both Key Stages, children can produce pie charts from data they have put into the database, without having to know how to construct the chart for themselves. They are then freed to concentrate on the more advanced thinking involved in interpretation and deduction.

However, the same key points relate to the use of computers as to learning about data handling in general: that is, to what extent can computer software help children in posing questions, setting up hypotheses, questioning, interpreting results and answering the questions posed? It is important that young children have opportunities to work with real objects in sorting and representing data and that

ICT should should not be used for its own sake but only where it contributes in ways that enhance learning.

Posing the question

The internet can be used to allow children access to real data, such as census data, to explore and interrogate. Comparing results in a local street now with the past could be aided by this, for example. Children in primary school will, in the main, be collecting, storing and retrieving their own data but the internet provides the opportunity to pose questions related to different curriculum areas with older Key Stage 2 children. For example, 'How has the weather changed?' might involve finding the data about the weather (rainfall, hours of sunshine, etc.) over the last 10 years.

Collecting the data

Data capture sheets can be discussed and modeled on a computer screen. Children can begin to evaluate different approaches to collecting data and making decisions. For example, which is easier to read – a table presented vertically or horizontally? Does it matter?

Representing the data

Computer software can quickly recall previous screens, allowing a comparison between different data representations and promote evaluation. From Key Stage 1 the teacher can encourage children to evaluate different representations and make decisions about the clarity of the graph or chart in answering the question posed. In Key Stage 2, children can be introduced to a wider range of representations to evaluate and examine the effect of changing one attribute (for example, the scale).

There is a range of content software for interactive whiteboards available through national websites (www.nrich.org.uk) that provide opportunities for children to become familiar with specific graphs and charts and explore technical aspects. Children can sort provided data into Venn or Carroll diagrams or work out how a bar chart should be labeled, given the title. In this case children need to understand what the graph is saying and relate this to the information given. The teacher can ask the children to justify their thinking by the use of questioning such as 'Why do you think that?' 'Why can't the blue bar represent …?' to promote mathematical thinking.

Simple counts: software allows straightforward inputting of data, such as preferred toy (choice from a list), or likes/dislikes (Computer games – yes/no) (see Figure 4.18). Results appear in a simple chart.

Using software of this type, children can produce various graphs and charts showing their results. They can be encouraged to compare the different representations and make statements about what the results show (see Figure 4.19). In this case children were asked to select the toy they liked best (one response only) and the pie, therefore, actually represents the number of children in the class.

Tree/sorting databases: depend on the logical asking and answering of questions to sort one item of data from another. In a database for 2-D shapes, for example, a question to distinguish a triangle from a square might be '*Does it have 4 sides?*' Children need to know about the subject they are addressing in order to frame questions in setting up the database. They will also develop their classification skills as they move from questions which have a range of possible answers (how many sides does it have?) to ones that can be answered 'yes' or 'no' (does it have three sides?). Once a store of shapes has been set up, other children can interrogate the database by answering, in turn, the questions offered in the search for the shape they are thinking of. If that is not found, the program requests a new question to distinguish it from the last object offered (see Figure 4.20). Children are developing logical thinking here in eliminating other possibilities in the search for a particular shape and experience in defining key discriminatory characteristics.

Through the search and through addition of their own questions, children are responding to questions from information they have gathered and are framing new questions based on their research.

teddies	6
dolls	10
bikes	4
computer games	5
board game	2

Figure 4.18 Toys table

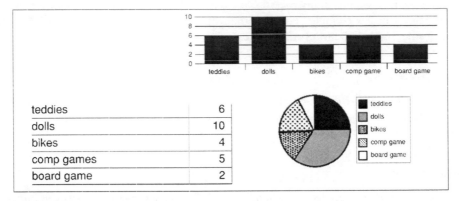

Figure 4.19 Block and pie charts produced from a database

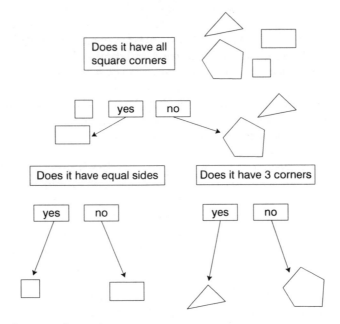

Figure 4.20 Tree diagram of sort shapes

A development in thinking with this type of database is to refine the sequence of questioning to identify the object in an economical number of moves – Can you find your shape with three questions?

The representation of the tree can be reinforced by making a physical representation of a tree using sticks (rulers) to link the objects being sorted on table tops or the floor. Pictorial representation can be made by drawing lines between objects on large sheets of paper. Labels for questions/choices would also be required (see Figure 4.20).

Databases allow the comparison of data and the search for relationships. Information is put into 'files' which can be thought of as index cards (Figure 4.21).

Field names are selected by the user as you set up the database, for example name, age or other personal details. If a card referred to a toy it could have material, power, etc. as field names.

In these programs, children need help to realise when they are operating on a subset of the data. They also need help on how to obtain the data showing the relationship they require, for example 'and' and 'or'. The word 'and' is used to narrow the search. This would produce only girls who like bikes for 'girls and bikes' The 'or' ('girls or bikes'), on the other hand, produces girls who like bikes, girls who do not like bikes and boys who like bikes. Children will need to experiment with the data to develop understanding of the structure (see Figure 4.22).

Spreadsheets have the benefit of showing all the data at once and performing calculations on it. It can produce a range of graphical representations (for example, bar chart, pie chart) quickly and allows children to make comparisons of the different graphical representations easily. If a number entered in a cell is changed, the graph which is based on the spreadsheet is automatically adjusted (see Figure 4.23).

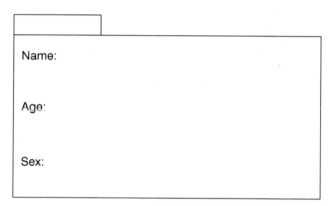

Figure 4.21 Files like index cards

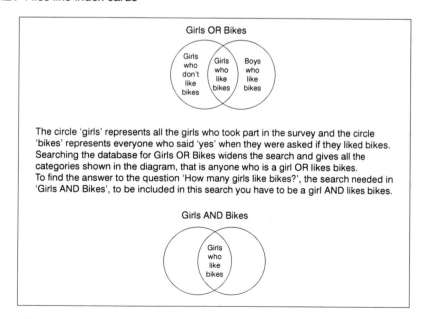

Figure 4.22 OR and AND

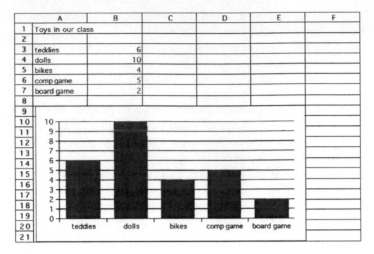

Figure 4.23 Graphical display on a spreadsheet

General points in using databases

Children at both Key Stages 1 and 2 need the experience of putting data into a computer database and producing representations of results to interpret. It is important that children have the opportunity to use physical objects and their written representations alongside the use of computer software to allow a more considered approach to understanding structures. The speed of the computer allows efficient sorting and the production of graphs and so on, but this very characteristic can mask the process by which these outcomes are achieved, and there are points where children may gain from a 'slowing down'.

For example, children can sort real objects on to charts like those produced by the programs by using floor grids. Large grid plastic-coated tablecloth fabric is available from department stores; or the teacher can draw up grids on paper or on the playground depending on what size of square is required. Once the children have placed objects or name cards or number cards to make a chart, the information could be transferred onto the database so that children might have a better understanding of what the computer is doing.

This procedure can also be applied to tree-type databases. Metre rules could be used for the branches on the classroom floor or playground, with objects and cards for questions and 'yes/no' choices, as detailed in the sorting program section above.

Interpretation

Interpretation and analysis of the data is often limited to identifying the least or most popular item, particularly when teachers feel constrained by time and the children have already collected and presented data of their own. Access to data and graphical representations available through software and the internet can provide opportunities to focus on interpreting specific data and making deductions. This may lead onto posing further questions and the data handling cycle can thus be entered at a different point.

Specific programs available nationally and commercially focus on reading and interpreting selected data. For example, a line graph presented with a title only, where children are invited to invent a story to match the line graph. The teacher's role in encouraging children to justify their answers and ideas is crucial and promotes both interest and higher level thinking. For example, looking at electricity usage in a town (Figure 4.24), can children come up with a story to match the line graph?

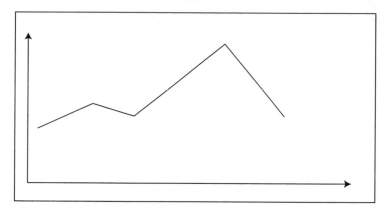

Figure 4.24 Electricity usage in a town

Key points to remember when children are using the computer

When it comes to using the computer:

- All children should have the opportunity to enter data into the computer. However, it can be extremely time consuming to enter all data in this way. Classroom help (classroom assistants or parents) could be brought in so that children are not demotivated by the size of the task.
- When children are having their turn, they should be encouraged to help each other so that their understanding is reinforced by explaining to someone else.
- The teacher needs to get to know the program well to avoid the frustrations children might have in losing data if they are not confident and the teacher is not aware how to retrieve mistakes.
- The teacher needs to find out how to make alterations or add information once a file is set up.
- Data should be saved at regular intervals, particularly if large quantities of data are involved.
- Inaccurate typing or inconsistent use of headings (for example 'dog'/'dogs' used interchangeably) can have unintended results. In the index-type database where children might type in 'dog' for some children and 'dogs' for others, two columns will be produced on a block graph, one labelled 'dog' and the other labelled 'dogs'. This can be a point for discussion, but can be frustrating. The teacher needs to find out about these effects through familiarisation with the program or be prepared to discuss them.

Activities

There are many different contexts in which data handling can be used and we can only give a flavour of the kinds of questions which might prove fruitful for investigation. In line with earlier comments, children will gain from handling data of relevance to them, and our experience tells us that motivation is encouraged if children genuinely have an interest or issue to pursue. This means that the teacher's role should be to identify starting points which will stimulate the children in the particular class, and note questions arising from planned work. The examples that follow provide general guidance for types of question and helpful resources.

Having stressed the need to take starting points close to the children, it is necessary to say something about topics which require sensitivity because they are too personal and might cause upset or embarrassment. It needs to be considered in advance, where possible, what these might be and how to deal with them. For instance, asking children to compare weight with others might cause more unease than asking them to compare their own height and foot lengths to look for a proportional relationship – 'Is it true that your feet fit about six times into your height?' Questions about parents or family circumstances are also areas of sensitivity. Differences between children (for example cultural background) can be dealt with positively if the climate in the classroom is conducive to open discussion, with the teacher as chairperson. Of course, as we have said, data handling can be used to examine issues, which might be controversial, such as children choosing to investigate dominance of the playground by football. In these ways children can begin to see how they can support a particular viewpoint with data and how data can be used (or abused) to show different viewpoints. The teacher's role is to consider issues of sensitivity during planning for work with children and to make professional educational judgements about the best way to handle them in the particular context. One condition, which might have an influence, for example, is how well the teacher knows the class.

Examples for Foundation Stage/Key Stage 1

Starter questions – problems, mathematics and other curriculum areas

Making decisions about classroom issues and curriculum areas

What story shall we read?
How shall we organise the books?
How can we make using the computer fair?
How many children are having dinner/milk today?
What is your favourite fruit?

Mathematics

Which number comes up most often when we roll the dice?
Which box holds the most?
What goes in my set (sorting/logic, for example with shapes)?
What shapes can you find with four sides?

Science

Which ball is the bounciest?
Which car goes fastest down the ramp?
Where did we find most minibeasts in the school grounds?

Other

What is the favourite book in this class?
Which is the most used letter of the alphabet?
How many brothers or sisters do you have?

Resources

Apparatus helpful in creating representations

Set rings/string/ropes/hoops – table top or children in hoops.
Abacuses (open at the top) to make physical block graphs.
Unifix or other cubes.
Grids of various sizes, some reusable (for example fabric with squares large enough to contain objects such as fruit). Some will have only two columns.
Reusable items to use as objects/symbols on graphs:

- small photos of children;
- name cards;
- matchboxes with children's names.

Examples for Key Stage 2

Making decisions about classroom issues and areas

Lost property, for example, How can the 'lost property' be made more efficient?
Use of classroom areas/resources, for example, How can we make using the keyboard fair?
What is the probability that the weather will be fine on sports day?

Personal issues

What is the average pocket money in this class? Which is most appropriate mean, mode or median?
Is my bedtime reasonable?
Do adults watch more television than children?
Can people with big feet run faster?

Other curriculum areas

What worked best in attracting particular birds to our bird table?
Which is the best waterproofing material?
What was the most common occupation of the people living in our street 100 years ago?

4.4 PROBABILITY

Probability in society

Many of the decisions we make in life involve a level of uncertainty. In order to make informed judgements we need to have some understanding of probability. As adults, our decisions are often informed by our experience and knowledge of a situation. For example, if we are planning a barbecue, we may have a back-up plan for the eventuality of bad weather. Children do not have such a repertoire of knowledge to draw on, and so may make decisions based on intuition. Of course, adults also use intuition, and the problem with this approach is that decisions based on it are often wrong! Examples of intuitive reasoning are: '*When I go to the supermarket the other queues always move faster than mine.*' '*It isn't fair to have to get a six to start a game because it's harder to get a six.*'

Young children are also likely to explain events in relation to themselves, for example, '*I like that number*' or '*That number likes me*'.

Early ideas of probability: usually centre on discussions about the likelihoods of different events happening in stories or in the child's experience. Here, prediction is involved in thought about appropriate possible outcomes, for example, '*What do you think will happen next in the story?*' '*Do you think Jenny will meet a dragon in the street?*'

A simple activity which can be set up to develop these processes (as well as to sharpen observation before an outing) is to ask children about what they expect to see '*on your way home tonight*', '*when we go to the park tomorrow*', '*when we visit the farm next week*' or '*on our outing at the end of term*'. What kind of ideas do children have about what they are likely to see? ('*What will we definitely see?*' '*What won't we see?*' '*What might we see?*').

Again, in discussion about everyday life, children could be asked what events they see as certain or unlikely? ('*I'll definitely get sweets tonight because we go to Sainsbury's every Thursday*' '*I'll never see an elephant in school!*'). Quite a lot of fun and imagination can be had in these discussions as children predict events and discuss possibilities in real life and in fantasy.

Another aspect of prediction is the role of chance, as in some games. Dice throwing or card selection, for example, could be the subject of debate. It is interesting to ask whether children (and adults) take losing very much to heart because they do not fully understand the role of chance and feel they have more control over events than they actually do. Games of chance (Snakes and Ladders) can be contrasted with games including an element of decision making (as in Monopoly), and children can design and make games which incorporate chance or strategy aspects. They will be aware of competitions such as at the school fair, raffles or the National Lottery and will be able to discuss their understanding of what you have to do to win.

At Key Stage 2 ideas of fairness, certainty, likelihood and terms such as 'probable', 'equally likely' will be developed. Ordering events in terms of likelihood, such as 'unlikely', 'possible', 'probable' and 'definite', will underpin the concept of a 'probability scale'. This experience should help children to move more smoothly on to the numerical scale, where absolute certainty is denoted by 1 (or 100%) and absolute impossibility by 0. Inbetween positions can be labelled as percentages, vulgar fractions or decimal fractions (for example 'evens' would be 50% or 5/10 or 0.5). The other main aspect of prediction is estimation. Activities here could involve conducting experiments to estimate (for example rolls of dice) or learning about situations where outcomes are equally likely (for example rolling a number 1 to 6 on a dice).

Activities

Key Stage 1

Preparing for an outing to the park, ask children to contribute to lists:

We will see …
We might see …
We won't see …

Encourage children to give reasons for their choices and you can make assessments of their reasoning.

On return from the park, compare observations with predictions. Ask questions such as, '*Why didn't we see many leaves?*' or '*How many things did we guess right?*'

Discussions about luck and games

(a) Ask children about luck, 'When you play games, are you lucky?' Probe to find out what children think makes them lucky. What do they think it means to be lucky?
(b) Observe children playing games with dice. What sort of comment do they make about the number they want? For example, one six year old when asked whether it is hard to get six, said, 'It's not hard for me … well sometimes it's hard. When I get bigger I think I will throw it better … (but it's broken now so I can't play it any more!)'. Children can develop some ideas of chance by experiencing different types of game, some based on chance and some with strategy.
(c) The following is a list of books that have been used to stimulate discussion on likelihood.

- *Anno's Hat Tricks*, Mitsumasa Anno, Bodley Head.
- *The Shopping Basket*, John Burningham, Picture Lions.
- *Time to Get Out of the Bath, Shirley*, John Burningham, Picture Lions.
- *The Tiny Seed*, Eric Carle, Hodder & Stoughton.
- *Dear Zoo*, Rod Campbell, Picture Puffin.
- *How Many Bugs in a Box?*, David Carter, Orchard Books.
- *Princess Smartypants*, Babette Cole, Picture Lions.
- *Rosie's Walk*, Pat Hutchins, Bodley Head.
- *The Doorbell Rang*, Pat Hutchins, Picture Puffin.
- *Clotilda's Magic*, Jack Kent, Hippo Books.
- *There's No Such Thing as a Dragon*, Jack Kent, Blackie.
- *The Tiger Who Came to Tea*, Judith Kerr, Collins.
- *Not Now Bernard*, David McKee, Sparrow Books.
- *On the Way Home*, Jill Murphy, Macmillan.

- *On Friday Something Funny Happened*, John Prater, Picture Puffin.
- *Alexander and the Terrible, No Good, Very Bad Day*, Judith Viorst, Angue & Robertson.

Key Stage 2

Find the Fairer Game (from NCTM 1981)

There are actually two games, based on scoring odd and even numbers with dice. Both need two people, two dice (numbered 1 to 6), paper and pen for recording and a watch or timer. For each game play three rounds.

One person claims 'odd' results and the other 'even'. Time each round equally, say two or three minutes.

First game: Roll the dice and find the difference between the two numbers. If the result is odd, the 'odd' person gets a point. If it is even, the 'even' person scores. Continue for the allotted time and compare results (count 0 as even). What do you notice about them?

Second game: play as the first but this time multiply the two numbers and record as before.

The winner in each game is the person with more points.

Questions: Which is the fairer game and why? Children can be asked to make a table of results to analyse. They will need to investigate what happens when you find the difference between or multiply odd and even numbers. It will be seen that finding the difference between two odds and two evens produces an even result while finding the difference between an odd and an even or an even and an odd number on the dice yields an odd number (i.e. there is an equal chance of scoring odd or even). With multiplication, however, the person seeking even results will score more because an odd result will only be obtained if two odd numbers are rolled. The other combinations produce even numbers. Thus, the first game is fairer.

Ordering events according to likelihood, leading to the idea of a scale

This can be done by suspending cards on a length of string or lining them up across a table top. It is some times helpful to make up some for children to use at first and then get them to make up their own (Figure 4.25).

These cards can be ordered, after discussion between children, by the degree of likelihood. The discussion will encourage children to give reasons for choices and the task requires agreement if done as a group. A scale can be introduced by first using labels such as 'certain', 'possible' and 'impossible'. Refinements can be made and more categories created – 'highly likely', 'likely', 'unlikely' and 'highly unlikely'. Then numerical scales can be introduced – 0 for impossible and 1 for certain. As ideas are refined, subdivisions will be needed and conventions of 'half' or 50% or 0.5 for only two equally likely outcomes can be added to 100% or 1 for 'certain'. Further subdivisions will be necessary as children discuss the relative likelihood of various events (see Glossary).

It will rain tomorrow	An elephant will walk past the school	I will win the Lottery	I will come to school tomorrow

Figure 4.25 Probability statement cards

Glossary

*This section is intended as a reference for teachers and not all of the terms
mentioned need be used directly with children.*

Attribute (also property): a quality possessed by an object or subject, for example soft,
battery operated, round, straight.

Average: we use an average when we represent a set of data by a single representative
value which typifies that set. At Key Stage 2 children should understand and use the different
averages: **'mean', 'median' and 'mode'** (see headings below).

Block graph or bar chart: in general there should be spaces between the columns (see Figure
4.26). Touching columns can be used to represent continuous or grouped data provided the
horizontal axis is marked like a ruler (see Figure 4.27).

Carroll Diagram: a two-way table that summarises a situation based on two different criteria
(see Figure 4.28). This is named after Lewis Carroll.

Charts/tables: large sets of data can be recorded in a way which makes the data more
accessible (see Figure 4.29).

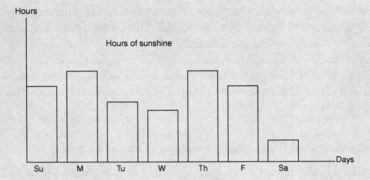

Figure **4.26** Bar chart: discrete data

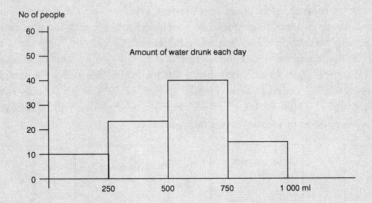

Figure 4.27 Bar chart: continuous data

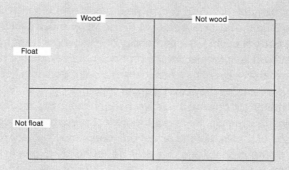

Figure 4.28 Carroll diagram

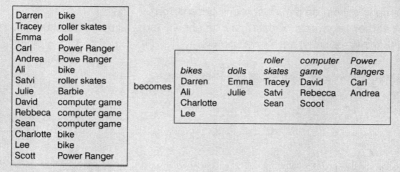

Figure 4.29 List/table

Class interval: often a set of data is too varied for direct tabulation and representation to be useful, so it is more convenient to group the data into classes. The class interval represents the range in any one class, for example heights of children, amount of pocket money, etc.

Table 4.3 Data grouped in classes

Cost of toys/favourite toys	Number of toys	Total
£0–£4.99	////	4
£5–£9.99	///	3
£10.00–£14.99	///	3

Continuous data (and discrete data): consider a running race. The number of runners taking part is **discrete data,** expressed in whole numbers (4, 6, 10 … contestants). It would not make sense to talk about 1.5 runners. The time in which they complete the race is **continuous data,** points along a range (47 secs, 47.5 secs, 50.8 secs …). Discrete data should be represented by non-touching bars on a bar chart and continuous data should have touching bars, only if the horizontal axis is marked like a ruler. Continuous data is usually grouped (for example in the race example, 45 to 47.59 seconds, 48–50.59 seconds …).

Data collection sheet: a table, chart, or even questionnaire, designed for organising the collection of data.

Discrete data (see 'Continuous data' above).

Event: a mathematical term to describe a situation which may have more than one outcome (for example in rolling a dice numbered 1 to 6 there are six possible outcomes of the event of rolling the dice). **Independent event** – where one event is not affected by the outcome of another event (for example if rolling a dice nine times had resulted in 6 each time, the probability of scoring 6 on the next roll is still 1 in 6 – however much it might be suspected the dice is loaded!). **Dependent event** – the probability of selecting a heart from a pack of cards is 13 out of 52. If that card is not replaced, the probability of selecting a heart next will be 12 out of 51. **Mutually exclusive events** – when tossing a coin, getting a head and getting a tail are mutually exclusive events, as they cannot occur together.

Experimental probability (or observed relative frequencies): the results obtained from an experiment or survey. For example, there is a theoretical probability of scoring 25 heads and 25 tails from 50 tosses of a coin, but the actual outcomes may be very different, particularly for a small sample. Some probabilities can only be found by experiment, for example the probability of being late for work.

Frequency diagram: the generic name for pictorial representation of relative frequencies (for example on a graph for how children travel to school, data recorded would show how many children came to school on particular forms of transport).

Frequency table: large sets of data may be shown more simply in a table recording the number of times (frequency) each value occurs.

Table 4.4 Frequency table for heights in a Year 3 class

110	115	121	111
111	130	119	113
115	135	126	132
121	123	135	113
135	128	134	118

This data could then be grouped (as it is continuous), for example 81–90 centimetres and frequency graphed (see Figure 4.30) from the following figures.

Table 4.5 Grouped continuous data

Class	Frequency
110–120 cm	9
120–130 cm	5
130–140 cm	6

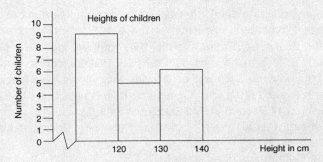

Figure 4.30 Frequency graph

Grouped data: data which is grouped into **classes,** as in the heights in the **frequency diagram** entry above. The group becomes the **class interval.** This usually applies to **continuous data.** It may also be convenient to group **discrete data,** for example 0–4 seeds, 5–9 seeds, 11–14 seeds, 15–19 seeds.

Line graphs: a line graph is used when representing two sets of continuous data. Remember each point on the line/curve must be meaningful, for example a graph to convert temperatures from Fahrenheit to Celsius (see Figure 4.31). Each point is meaningful and the line joining them shows a proportional increase.

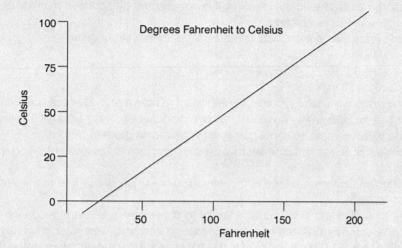

Figure 4.31 Line graph (Fahrenheit to Celsius)

Mean: the mean, sometimes referred to as the arithmetic mean, is found by totalling all the data values and dividing the total by the number of data items. The mean value tells us how much time each child would spend playing with their toys if they each played with them for the same amount of time, or how much pocket money they would each have if they all had the same.

Time in minutes:

10, 10, 10, 15, 15, 30, 30, 30, 30, 30, 60, 60, 60, 60, 120

Arithmetic mean (as shown in Figure 4.32):

$$= \frac{10 + 10 + 10 + 15 + 15 + 30 + 30 + 30 + 30 + 30 + 60 + 60 + 60 + 60 + 120}{15}$$

Figure 4.32 Calculating the mean – equals 38 minutes.

Median: the median is the element which occupies the central position when the data has been ordered. In a survey to discover how much time children spent playing with their favourite toys, the median would be found by arranging the times in order of magnitude, taking account of each score, and finding the value which occupies the central position.

Time in minutes:

10, 10, 10, 15, 15, 30, 30, 30, 30, 30, 60, 60, 60, 60, 120

Median value equals 30 minutes.

Where there is an even number of values the median value need not be one of the amounts but would be the middle value for the two central values.

Time in minutes:
10, 10, 10, 10, 15, 15, 30, 30, 40, 40, 40, 60, 60, 60, 60, 120
Median value (as shown in Figure 4.33):

$$\frac{30 + 40}{2} = 35 \text{ minutes}$$

Figure 4.33 Calculating the median – equals 30 minutes

The median can be preferable to the mean as it is not affected by spurious data values, for example extreme values have no effect.

Mode: the mode is the element that occurs most frequently in a set of data.
     Time in minutes:
     10, 10, 10, 15, 15, <u>30, 30, 30, 30, 30,</u> 60, 60, 60, 60, 120
     The modal value is 30 minutes.
     Although the mode is a useful average it is important to note that it does not take account of the other values and there may be more than one modal value. It is particularly useful for non-numeric data, for example colour of hair/eyes, examination grades.

Outcome: the result of an event. There are six possible outcomes to the event of rolling a dice numbered 1 to 6.

Pictograms: a graph using repetitions of the same symbol to show the size of the variable (see Figure 4.4 (p. 119)).

Pie chart: this type of graph is particularly useful to show how a whole is made up from its parts. It is probably more difficult to construct than to interpret. Computer database and spreadsheet packages can allow young children to produce data in this form without the need to deal with its construction. (See references to pie charts in earlier parts of Section 4, including the Key Stage 2 case study.)

Probability scale: the probability of an event occurring is a measure of how likely it is to occur. Events can be categorised on a continuum between impossible and certain, on a scale from 0 to 1 (see Figure 4.34):

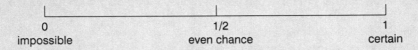

0	1/2	1
impossible	even chance	certain

Figure 4.34 Probability scale

Range: the range indicates the spread in a set of data values. It is the difference between the smallest and the largest value.

Scatter diagram (or scattergraph): a scatter diagram is used to show whether there is any relation between two variables (see Figure 4.6 (p. 120)).

Tallying: a tally is made by recording a series of single strokes. Usually every fifth stroke is a bar to the other four for easy counting.

Theoretical probability: a description of the probability that an event will occur based on a knowledge of *equally likely* outcomes. The theoretical probability of picking an ace from a pack of playing cards is 4/52 or 1/13.

Tree diagram: this is the result of the sorting and classifying of data using a decision tree structure. It is used in identifying specimens in science for example, often using questions to which the answer can only be 'yes' or 'no' (see Figure 4.20 (p. 134)). It is also used for summarising outcomes in a probability experiment, for example two coins (see Figure 4.35):

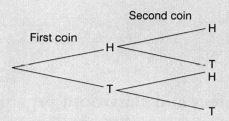

Figure 4.35 Tree diagram

There are four outcomes HH, HT, TH and TT.

Venn diagram: this is a pictorial representation from the sorting of data using two or more attributes. The Venn diagram (see Figure 4.36) here shows a sorting of a collection of shapes, including triangles, which have right angled corners. The shapes have been sorted according to whether they are triangles and have right angled corners but are not triangles. The section in the overlap between the two sets contains shapes which have both attributes – triangles with a right angle.

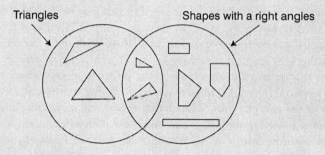

Figure 4.36 Venn diagram

Planning, assessment and classroom organisation

5.1 PLANNING AND ASSESSMENT

Mathematics lessons can involve a variety of activities. They might be structured in parts with a mental and oral starting activity, a main activity and a plenary session. There might be a mathematics investigation workshop with all the children working from the same starting point where different outcomes will be anticipated by the teacher, based on knowledge and observation of the children, as in Section 2.2 in the How many ways? activity.

Other stimuli can lead into mathematics work in the classroom such as enquiry that can arise in cross-curricular contexts. If young children are engaged in role play in the home corner for example, counting might be used in laying the table. In the case study in Section 4.2, data handling was addressed at Key Stage 1, arising from the reading of a story. With older children work on number might arise in calculating how long ago something happened in history. Sometimes these will be taken up at the time by the teacher and sometimes inform the planning of experiences to address a lack of understanding or to extend thinking. Children might be designing and making (a block construction, notices for the shop in the role play area, vehicles that move) and comparing and measurement are needed in the process of achieving the design aim and these skills might usefully be anticipated and taught in preparation. Some mathematics may be taught as a result of a problem arising in the context. For instance, in Section 3.4 in the packaging case study, the teachers made use of the opportunity for children to explore equivalent ways of expressing weights of objects, involving decimals and place value. This may arise in a design and technology context. In Section 4.2 the Key Stage 2 data handling case study could have arisen from a study of looking after ourselves, linked with science or health.

Early years settings

In the Foundation Stage mathematics may be planned as an area of experience, mainly addressed in particular aspects of the provision, such as block play or group singing times. It may also be planned as a result of observation of individual children's needs and interests, such as an interest in big numbers.

A useful starting point for this stage of education is identifying the mathematical potential in existing provision. One aspect may permeate a range of areas. For instance children might not learn about volume and capacity only at the sand and water trays. There will be other contexts for addressing capacity such as in pouring 'cups of tea' in the home corner 'How many cups can we get from this tea pot?' – or in real contexts like 'juice time', sharing juice between children. The water tray can also be the site of other aspects, for example, if children are testing how many puffs of breath send boats across the water, counting is involved. The teacher can observe and encourage the child in this context: 'Which one was best?' 'How many puffs did you do?'

The teacher's planning and interaction with the children is crucial; for instance a judicious choice of containers will encourage discussion about the relative capacities because tall thin containers and wide flat ones can all hold the same.

Counting books and stories such as 'The Great Big Enormous Turnip' can encourage children to tackle number in a context. Children can be asked to predict how many people there will be next.

Enactment can make this even more memorable. It is important that stories like this are chosen to allow children to encounter numbers beyond 3.

Board games with simple tracks and dice are good practice for counting and may have been experienced at home. The shopping game described in the case study in Section 2.2 is an example of a different sort of game which also gives opportunities for counting and prediction as well as shopping role play and turn taking.

Everyday contexts in the nursery can be used to give mathematics a real purpose, for example 'Can you get aprons for these children?' Observing a child's response to this can be informative – does the child grab an armful, match or count to do this? There are also many opportunities in the organisation of the day – tidying blocks away and making sure they fit the right way in the box (shape, space and measures), sorting objects into the right places (sorting and classifying). Children can see whether they have all the pieces needed for a game (for four children to play the Insey Winsey Spider Game (Orchard Toys) there need to be four spiders) or put pieces away in relation to numbers on tins or boxes. Signs such as 'four children may play with the sand' are also good reference points for children in learning about number and numerals. The discussion with the teacher in these contexts will help children to articulate their ideas and allow assessment of understanding.

Planning and assessment

It is usually considered that planning and assessment follow the cycle shown in Figure 5.1. We would suggest, however, that the activities of planning, teaching, assessing and evaluating are not separate and sequential in practice. Assessment needs to be built in at the planning stage, so that the teacher knows what, who, how and when to assess. For assessment to inform teaching (Assessment for Learning) it needs to be undertaken on a day-to-day basis. This will also contribute to the evaluation of teaching effectiveness. The key steps are:

- identify the learning objectives;
- read about them;
- consider possible activities;
- identify assessment points;
- refine to weekly or daily plans.

What is to be taught will come from long-term planning, that is what is planned for a particular year group in a particular year. Here it will also be necessary to make provision for transitional (summative) assessment. Longer-term planning will need breaking down in medium term plans (usually a half term) where it will be clearer when and in which order mathematics will be taught for a particular class or year group and periodic assessment will be planned. Finally teachers will draw up short-term plans (for example, weekly) to identify more specifically what activities and contexts will be used.

Teachers need to be confident in their own knowledge of key mathematical ideas, language and the misconceptions children might display. To address this, teacher handbooks of published schemes, sections of this book or other reference and resource books will be helpful. Awareness of these aspects

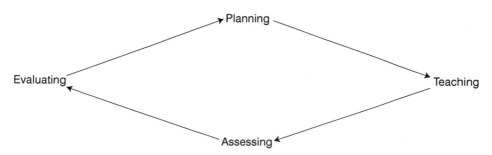

Figure 5.1 Planning and assessment cycle

will inform the teacher in selecting activities and contexts to stimulate mathematical thinking, apply mathematical knowledge, consolidate learning and so on.

For example, a teacher may be planning to address the learning of number bonds as key facts in supporting mental strategies. Encouraging children to spot and articulate the pattern in, say, 1 + 9, 2 + 8, 3 + 7 ('one side goes up and the other side goes down'), should help in the memorisation of these facts or to support them in deriving new facts and check 'wobbly' ones. The How many ways? activities in Sections 2.2 and 2.6 would address this and more, in helping children to spot patterns in number bonds and extend into other ways of making a particular number. Taking this through each of the planning stages listed above for children in Key Stage 1, it might address the following.

Identify the learning objectives

These might include children identifying pairs of numbers for ten in a variety of contexts, being able to represent these pairs with their fingers and being able to use commutativity to see that the facts can be reversed to produce the same result (9 + 1 = 1 + 9). In addition they will be encouraged to generalise the pattern, using talk and appropriate language ('*2 is 1 more than 1 and 8 is one less than 9*'), and apply the facts in the context of problems.

Objectives may also relate to collaborative working – discussing and reaching agreed solutions such as convincing a partner that all combinations have been identified

Attitudinal objectives are also important – are curiosity and enthusiasm promoted?

Read about them

Here teachers need to be aware of the place of number facts in supporting confident calculation. In Section 2 the key idea of number bonds was illustrated through images produced in the how many ways activities. Children's learning may be supported by building mental pictures from activities using arrangements of objects or dots. Then the role of recording and moving to the use of symbols needs to be understood. For example, encouraging children to find their own ways of recording may offer an insight into children's understanding of number patterns and knowledge of conventional symbols.

Consider possible activities and groupings

Reading about key ideas should support the choice of appropriate activities and resources – the How many ways? activities in Section 2 include the use of various resources, for example, cubes in two colours to allow the number pairs to be highly visible. Children would be asked to find as many sticks of 10 as they can, using the two colours. Having those arrangements in front of them is intended to give a clear visual image of the pairs and asking children to find an order would be aimed at their spotting the increasing and decreasing pattern. For reasoning, questions might include '*Have you made them all?*' '*Are they all different?*' '*What do you notice about these two (for example, sticks with four red, six yellow and six red, four yellow)?*' '*How do you know you have made them all?*'

Deciding whether:

- children to work individually or in pairs to find all the ways (or 'think, pair, share'). What kind of grouping would support the learning?;
- would children benefit from individual working to spot patterns?;
- what kind of talk would help learning?;
- how would talk or recording support this activity?

Identify assessment points

As children work on these problems, do they:

- work systematically and find patterns (notice that as one number increases the other decreases)?;
- use symbols or drawings to record (numbers, dots, equations)?;
- explain patterns they see (*'if you add one here, you take one away here'*)?;
- have difficulty in maintaining the total amount (lose track of the total always being 10)?;
- make predictions (*'I think it will be 2 because with 7 it was 3 to make 10 and now 8 is one more'*)?

Teachers will ask questions as children work to make assessments of these and other possible understanding. If there is written recording, this can provide evidence of understanding. This might require discussion with the children, too. Asking children to share their findings with others can also provide the opportunity for teacher assessment.

Refine to weekly or daily plans

The spread of objectives and activities in short-term (weekly or daily) planning will depend on knowledge of the class and the wider curriculum being provided. Weekly plans will need to be adjusted daily as teachers observe children's responses and identify learning needs as work progresses. For example, with the child's work in Section 2, Figure 2.7, following discussion with the child and the assessment that she had begun to see a pattern, the teacher intervened to discuss recording and to prompt the writing of the number bonds in symbols. The intervention also supported the recognition of the pattern.

Addressing assessment and following on from the identification of assessment points in planning, the ways in which judgements will be made about learning need to be planned too, through identifying strategies and setting up systems for recording.

Some useful assessment strategies

- Asking children to talk through what they have just been doing; this can allow children to spot mistakes for themselves as well as giving insights into their strategies.
- Asking a group of children to solve the same problem, then asking individuals to explain methods; an example of this is the children explaining methods for working out six nines (see Section 2.3, circle game case study).
- Asking a group of children to solve a problem collectively, then listening to the discussion (for example, Section 3.4, packaging case study).
- Asking children to report back to the whole group at the end of the session. This gives them opportunities not only to communicate findings, but to explain their thinking to support the development of their reasoning. They can be asked to explain methods used, and to justify choices they have made about methods and apparatus (for example, Section 4.2, Key Stage 1 data handling case study).
- Giving children a choice of apparatus which includes some unsuitable equipment. For instance, offering children shells of different sizes and Multilink for weighing allows the teacher to see if children appreciate the need for equal units. Questioning them will help in ascertaining whether they have chosen the unsuitable materials just on a whim, or because they really do not understand.
- Asking children to record a practical or mental activity in their own way. What they choose to stress or ignore, and the use of abstract symbols or language used will give clues to be followed up by questioning. For examples of children's recording see Section 2.2, Figures 2.5 to 2.9.
- Giving children a range of examples to sort, which includes a variety of non-standard possibilities as well as more common ones, together with 'nearly but not quite examples' will help to show whether they are focusing on significant features. An example of this is discussed in Section 3.1, introduction to the shape and space section.
- Making deliberate mistakes, or examples which follow children's incorrect reasoning, in an atmosphere which invites them to correct the teacher. One example might be cutting unequal 'halves' and

seeing if children spot this. A useful strategy with very young children is to have a puppet or toy that is not very expert and known to get into muddles, and invite the children to help out, for instance in sorting letters from numbers, or making number sentences.

- Asking children to give instructions to someone else, as with the drawing activities in Section 3.2.
- Asking children to use an idea in a different context: care needs to be taken that the context is one in which the child feels confident, and that the level of difficulty is not too high, or the accumulation of unfamiliar challenges may make the problem overwhelmingly difficult. Examples of this are the problems for multiplication and division of converting currencies and scales, or costing drinks for a party in Section 2.3.
- Asking children what they thought about doing an activity; this may range from asking children to select from a smiley face or a frowning face, to choosing statements such as '*I did my best*' or '*I could have tried harder*' or asking children what they found difficult or easy. Older children might keep a mathematics diary, in which they record activities and reflections on them; this can form the basis for a written or verbal dialogue with the teacher.

Recording assessments

Some different kinds of recording

- Identifying particular needs during a session: the teacher notes these in a daily diary and refers to them when planning the next stage of the work. In Section 2.2 in the nursery shopping game case study, a group of children could already confidently read numerals to 6 on a dice and the teacher could build on this in making future provision for these children.
- A child makes a significant breakthrough in understanding, revealed by a comment; the teacher has a record book with a page per child and, as part of a regular routine, notes this at the end of the day. This is referred to when writing a summative report for parents. If the significant remark was in relation to some work on paper, this (or a photocopy) is put in the child's file, with the context and the remark written on the back. If this is the main mode of record keeping, it is useful for the teacher to keep a review chart (see Figure 5.2) at the front of files as mentioned above. If this has the children's names down the side, and date when entries are made, the teacher can check all children are receiving attention.
- Making observations of very young children. The teacher may spend 10 minutes of each session observing a particular child, as well as noting significant incidents. Usually such observations will cover social, emotional, physical and cognitive aspects of learning, including more than one area of learning, such as language and communication and mathematics. Sometimes the focus will be more mathematical, perhaps because the child is playing a game, or solving a problem involving mathematics. Where the teacher works as part of a team, the observations are usually shared, before being filed, by placing them in a central location, and implications for planning are identified by the team.
- Working with a focus group. The teacher may prepare a sheet to record observations for the group,

Names	Using and Applying	Number	Shape and space	Data handling

Figure 5.2 Review chart

with headings. This can be photocopied to put in each child's file. At intervals they can be reviewed and patterns of development identified. Figure 5.3 is an example from the packaging case study in Section 3.4. The headings are adapted from A Guide to the Primary Learning Record (Hester et al. 1993).

- Noting responses of the whole class in a record book with children's names listed down one side of each page; the teacher will record one line of observation and comment against each child's name (see Figure 5.4). This is particularly useful for regular written work from the class which needs to be analysed after each session, noting children with difficulties or needing further challenge. This allows the teacher to modify work in the following session. Developments can then be followed through easily by following an individual child's name across several pages. These record formats can also be printed on the back of weekly plans, or interleaved with them, so they can be easily referred to when planning and tracking progress. Entries might look something like this:
- Children make their own responses and self-assessments. Children learn more effectively when they are involved in assessing their achievements (against learning objectives) and in setting targets for themselves. For older children, written feedback may be part of a written dialogue with the child, which includes their self-assessment and targets, and in some schools children keep notebooks or mathematics diaries for this purpose. Younger children may be asked to pick smiley or frowning faces to reflect their feelings about an activity. Whatever their age, children will need to discuss their achievements with their teacher. Children need careful support from their teacher in this process.
- Keeping a class progress review sheet for a particular topic: this may simply help the teacher to keep track of who has done what, but it may also allow the teacher to summarise progress and note children having problems, in coded form such as ticks and stars, plus one-phrase comments where needed. This acts as a reference when planning work and future assessment, and helps to identify

CONTEXT	Designing packaging for delicatessen items
NAMES	
ATTITUDE AND APPROACH	
STRATEGIES Estimating Measuring	
UNDERSTANDING Calculating volume Making nets	
CHILD'S COMMENT	
SIGNIFICANCE AND PLANNING	

Figure 5.3 Recording observations

Date 13/11/07 investigating nets for cubes (page 35, Book 4)	
Fadilah A.	No problems. Go onto nets of other 3-D shapes.
Tom C.	Found it difficult to predict which nets would fold into cubes. Use polydrons.
Rheem S.	Had system for checking all possibilities: 'You have to have one sticking out on each side'.
Tracey W.	Found all possibilities but hadn't explained system. Talk to her.

Figure 5.4 Entries in record book

groups of children with similar needs in a particular area. This would supplement but not replace evidence of what children say, do and produce. For the multiplication work described earlier the review sheet might have these headings:

Names	Use and apply	Repeated additiong	Recall factors	Multiplication and divison by 10	2 digit multiplication

Figure 5.5 Class progress review sheet

Reporting

Reporting methods will depend largely on school policies and national requirements. Normally teachers summarise children's progress at the end of the topic, term or year and keep samples of work. This needs to reflect a broad spectrum of mathematics and to include attitudes. The acid test for an assessment and record keeping system is, if at any time of the year a parent asks about a child's progress in mathematics, can the teacher provide a detailed answer, with some examples, relating to different aspects of mathematics, and with indications of the child's mathematical needs? If a child has particular learning needs, then more detailed evidence of patterns of behaviour will be required. Parents can make a positive contribution if reports advise them on the types of activities they could pursue with the children at home.

5.2 CLASSROOM ORGANISATION

Atmosphere and ethos

It is essential to consider what kind of messages are transmitted, explicitly or unintentionally, to children about mathematics learning. In the case studies, for example in Section 3.4 on packaging, teachers have tried to set up situations in which the children were stimulated by the nature of the tasks and experiences and given opportunity to think for themselves. At times the teachers saw the need to impart information or teach skills to move thinking on or to support an observed need. For example in Section 4.2 in the reception class data case study, children needed help in preparing a data collection sheet. In the conversations described, the questioning is significant in the degree to which there is challenge to children but respect for their developing ideas. The Key Stage 2 case study in Section 1 explicitly identifies the kind of atmosphere that helps to develop children's mathematical thinking through the encouragement of prediction and conjecture. There is also an element of risk taking for the teacher in the more open ended work. Likely outcomes for the children can be identified but the teacher will need to keep an open mind in looking for particular approaches or unexpected strategies which require continual reflection on the children's development.

The atmosphere or ethos of the classroom should be aimed at being inclusive so that all children can engage with the learning. This might mean making special arrangements for particular children to be able to take part. Teachers need to be prepared to adjust their teaching in order to support and extend the thinking of all the children in the class. For example, in Section 2.3 in the Key Stage 2 case study featuring the loop card activity, children were given the task of making up their own loops and this allowed individual children to approach the task in different ways. The teacher was planning for differentiation by outcome. One child, a boy with special learning needs, was able to come up with a different idea which was respected by other children. The nature of the task allowed him, with his support teacher, to have access to the work of the class and to respond with his own ideas. The valuing of children's ideas is crucial. Teacher expectation must not limit the possibilities for children in individual tasks. In the nursery shopping game context, in Section 2.2, some children would benefit from the opportunity to work with a dice with numbers 1 to 10. The particular case of those having difficulties in learning mathematics is addressed further in Section 5.3.

The teacher would, similarly, need to consider children at different stages in learning English as an additional language (EAL). For example, would it help to begin with a more practical or body task where children can follow actions, accompanied by appropriate language, before embarking on an oral or written context? (see the comments on 'body activities' later in this section). Another type of activity supportive of these children is a game with a repetitive structure of moves. This and the accompanying language allows reinforcement and a model for speech. For example, board games involving rolling dice and counting spaces and responding to simple instructions such as 'go back 4' or 'move on 3' provide repeated occurrences of speech and physical moves which children can observe and hear before participating. Other strategies to support children with EAL could include the following:

- ensuring that class activities are clearly demonstrated and modelled with appropriate physical resources, for example showing jumps on a number line on an interactive whiteboard;
- making classrooms displays with mathematical vocabulary and clear visual images or physical apparatus;
- pairing children with others who have the same home language but who are more fluent English speakers, who can translate and model speech where appropriate;
- pairing children with EAL and native English speakers as talk partners in whole class activities, to allow children to rehearse responses to questions before answering publicly.

The teacher's role is central, and has been examined in particular contexts in this book. The next sections discuss how the teacher can organise overall for successful mathematics learning. Key aspects in this context are:

- starting work in stimulating ways;
- encouraging and facilitating talk about mathematics;
- grouping children in a variety of ways to suit different purposes;
- selecting and using resources and displaying images to provide mental models.

The intention is to suggest how all of these considerations can be drawn together in providing for a context in which challenging work and confidence building can be developed.

Starting an activity in stimulating ways

Engagement with a task

How can teachers make the experience one which children are able and eager to tackle? The initial presentation and questioning is crucial. If the teacher is introducing a new topic, how can children's current understanding be built on? In teaching fractions to a class of children, they may be asked how they would explain or 'make a picture' to show a half to someone else. It is useful to consider what they may do in response. If the teacher expects and encourages creativity in showing half a shape in many different ways, the activity will begin to develop momentum. Children may draw illustrations of halves of everyday objects such as half an apple or half a sandwich. They may draw a set of objects separated into two equal sets by a line. In another context described in Section 3.4, 'Aspects of Measurement', children working on reading clocks were asked to recall from memory '*a clock you know*' and draw it. Their drawings and accompanying discussion involved the children in describing something familiar to them and allowed the teacher to make informed judgements about how to proceed. Children are then put in the position of sharing knowledge they have and experiences related to the topic under consideration. The teacher can challenge them further in an appropriate way if they have demonstrated what they know already. If a child writes 12 at the top of the clock they have drawn, how do they add the rest of the numbers? Do they place them randomly around the face, continue past 11 if they do not fill the space, know where to put 3 and 9? Children could compare and discuss their pictures and share their ideas. Another stimulus for mathematical work is story books and examples have been given throughout this book, looking at counting books, stories used to think about the probability of events happening and the data handling work prompted by the Three Billy Goats Gruff tale in the Reception class (Section 4). Many of these are most appropriate for younger children but there are also some stories that present opportunities for work with older children, such as Anno's *Mysterious Multiplying Jar* (Anno and Anno, 1983) where ideas of multiplication and factorials can be explored in an interesting way as numbers increase through the beautifully illustrated story. *One Hundred Hungry Ants* (Pinczes, 1993), most suitable for children in KS1 learning about multiplication and division, is about the journey of one hundred ants to a picnic and explores the various ways in which the ants can be grouped to march and reach their destination most quickly. Again ideas related to multiplication and division such as arrays, multiples and factors can be explored in an enjoyable context.

Puzzles or questions

Setting challenges like, 'Who can find the biggest number in the newspaper?' or 'How many sweets are in the jar?' can encourage thinking about the possible outcomes and also about how to tackle the question. 'Magic squares' is an example of a puzzle: 'Can you fit the numbers 1 to 9 in a 3 by 3 square so that each line adds to 15?' which can again be used to stimulate thinking, 'Can it be done? How can we find out?' When a solution is found, can children find any others. How will they know if they have found all the possible solutions? Could the activity be extended to consider other sets of numbers or sizes of squares?

Focusing children on the questions rather than the 'answer'

This is quite the opposite of what many of them may expect and can be profitable in creating interest. For example, 'The answer is 24, what is the question?' Here the children work in pairs. Initially, they identify calculations which will give the answer 24. Later they can be asked to provide challenges for other children by imposing constraints on the activity. For example 'The answer is 24. What is the question? Your questions cannot involve addition' or 'Your questions must involve division and at least one other operation'. As all good quiz-setters must know the answers themselves the children designing the activity will need to have addressed some of the issues that may arise before they challenge their friends! For example, if you 'mix' multiplication and addition does it matter which operation you do first: 4 + 4 x 5? What happens if you use division and subtraction together? The children can also be given the task of 'marking' their friends' efforts and feeding back to them. This gives rise to questions such as, 'Why does it matter what order the calculations come in?' and 'How will you explain ...?'

Drama or role play

Using drama or role play to stimulate mathematical ideas is another possible approach. For example, young children might arrive in school one morning to find a pile of boxes in the role play area (set up as a shop) and a letter from the shopkeeper who has been unexpectedly called away and had to leave stock unsorted: 'Can the children please sort the shop out and open up until she returns' (see Figure 5.6) This would lead into sorting items on shelves, setting up a till, labelling prices and so on which can support play in the shop. Older children, given a similar task, could work in pairs or small groups, to identify a range of goods in which their peers would be interested. They would then have the task of researching accurate prices for the items. What would be the sources of such information? Given accurate prices, what denominations of money would customers be likely to offer in payment? How would they ensure that they had the means of giving the necessary change? For example, '*If a customer buys a book costing £6.99 and offers a £10 note what coins or notes will they have to have in the till as change?*' '*Is there only one possible solution?*' Clearly, much decision-making will be necessary throughout and those offering solutions will be called on to justify and explain their ideas so that possible outcomes can be agreed and an appropriate 'float' assembled.

Enacting number stories or rhymes can be effective in making mathematics more vivid. The rhyme 'Five Currant Buns in the Baker's Shop', where children can 'buy' a bun and pay with a penny can be experienced by a group of children so that the operations of exchanging and subtraction are modelled by the actions in the rhyme.

Whole body activities can provide another approach in which children can experience mathematical ideas physically. Children can be labelled as numbers, for example with hats or numeral cards.

> Monday 5 September
>
> Dear Class 1
>
> I have gone home to fetch some more things for my shop.
> I have to open these boxes, set up my paper shop and write out the prices with my big red pen.
> Please can you help me. I will be back at 12 o'clock.
>
> Your friend
>
> Berty

Figure 5.6 Letter found by children

They can then be asked to make relationships between the various numbers, depending on stage of understanding. Children could sort themselves into number order, pairs could get together to make two digit numbers or bonds for ten or two people could stand on either side of a 'decimal point person' and make numbers with one decimal place. Numbers could relate to the number of children in the class or be varied to suit particular purposes (see Figure 5.7).

Making shapes with the body in PE activities are another example. In Section 2.2 in the corners activity children can stand in groups at the corners of a PE mat and move to the centre to answer,

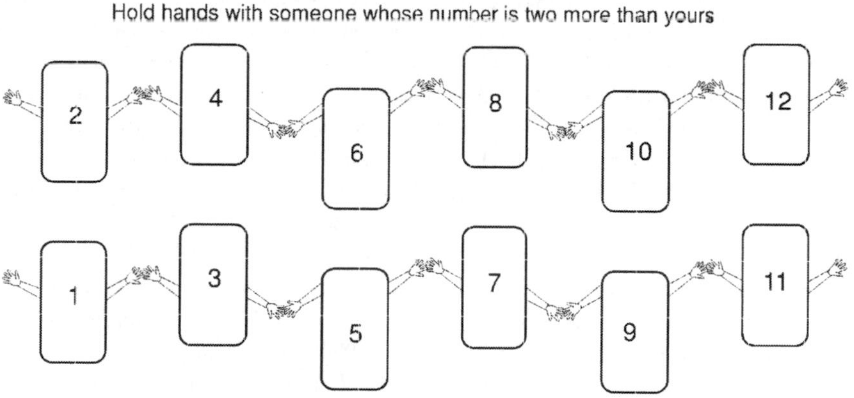

Hold hands with someone whose number is two more than yours

Figure 5.7 Activities for children wearing number cards

'How many are there altogether?' This can lead to finding totals by using cubes on paper shapes. At Key Stage 2 numbered children can move across a decimal point when multiplied or divided, as described in Section 2.4 (see Figure 5.8). Questions such as '*What will happen if the number is multiplied by a hundred?*' require children to predict the new position of the digits and reason about what is happening. For factors, 24 children from the class can be asked to group themselves in twos, then move into threes, fours, etc. to illustrate which numbers work and which do not. EAL children can be helped to see the nature of the mathematical ideas by being involved and work can then move onto arranging objects on table tops. For all children the physical experience can be recalled in assisting the development of mental images.

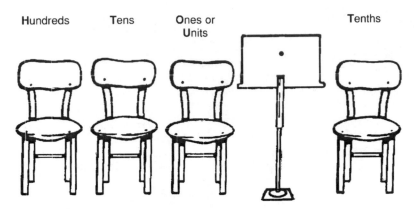

| Hundreds | Tens | Ones or Units | | Tenths |

Figure 5.8 Apparatus for whole body activities

Encouraging and facilitating talk about mathematics

Planning for children's talk

Stereotypically, mathematics has been thought of as an isolating or solitary activity; learning about it meant listening to exposition by the teacher followed by the learner practising relevant examples. Certainly, we would wish our children to listen to their teachers. There *are* times when it is profitable to work alone and to think independently and the practising of skills is important. Every learner has experienced uncertainty and confusion, however. They can arise at the beginning of trying to solve a problem – we cannot 'get going'. We may get so far and then not be able to think of what needs to happen next. We can fail to recognise a misconception on which we base our reasoning. Having arrived at a possible solution we may not be clear about how effective a solution we actually have. In other words, making sense of and understanding ideas does not necessarily occur as a result of this model of exposition and practice. It is often not until we interact with others that our thinking is clarified and our reasoning exposed and challenged. The most common type of interaction, of course, whether between children or between teacher and children, is talking. Hence, one of the themes of this book has been the importance of talk in mathematics. This has been exemplified by the kind of questions teachers ask to elicit explanations and reasoning from children and by the examples of talk generated in the case studies. Most recently the 2008 Williams Review has supported the importance of discussion in mathematics, for example in paragraph 237 where it is stated, 'The critical importance of engaging children in discussing mathematics is widely recognised' (Williams 2008).

Merely challenging children to talk about or discuss their mathematics is not enough in itself, however. Teachers must be mindful of the type of talk taking place and the fact that children may well need support concerning *how* to hold a profitable discussion. Disagreement between children can occur; they can respond to each other merely by making counter-assertions and without considering the value of what has been offered and these exchanges tend to be brief and relatively superficial. These factors are some of the characteristics of what is sometimes referred to as *disputational* talk (Wegerif and Mercer 1997) and far from being helpful it can lead to children losing sight of what they are trying to achieve. The disagreement itself can become the focus or what was a potentially profitable suggestion can be lost and some children simply tell others what to do, and they comply! Nor is it rare for children simply to accept unquestioningly what is offered by one child and to build on it. They simply repeat and confirm what has been suggested and perhaps make minor amendments. These are some of the characteristics of *cumulative* talk, according to Wegerif and Mercer. Should the original idea put forward be flawed then in mere acceptance, there is the obvious danger that any resulting solution will be inaccurate. What teachers must plan to stimulate, therefore, is talk that deepens the children's engagement with the mathematics i.e. discussion involving reasoning. In order to encourage purposeful discussion, it may be helpful to identify some features and strategies.

Firstly, teacher questioning is crucial in drawing out children's thinking. At times closed questions are appropriate, for example in assessing whether particular facts are recalled (*'How many sides and angles does a triangle have?' 'What does the 5 in 56 represent?'*). However, to allow children to explore ideas, share meanings and develop reasoning, questions are needed which require more elaborated responses. Examples of these key questions are included in Section 1, for instance, *'How do you know that?' 'How can you be sure?'* There are also many examples in the case studies of teachers questioning to encourage reasoning, The skill of the teacher is to follow children's responses and model ways of talking which will help them develop the skill of saying what they mean through the use of more precise vocabulary, for example.

The aim is to promote a more active involvement in mathematical thinking and to promote what has been described by Wegerif and Mercer as 'exploratory talk'. This involves children considering different hypotheses, constructively challenging the ideas of others and agreeing conclusions based on clear reasoning. In order to achieve this, children need confidence and social skills, which can be developed through ground rules for group work. Activities need to be carefully selected and planned to require children to discuss between themselves. There also need to be relationships of trust with safe risk-taking according to Howe and Mercer (2007) and Wheeldon (2006).

Two examples are offered below to illustrate this point.

Activity 1: Classifying shapes

A group of children are challenged to classify shapes and then to explain and justify their decisions. The teacher chooses carefully which examples are provided for the children and in doing so thinks carefully about how effectively productive talk might be stimulated. The kind of experience is key; it is collaborative (the sorting has to be agreed) and open to different criteria for sorting, so discussion is needed to air and resolve differences. It may create more discussion if the criteria are closed and the shapes are tricky.

The shapes in Figure 5.9 could be sorted in a variety of ways, initiated by the children or the teacher, for example, angle properties (triangles or shapes with obtuse angles) or number of sides. Misconceptions may manifest themselves through the justifications children give, for example, seeing the irregular pentagon as a triangle because it has an acute angle. The teacher can choose shapes that will challenge, according to the age and understanding of the children, for example, using either triangles or quadrilaterals on their own with older children, including 'nearly but not quite' examples such as the pentagon or quadrilateral in Figure 5.9 which children might take for triangles because of the acute angles.

The teacher's role in this activity is to encourage and model responses such as, *'I think that goes there because…' 'That can't go there if …' 'I don't know why you've put that there …'* Productive talk will involve children questioning each other in this way, rather than simply accepting a conflicting idea. They will be prepared to ask for and give reasons for choices of sorting. For example, *'No, I don't know why you put those shapes together. Can you explain to me?'* A response might be *'Because these all have a right angle and these don't'*. The child may support the explanation by showing where the right angles are. In responding to a misconception, for example a child's suggestion that a shape is a triangle because *'it has a point at the top'*, the teacher can ask others to say whether they agree or disagree and why.

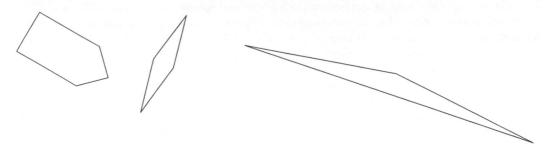

Figure 5.9 Classifying shapes

Activity 2: Odd and even numbers

Working in pairs or small groups children have already been working on what happens if you add an even number to another even number. They have decided that the answer is that you get an even number. They are now asked to respond to the statement, '*If you add an odd number to another odd number the answer is an even number*'. Here the children must decide on how to get started. Left alone they might choose to work on some examples in order to gather data. Which ones should they use? Consider the scenario below:

Fatima: '*7 and 13 are odd. Let's do those.*'
Maya: '*Okay.*'

After working for a short time on some numbers chosen at random one child pauses:

Fatima: '*It works for all the ones we've done.*'
Maya: '*Yes, but we haven't done them all. Let's do them all. We have to do them all because otherwise we won't know.*'
Fatima: '*We could do 1 and 3 first then 3 and 5.*'
Maya: '*We could but we've already done bigger ones. If it works for bigger ones it will work for 1 and 3.*'
Fatima: '*How do you know?*'
Maya: '*...well it does, it's 4.*'
Fatima: '*...but you can only tell because you've done it. And anyway I don't know which ones we've done 'cos it's all mixed up. If we start with the smaller ones and work up, then we'll know.*'

Given the same task, the teacher may choose to be involved from the outset:

Fatima: '*It's an odd and an odd now.*'
Teacher: '*Does what you learnt from the task of an even add an even help?*'
Maya: '*It might do ...*'
Fatima: '*An even add an even makes an even so ... an odd add an odd must be ... an odd.*'
Teacher: '*What makes you think that?*'
Fatima: '*Cos it's the same when you do evens and evens (you get an even number) so it will be when you do odd and odd (the answer will be an odd number).*'
Teacher (to Maya): '*What do you think?*'
Maya: '*Yeah, it could be ... even and even, even ... odd and odd, odd. But 3 add 5 is 8 and that's even ... so ...*'

In both scenarios it is clear that the most productive talk is that which challenges the ideas put forward and requires the speaker to justify an opinion. In short, whatever the strategy chosen by the children, and whether the teacher is involved or not, we can see that the most profitable talk is that which involves comments such as, '*I think we could ... because ...*' and responses in the spirit of, '*Yes that might work but what if we ...?*' The main point is that the activity is good and the response is productive if it prompts children to use the word 'because'.

This is where ethos and agreed ways of challenge are crucial in making it possible to take risks in mathematics lessons. Children can be explicitly encouraged to ask for further clarification if they do not follow an explanation. Teachers should also be very considered in response to children's suggestions or answers to questions. Pratt (2006) argues the importance of giving children time to frame their answers and of not expecting that children will necessarily be able to provide complete responses at their first attempt. Perseverance on the part of the children is a requirement and this will not be encouraged if the teacher takes over the children's ideas and re-phrases or tidies them up for the benefit of others or so that things can 'move on' quickly. Equally, if the children are to continue to think, the teacher must beware of responding in such a way that a 'right' answer is immediately signaled. Rather, it is the responsibility of the teacher to elicit further engagement by responding in a more considered or 'neutral' way. For example, '*What do people think?*' will continue to press children to remain engaged whilst '*Good, well done*' can have the effect of signaling that a conclusion has been reached and that no further thought is necessary. It is also worth considering, here, whether teachers can sometimes model most effectively if they and the children are involved with scenarios to which the teachers do not have a previously worked out solution. Here teachers must have sufficient confidence in their own subject and pedagogical knowledge to let the children 'run' with an activity without worrying that they have to know precisely how things are going to turn out. They will at least have to resist the temptation to lead the discussion too strongly in the direction they might have followed themselves.

Following from the modelling of responses explicit agreed ways of working or rules can be set up and publicly recorded. For example '*It's OK to change your mind*' or '*Make sure everyone gets a turn to speak*'. Monaghan (2005) suggests that the following are helpful:

- everyone is encouraged to contribute;
- everyone listens actively;
- information is shared;
- ideas and opinions are treated with respect;
- challenges are welcome;
- reasons are required and given;
- contributions build on what has gone before;
- alternatives are discussed before decisions are taken;
- groups work towards agreement before an action is taken;
- it is possible for participants to change their mind;
- discussion is understood to be a way of learning.

Children can then be asked to reflect on whether those rules were adhered to successfully. Wheeldon (2006) discovered, also, that her children were able to refine and develop these 'ground-rules' for themselves as they became more used to working in this way. Collaborative talk is an area that has to be worked on and it will not happen quickly. In passing, it is also worth considering the use of such an approach in the classroom generally, and not merely in the context of mathematics. Children can benefit from constructive and profitable talk throughout their learning, of course.

In addition to having identified general ways of working, particular strategies can be employed to support collaboration. Some examples are:

- *Setting up talk partners*: so that children have someone to share ideas with before opening them up for wider discussion. Aplin (2006) argues that variety in the make-up of pairs will be helpful for the children. Working with a friend is sometimes appropriate; children with different levels of attainment can be paired so as to learn from each other; and working with someone less well known can challenge them to be more considered in their responses.
- '*Back to back*' activities: where one person gives instructions and the other follows while neither can see what the other is doing, for example, making a model with five interlinking cubes. Here the children must address the issue of shared understanding of the vocabulary and the accuracy of the instructions they give or receive.

- *Thought shower*: asking groups or individuals to note down (this could be in the form of a network of ideas) what they know already at the start of a new topic. This can be returned to and reviewed at a later stage
- *Solver/recorder*: one person (solver) works on a problem (for example, calculation) talking through each step. The other person (recorder) writes down the steps as described. At times the recorder will need to check on detail which means the solver will have to elaborate or repeat explanations.

(For more examples see Aplin's 'classroom techniques' in BEAM's *Maths Out Loud* series, Year 6.)

In order to emphasise and embed working rules and key questions, these could be displayed in the classroom as a reference point to remind children to employ them as a matter of course.

Groupings

According to the purpose of the mathematical task or activity, different groupings may be appropriate.

Whole class

This can be used to set the scene for new work, draw points together, ask children to report findings or set up a common starting point. Quick oral games and activities such as Fizz Buzz or rhymes can also be tackled in this context. One concern with a common starting point is that not all children will understand what is aimed at a whole class but it is possible to plan so that different children will gain different things from the experience. As long as the starting point is initially accessible to all the pupils, particular groups or individuals can respond in different ways. The teacher needs to be clear what the range of responses might look like and about the kind of that will be offered based on knowledge of the children. Some examples of activities suitable for the whole class are 'How many ways can you make …' (choose a number, amount of money, arrangement of squares, etc. to suit the class or allow children to choose their own, see Section 2.6, Activity 2). There is also an example of 'How many different …?' in Section 3.2 in the shape and space activities section). Children can respond in different ways, however:

- solutions they suggest, for example, for '10' might be pairs adding to 10, answers involving a wider range of operations or fractions/decimals;
- approaches they use – do they systematically work through ways of arranging five squares?;
- different ways of recording and explaining findings.

Feedback or plenary sessions are very valuable. If different groups have worked on different aspects of the same theme, reporting back gives an opportunity for children to articulate their findings and listen to the ideas of others. The teacher can listen and make assessments as well as participate by drawing out key teaching points. When a task has been completed by a group, members can be challenged to explain what changes they would make in how they tackled it if they were asked to do it again. Children can be encouraged to present their findings in posters that can be displayed and discussed, with the 'audience' of peers asking questions to clarify. Groups may present different ways they have solved a problem and the class can think about and comment on the methods.

'Maths on the mat' times are useful for practising and consolidating mathematical skills and ideas. Helping the teacher calculate register numbers, adding up the dinner money, playing games and rhymes, responding to mental challenges in geometry and number are all possibilities. Children could be asked to hide behind a screen and hold up hands while others work out how many children are hidden from the number of hands they can see. The teacher (or a child) can hold up a shape, but show only part, such as a corner. Can children guess the shape and say why? Then a bit more can be revealed. Do they want to revise their guess? Why?

Small groups

Children are usually organised into groups within the whole class lesson but at times the teacher will need to group children for particular purposes and these will inform the size and composition of the groups. In Section 3.4 in the packaging case study, children were grouped so that a range of roles could be covered, including the keeping of a diary. For example, the class might be planning an event – a picnic or a party – and groups will address different aspects, identify approaches and gather necessary data. Some might be responsible for considering the food while others may have to plan the games, and so on. The groups are required to collaborate in solving a problem, using mathematical knowledge, skills and understanding. Other groups may be set up by the teacher, based on observations made of a particular learning need. For example, some children may be having difficulty with using measuring tools in a design and technology activity so a group is formed to focus specifically on the relevant aspect of mathematics which might be reading the scale on the ruler and noticing where to read the measurement from – zero or one? The teacher may have observed several children who could be taken further in a topic and so gives them a particular extension task to work on together.

Gender can be an issue and needs to be taken into account in planning group composition. In Section 4.2 in the Key Stage 2 handling data case study, girls and boys chose to work separately and the teacher did not interfere. In some contexts, perhaps where particular girls feel less confident, single sex groups might act as support to the development of expertise free from the pressure of more confident peers. Bennett and Dunne (1992) suggest that the mode of the task needs to be taken into account and that in tasks such as computer work girls may be less confident. In addition the teacher needs to monitor the composition of groups to see if all children have equal opportunities for involvement and to ensure that everyone has the chance to be the 'expert' or the 'teacher' at some point.

For children with EAL the teacher will need to consider how to involve any support teachers with groups, as well as different ways of pairing children, in order to support understanding and to develop confidence in mathematical reasoning and using mathematical vocabulary.

Organising for group work also means planning teacher focus to avoid the pressures of having to respond superficially to the needs of groups. How many groups will there be? When and where will teacher attention need to be greatest? Which groups can work without teacher help? All the children need to benefit from teacher support at times and so groupings will need to vary to ensure that all attention is not focused on one group. The likely times at which teacher support will be needed should be identified in advance. If a group is to be started on a new activity teacher input may be required at the beginning and other groups will need to be fairly independent to allow this to happen. Similarly, if all groups finish at the same time or need moving on at the same time, the teacher will be unable to give sufficient attention to each. Groups need to be planned so that while one group is starting on a new activity, other groups are working on tasks they have started previously or on follow up which they can work on independently.

When children are working in groups the teacher can maximise teaching opportunities by planning the support for different groups. For example if four groups are working two groups could be involved in reinforcement work requiring little teacher intervention. Of the remaining two groups one might need attention to start a new activity and the other might need intervention after beginning a task. The main point is that the teacher plans interaction with particular groups and sets up other tasks which require less explanation or teacher support. The teacher will need also to anticipate which groups or individuals will require support immediately after a whole class introduction to enable them to engage with the task.

Individuals

It is often necessary for the teacher to help an individual child who needs immediate attention to be able to continue with the task. There will also be times children tackle work individually, making records, or practicing mathematical skills. Some children have particular needs and may have special teacher support. The class teacher can work with the support teacher to integrate the child into the mainstream work of the class. It is as important to provide special needs support for mathematical work as for literacy. As in group work, although this allows for more focused attention and observation by the teacher, it is essential that others in the class can work independently.

Selecting and organising resources

We have selected examples of resources we feel would support the tasks described in this book. They are not exhaustive but aimed at exemplifying appropriate material to support our aims. It is worth mentioning here that there is a need for teachers to resist the temptation always to put out the resources needed to tackle a task. There is value for the children in trying to decide what resources they will need and they cannot do this if the necessary equipment has already been provided by their teacher. Sometimes children are guided towards a particular strategy or approach because of the resources the teacher has chosen.

A wide range of equipment will be used in all phases but there are some items which will need to feature particularly at different stages. Messages can be communicated unconsciously if practical equipment is kept in classes of younger children and older children have to go to those classes to fetch equipment. Apparatus such as Polydron may be used in a structured way with older children and it can be extremely helpful in developing spatial ideas, such as nets of 3-D shapes.

Early years settings

Some Foundation Stage learning environments will contain a designated mathematics area, but this may be more common in later stages of school. Much of the practical equipment suggested for older children is to be encouraged at this stage but it may be integrated into the provision in a variety of areas. For example, in a shop role play area a till with coins, calculator, telephone, tape measure, height chart and scales can all be made available to support the play. At the same time these will stimulate experience with number, measures, money and so on. Just as a notepad by the telephone will encourage young children to engage in writing so numerical recording of mathematical experiences can be stimulated by appointment books and making party invitations. Large floor or wall hundred squares or lines would stimulate interest in larger numbers.

Sand and water experience, whether indoors or outdoors offer opportunity for exploration with containers but also building and also counting: 'How many bucketfuls of sand did your castle need?' Numerals can be quite naturally displayed and discussed on calendars, clocks etc. In addition more structured play equipment can be introduced, for example numeral floor tiles and number rhyme and story books. Large wooden numerals for floor or table top use can encourage recognition, ordering and so on. Calculators can be incorporated in play but also explored in their own right through questioning, such as '*What happens if you press this button?*' Programmable toys, such as Roamer can also be explored in developing early spatial and measurement ideas through activities such as, 'How can you make Roamer come to you?' Number games and puzzles such as children experience with family members at home can also be included as table top activities, involving spatial and numerical experience but these will need to be supported by an adult. A variety of construction material, including building blocks, is commonly found in nurseries; building and talking about their constructions will offer contexts for children to manipulate shape and space and also to develop their mathematical language in describing and explaining their building. Shapes or pattern blocks can offer stimulus for pattern making. Cooking and gardening are other contexts which can offer opportunity for number and measures. Equipment which may not at first appear to be 'mathematical' also needs to be considered, for example, musical instruments for developing patterns of sounds. There is a variety of computer software which supports number recognition and develops spatial awareness; interactive whiteboards can be used to illustrate number rhymes, emphasising the patterns and relationships.

Key Stages 1 and 2

Number

- Counting material can include structured as well as more everyday objects such as Unifix, Multilink, coloured sticks or rods and teddy counters (they come in different sizes and weights) and counters, acorns, conkers, shells and buttons. It is useful to have quite large collections of objects for '*How many in the jar?*' type estimation and counting activities.
- Games could be commercial such as Snakes and Ladders, dominoes or the variety on offer in toy shops with potential for number or home made with a simple track for filling up with favourite objects.
- A range of dice allows flexibility in game design, both commercially produced with dots, numerals or different numbers of faces, and home made with colours, shapes or money, for particular games.
- Digit cards, number cards (1 to 100) and also playing cards and blank cards allow children to make their own games.
- Place value cards to allow children to see how numbers are numbers are made up ones, tens and hundreds, and include decimal and money versions.
- Number lines and squares are useful for reference (0–1000 or fractions, decimals, negative numbers).
- Base 10 apparatus show relationships between ones, tens, hundreds, thousands.
- Calculators – as well as hand held ones, it is useful to have some table-top or on-screen versions so that the teacher can focus children's understanding by getting them to give instructions for key sequences.

Shape and space

- puzzles (for example, tangrams);
- Multilink and mats for building, translating 2-D plans into models and representing models as plans;
- mirrors – different sizes, hinged pairs;
- pattern blocks for tessellation, forming and dissecting shapes;
- paper, various – with squares of different sizes, dotty;
- 2-D/3-D shapes/recycled boxes, for example, a collection of interesting packets with Easter egg boxes;
- programmable robots for giving directions and devising routes.

Measures

- rulers and tapes marked in different ways to allow comparisons and discussion;
- real coins as well as 'pretend' so children can feel the weight, see the colour, etc.;
- capacity containers, standardised (as well as recycled) containers from home;
- varied scales, balance and hanging including some with see-through buckets and spring balances;
- clocks including real working clocks – geared analogue and digital;
- timers – sand, digital and analogue, clockwork pingers, tockers and water, candle, marble timers, sun dials, etc.;
- calendars and timetables.

Data handling

- sorting/Venn sets and sorting material – with shapes and number cards;
- collection of buttons, bought in shop or boot sales (excellent for sorting and counting);

- cubes and spike abacus, Unifix and Multilink for 3-D graphs;
- large floor grids for real graphs.

General

- mathematics dictionaries, commercially produced and made by the children;
- variety of papers for exploring and recording (different sized squares, dotty, 100 squares etc.);
- 'thinking paper' for children to record in their own ways and draft mathematical ideas;
- topic collections, for example, pattern (wallpaper, wrapping paper, photos from the environment) all from a range of cultures.

ICT

Various activities have been described in earlier sections which involve the use of calculators and computers – spreadsheets, databases and calculation. In addition the major ICT development more recently has been the introduction of interactive whiteboards (IWB). These allow a range of opportunities for teachers to model and demonstrate mathematical ideas but also for children to interact with mathematical ideas and resources on the internet. There is a wide range of software and ways in which material, such as from the Internet, can be imported into the classroom and some examples are:

- images of resources such as place value cards or base 10 apparatus to be displayed and moved around the screen with a pen or fingers. Children can be involved in such movement so that, for example, they can separate and combine parts of a number while other children can observe what is happening and then explore with the practical apparatus or use the IWB to report findings from practical exploration;
- images of mathematical paper such as squared paper or dotty paper upon which figures can be constructed in displaying geometrical figures to children;
- downloadable software which allows geometrical images such as tessellations to be constructed or figures to be reflected or rotated, again to introduce or discuss practical investigations;
- display of short programs demonstrating mathematical ideas such as multiplying and dividing numbers by powers of ten on a place value column chart so that the movement of digits is shown.

While it may be too soon to judge the impact of IWBs on the longer term learning of mathematics, their use appears to enhance the presentation of ideas to children and engage and focus their attention as well as allowing their interaction with those ideas as presented in this way. However, it is important that virtual images do not replace opportunities for children to handle resources practically and to talk while doing this.

Display/environment

The learning environment can be set up to encourage mathematical thinking through the organisation of resources as well as through displays of children's work or stimulus material. For example, labels on drawers can be made with numbers and pictures from catalogues for young children to encourage counting and calculation of missing items. Older children can make plans of places of furniture and equipment in the class if rearrangements are common. This can also serve the purpose of making children's self-selection of apparatus a possibility. Plans for the bases of containers of equipment can be drawn on cupboard surfaces so that children can match the container to its place by matching shape. Cross-curricular work based on improving the school environment and on organising events could act as powerful stimuli to mathematical work.

Permanent displays in school can be introduced by the teacher or made by children. Days of the week or months suspended from the ceiling in vertical order can be used as references by the children.

Posters and dictionaries set up by the teacher or made by children provide another source of reference material. Number friezes can again be displayed and varied according to the age of children (for example, 0–20, 0–100, 0–1,000) and very large numbers can be represented by colouring in blocks of 100 squares on fine scaled paper. Commercial posters help to stimulate ideas or provide reference. Children can write 'help' procedures for other children to use for Logo or the Roamer.

Stimulus collections and interactive displays contribute to the atmosphere of a mathematical learning environment. For example, a collection of patterns from wrapping paper, wallpaper and fabric can act as a focus for children to discuss pattern. Then they can add examples to the collection such as beads on thread or records of musical patterns they have made. Children could be asked to match nets to shapes or 'spot the odd one out'.

Other kinds of stimulus might include numerals taped to the backs of chairs. Children will start to talk about them and notice that theirs is 'two more than' their friend's. Questions of the week can be displayed to initiate discussion, such as 'How many marbles do you think are in this jar?' Children can work at this over a few days and parents and brothers and sisters are likely to get involved when children are collected! Questions can be varied according to the age of children. For older children a challenge might be '*What is the largest number you can make using the digits 1, 2, 3, 4 with multiplication signs? Is it 12 × 34 or perhaps 231 × 4?*' These challenges can encourage discussion across a number of classes or act as the introduction to developing a new idea or extending an old one. Further challenges could be: How far is it to the moon? How tall is Everest? How old is the oldest fish? How long/old /far is that in familiar units like heights or life spans of people?

5.3 CHILDREN WITH SPECIFIC MATHEMATICS LEARNING DIFFICULTIES

In the spectrum of mathematics performance, it is inevitable that some children will do better than others, and some children will find learning mathematics harder than others. However researchers such as Dowker (2004) have found that children who have difficulty with all aspects of mathematics are extremely rare. Even children with difficulties in learning number find different things hard: some may have difficulty remembering facts, but have good conceptual understanding, while others may remember facts, but have poor understanding. Some may have difficulties in solving problems: they may not easily make connections, have a limited range of strategies or they may be extremely slow but can get correct answers given time. Quite often children who get behind in mathematics have gaps in their understanding, for instance with place value. The commonest problems amongst those who are low attainers is a difficulty in remembering number bonds and multiplication facts, usually accompanied by a reliance on counting in ones, often using their fingers. There may be a variety of reasons for these difficulties.

For those children who are in the bottom 5% of the class for mathematics there are various possible reasons for their difficulties, which may affect all aspects of learning or just mathematics. They may be 'educational casualties' with gaps in their previous learning or poor confidence, or they may have specific learning difficulties which are neurological in origin, such as dyslexia or ADHD. Children with specific learning needs pose challenges for class teachers in terms of inclusion: is an inclusive curriculum one which is basically the same but provides access in a variety of ways, for instance by emphasising multisensory learning? Or do individual children's needs mean they should be given different activities or teaching methods? This is particularly pertinent when children are operating at a level two or more years behind the rest of the class or lack skills and understanding of concepts which should have been learned several years previously.

What are the possible causes for mathematics difficulties? And how can teachers help to compensate for these? Just as importantly, are there predictors of mathematics difficulties which we can identify and so prevent children falling behind? This section will attempt to answer these questions.

A major cause of children being 'behind' others is that they were behind to start with, due to social disadvantage. Class or socio-economic status is still the main determinant of mathematics achievement in Britain. Hughes in the 1980s found that working class three year olds tended to be a year behind middle class children, and stayed that way. More recent research in the USA has found huge differences at the start of kindergarten in children's number understanding, for instance in knowing that the counting numbers are worth one more than each other, for example, that 5 is more than 4 (Gersten *et al,*, 2005). If teachers assume that children have this understanding and move on, it is not hard to see that children's lack of understanding will grow exponentially and their mathematical confidence will decline. Therefore a key issue is the accurate assessment and monitoring of children's learning in order to identify and remedy gaps before they grow. Happily there is evidence that schools and pre-schools can make a difference, and an effective early years setting can prevent the 'start behind, stay behind' social trap.

One of the major causes of mathematics difficulties seems to be memory related. Some children may have particular difficulties in remembering words: this will make remembering multiplication facts difficult, as these tend to be stored in verbal memory. It will also make learning to count difficult, especially in English, where there is no consistent pattern until after 20. Children who have poor spatial memory, or who have dyspraxia and poor co-ordination, will also find it hard to learn to count. They may find it difficult to synthesise saying the counting words and pointing to objects, one at a time. They may also find it hard to remember which ones they have counted and need help to become rhythmic and systematic counters. If children have not become fluent counters, it may also take them longer to associate the final number with the quantity of objects or to understand the cardinal value of the total. Having to focus more on the mechanics of counting may also prevent children realising that the point of counting is to get a specific number of things. The ability to use counting to get a specific number of objects (for example '*Fetch me five pens*') has been found to be a strong predictor of number ability for five year olds. It is likely that children who take longer to learn to count will take longer to learn to add and subtract: if you do not always get the same total when counting, you may not realise that the total stays the same when partitioning a number in different ways. With traditional 'sums', which involved getting numbers of objects and counting them altogether, counting may be so laborious that children have forgotten the starting number by the time they reached the answer, so the number facts involved pass them by. Therefore we need to check that children with difficulties have learned to count confidently and with understanding, before assuming that they can use counting to solve problems. For instance, some nine year olds with mathematics difficulties thought that you could only count from left to right and that counting from right to left was wrong: they had learned counting as a procedure, without understanding how it worked (Gersten *et al,*, 2005). This suggests that there may have been other mathematical procedures they had learned without understanding.

Children with stronger visual or spatial memories, like most young children, find spatial patterns easier to remember than words. This is a strong argument for encouraging children to recognise numbers as dot patterns, particularly as the familiar dice or domino patterns also emphasise the highly memorable doubles facts (see examples in Section 2). Apparatus such as Numicon, Stern or Cuisenaire also offer spatial patterns for numbers. Children with strong spatial memories will also find fingers useful to represent numbers, especially as 'finger numbers' also involve muscle memory. Arranging counters in dot patterns, putting plastic bears on the floor dominoes or plugs in the Numicon holes also involve kinaesthetic learning and spatial memory. Older children can also use arrays and dot patterns to learn multiplication facts, for instance using multiples of four or five dot patterns.

An important principle for children with memory difficulties is to minimise memorisation and maximise calculation strategies based on reasoning. If children can recognise ten as a five and five pattern, they can see that moving one dot can create a six and four pattern without altering the total. Similarly if they can see three fours as 12 in an array, they can also see that four threes are also 12. (See examples relating to number bonds and multiplication in Section 2.) Even children with poor spatial memory benefit from learning number facts as visual patterns. Reasoning with visual patterns, explaining why numbers are the same, requires children to verbalise their understanding. For those children who are verbally strong this will tap a strength, for others the visual image will support their understanding and verbalisation. Using key facts to derive other number facts, using pattern and reasoning strategies, is therefore an inclusive teaching approach which minimises memory demands and encourages understanding of principles. For instance:

You know 5 + 5 = 10
So what else do you know?

6 + 5 = 11	one more, total increases by one
6 + 4 = 10	one more, one less, total stays same
10 – 5 = 5	inverse
50 + 50 = 100	place value
5,000,000 + 5,000,000 = 10,000,000	
15 + 5 = 20,	
25 + 5 = 30	pattern

You know 4 x 3 = 12
So what else do you know?

5 x 3 = 15	add another 3
How many 3s in 12?	inverse
8 x 3 = 24	8 times is double 4 times

Teaching children reasoning strategies also helps to build networks of connected facts, which makes the individual facts more memorable as well as providing several routes for retrieval and checking.

It seems that people who are strong spatial thinkers with weaker verbal abilities and also people who are stronger verbally than spatially, can all be high attainers in mathematics. There are different routes to understanding and children can learn to compensate for difficulties, by talking things through or using fingers and images. However, it seems it is very difficult to learn entirely in one mode: understanding involves the connecting of different sensory inputs, visual, auditory and kinaesthetic, and number understanding involves connecting words, images and symbols (Goswami and Bryant 2007). Poor numeral recognition can also predict mathematics difficulties, whereas familiarity with words and symbols seems to support understanding. It is therefore not useful to teach to one learning mode, according to a child's strength: it is better to help children develop all learning modes and connect them.

Working memory is another kind of memory which can affect mathematics learning: it involves holding several things in mind at once, both verbally and spatially, and monitoring one's thinking. Difficulties in counting backwards can be an indicator of poor working memory. For instance, mental addition using partitioning makes considerable demands on working memory:

48 + 35 =
40 + 30 = 70, 8 + 5 = 13
70 + 13 = 83

Adding the tens and units separately involves 'parking' the tens total, while calculating the units, then retrieving it to get the final total. You have to monitor the process of parking and retrieving while performing the subtasks, deciding where to focus attention. This places considerable demands on working memory. The monitoring of the procedure involves metacognition or thinking about thinking: this may be strengthened by language, as talking about thinking processes and strategies helps children become aware of these and able to control them. Using strategies which are less complex and place fewer demands on working memory space are therefore more inclusive. For instance, the 'jump' strategy involves fewer steps and is progressive, with no 'parking' and retrieving and can also be supported by a number line image:

48 + 30 is 78, + 5 is 83

Encouraging children to use informal jottings will also help to reduce demands on working memory.

The actual size of working memory expands considerably after the age of about six, and affects children's ability to deal with complex information. It has been suggested that very young children are not good at map reading, because it involves processing varied information and making multiple adjustments. Working memory is also affected by anxiety which fills the available space and blocks learning, having the same effect as a learning disability. Of course, children having difficulties with mathematics are also likely to suffer from anxiety, which will compound their learning difficulties.

Children who have dyslexia and dyspraxia may also have general learning difficulties which affect their mathematics. For instance, they may get confused about left and right, which can inhibit their place value understanding. They may have problems with sequencing or remembering instructions, which can make learning procedures difficult. The implications are that teaching approaches which emphasise understanding rather than memorising algorithms are likely to make mathematics more accessible to more children. In general, inclusive teaching approaches are multisensory and help children to connect actions, images and symbols through pattern spotting and explaining. What also works with children with mathematics difficulties seems to be extra time and attention, combined with detailed assessment and monitoring of progress: another vital ingredient may be the raised self-esteem and confidence of children who have found they can learn mathematics after all.

The profiles of children with specific difficulties in mathematics can vary. Identification of children with total 'number blindness' or dyscalculia, but who have no other difficulties, is extremely rare. Researchers have found that identifying children as 'dyscalculic', using tests or a computer screening programme can be unreliable: children may be just very slow, compulsively checking, with inefficient strategies or have other difficulties such as left-right confusion. Children can also get good scores on screening tests, but have worrying gaps in understanding. Some improve a year or two later, with or without intervention. Here are some examples of children identified with mathematics difficulties: the challenge for teachers is to decide what to try next with them.

Case studies

Two children with mathematical learning difficulties: Ben and Amanda

When Ben was nine, he was assessed as two or more years behind his peers, with great difficulties in memorising number facts. He was articulate and a high achiever in English, from a middle class background. At age ten he still had extreme difficulties in telling the time and putting numbers on a number line: he thought there were 10 minutes in a quarter of an hour and put 15 as halfway between 0 and 50. However, he learned times tables through lessons with a tutor, who used lots of games. He could use checking strategies like *'multiples of five end with 5 or 0'* but he did not use multiplication facts to solve division problems. Ben said he had got behind in year one, but teachers had ignored his difficulties because he was otherwise capable and he had lost confidence. With the help of a sympathetic class teacher and his tutor, Ben achieved an average level at the end of year six. However, his parents remained convinced he had serious problems.

Amanda was nine, low achieving and very anxious about mathematics, but reading at an average level. She had difficulties with place value and counted back in ones to solve 36 – 6. While she had quick recall of some number facts, she did not use addition facts to solve subtraction problems or employ strategies such as near doubles or bridging through ten. Amanda also confused left and right and was later assessed as having dyslexia: it seemed she had overcome this in order to read and memorise number facts, but it may have caused other difficulties with mathematics. Her lack of understanding of general principles had probably contributed to her lack of confidence. She later benefited from using place value apparatus and learning reasoning strategies in intensive, small group sessions.

These case studies underline the diversity of individual children with mathematics difficulties. Some with specific learning difficulties seem to overcome them in relation to reading more easily than with mathematics. A key feature is low confidence and anxiety, which inhibits progress. Both of these children needed to build belief in themselves as mathematics learners. A variety of multisensory and reasoning strategies was appropriate for both children, including visual models and games. However, they also benefited from intensive one-to-one or small group teaching, and arguably this was needed to compensate for several years of mathematical deprivation. A worrying aspect of these stories is that basic difficulties with number facts or place value were overlooked for so long, emphasising the need for informed and formative assessment to ensure that all children are making progress confidently.

Conclusion

Mathematical experience planned within the primary curriculum needs to demonstrate its distinctive nature but also to link with and reflect overall primary practice. There needs to be a stimulating environment showing its cross-curricular links but also addressing mathematical tasks for their own sake. A questioning, conjecturing atmosphere can be fostered by encouraging children to see that mathematics can be presented in different ways and that a variety of methods can be employed in solving problems. There needs to be a variety of approaches and teaching strategies according to clear aims and the organisation of the learning environment needs to reflect these aims. Above all children need to be actively engaged in mathematical thinking:

- solving purposeful problems that give access to mathematical thinking;
- communicating through talking about mathematical ideas with each other as well as with their teacher and as well as through written recording;
- reasoning about mathematics from rich tasks which engage and challenge thinking.

This takes us back to the aims of the book which are to support teachers in developing approaches which we believe will work towards this kind of experience for children.

Resources

(in addition to those contained in the References)

Classroom practice

Askew, M. (1988) *Teaching Primary Mathematics,* London: Hodder & Stoughton.

Ball, G. (1990) *Talking and Learning,* Oxford: Blackwell.

Baratta Lorton, M. (1976) *Mathematics Their Way*, London: Addison Wesley.

—— (1979) *Workjobs*, London: Addison Wesley.

BEAM (1994) *A Feel-for Number: Activities for number recovery programmes*, London: BEAM; and other BEAM publications, including:
Exploring Place Value;
Spot the Pattern;
Triangles and Quadrangles;
Start from Scratch Series –Measures.

—— (1995) *Number at Key Stage One*, BEAM/King's College London/Tower Hamlets.

Bell, R. and Cornelius, M. (1988) *Board Games From Round the World: A source book for mathematical investigations,* Cambridge: Cambridge University Press.

Bird, M. (1992) *Mathematics for Young Children,* London: Routledge.

Bloomfield, A. (1990) *People Maths,* Cheltenham: Stanley Thornes.

Griffiths, R. (1988) *Maths through Play,* Hemel Hempstead: MacDonald Children's Books.

Gura, P. (1992) *Exploring Learning, Young Children and Blockplay,* London: Paul Chapman Publishing.

Hansen, A. (ed) (2005) *Children's Errors in Mathematics: Understanding Common Misconceptions in Primary School,* Exeter: Learning Matters.

Haylock, D. and Cockburn, A. (2003) *Understanding Primary Mathematics in the Lower Primary Years,* 2nd edn, London: Paul Chapman Publishing.

Merttens, R. (1996) *Teaching numeracy: mathematics in the primary classroom,* Leamington Spa: Scholastic.

Mottershead, L. (1985) *Investigations in Mathematics,* Oxford: Basil Blackwell.

Open University (1990) *Supporting Primary Mathematics, A course for teachers which includes titles on probability, shape and space, data handling and algebra.*

Pennant, J. with Bradley, R., King, C., Thompson, J. and Walters, J. (2005) *Talk it. Solve it, a set of books for talk in primary mathematics 5–11,* London: BEAM.

Ross, A. (1984) *The Story of Mathematics,* London: A & C Black.

Straker, A. (1993) *Talking Point ,* Cambridge: Cambridge University Press.

Thompson, I. (e.) (1997) *Teaching and Learning Early Number,* Buckingham: Open University Press..

—— (e.) (2003) *Enhancing Primary Mathematics*, Buckingham: Open University Press.

Books to support teachers' subject knowledge

Haylock, D. (2006) *Mathematics Explained for Primary Teachers, 3rd end,* London: Sage.

Hopkins, C., Pope, S. and Pepperell, S. (2004) *Understanding Primary Mathematics,* London: David Fulton.

Suggate, J., Davis, A. and, Goulding, M. (2006) *Mathematical Knowledge for Primary Teachers, 3rd edn,* London. David Fulton Publishers.

Robots

BeeBot, Beebot.org.uk, Burghley Road, Lincoln LN6 7YE
Pip & Pixie, Swallow Systems, 134 Cock Lane, High Wycombe, Bucks HP13 7EA.
Roamer, Valiant Technology, Myrtle House, 69 Salcott Road, London SW11 6D.
Strategies: Maths and Problem Solving, Magazine, 27 Frederick Street, Hockley, Birmingham B1 3HH.

Software/websites

Association of Teachers of Mathematics, 7 Shaftesbury Street, Derby DE3 8Y(, tel 01332 4659).
BEAM: www.beam.org.u– has a wide range of mathematics resources.
Longman Logotron, 124 Cambridge Science Park, Milton Road, Cambridge, CB4 4ZS, tel(01223 42555).
MathsNet: www.mathsnet.net has a wide range of mathematics resources.
National Centre for Excellence in the Teaching of Mathematics: www.ncetm.org.uk
www.mathsonline.co.uk/freesite_tour/resource/whiteboard/decimals/dec_notes.html
www.nrich.org.uk is full of problems, puzzles and resources for teachers.
www.standards.dfes.gov.uk/primaryframework/downloads/SWF/fractions.swf
www.standards.dfes.gov.uk/primaryframework/downloads/SWF/coordinates.swf
Shodor Interactive: www.shodor.org/interactivate/activities/tessellate/

References

Anno, M. and Anno, M. (1983) *The Mysterious Multiplying Jar*, London: Bodley Head.

Aplin, R. (2006) *Maths Out Loud (Year 6): speaking and listening activities for primary maths*, London: BEAM.

Bennett, N. and Dunne, E. (1992) *Managing Classroom Groups*, Hemel Hempstead: Simon & Schuster.

Dickson, L., Brown, M. and Gibson, O. (1984) *Children Learning Mathematics*, London: Cassell.

Dowker, A. (2004) *What works for children with mathematics difficulties?*, London: DfES, available at http://publications.dcsf.gov.uk/default.aspx?PageFunction=productdetails&PageMode=publicatio ns&ProductId=RR554& (accessed 6 December 2008).

Gersten, N., Jordan, C. and Flojo, J. R. (2005) 'Early Identification and interventions for students with mathematics difficulties', *Journal of Learning Disabilities* 38(4): 293–304.

Gifford, S. (2005) *Teaching Mathematics 3–5*, Maidenhead: Open University Press.

Goswami, U. and Bryant, P. (2007) *Children's cognitive development and learning* (Primary Review Research survey 2/1a), Cambridge: University of Cambridge Faculty of Education, available at www.primaryreview.org.uk/Downloads/Int_Reps/4.Children_development-learning/Primary_ Review_2-1a_report_Cognitive_development_learning_071214.pdf (accessed 6 December 2008).

Graham, A. (1990) *Supporting Primary Mathematics: Data Handling*. Milton Keynes: Open University.

Harrison, R. (1987) 'On fullness', *Mathematics Teaching*, 119.

Hester, H., Ellis, S. and Barrs, M. (1993) *A Guide to the Primary Learning Record*, London: Centre for Language in Primary Education.

Howe, C. and Mercer, N. (2007) *Children's Social Development, Peer Interaction and Social Learning Research Survey: The Primary Review(2/1/a Briefing and 2/1a Report)*, available at www.primaryreview.org.uk/Publications/Interimreports.html (accessed 9 February 2009.

Hughes, M. (1986) *Children and Number*, Oxford: Blackwell.

ILEA (Inner London Education Authority) (1976) *Checkpoints Cards*, London: Harcourt, Brace & Jovanovitch.

Kerslake, D., Burton, L., Harvey, R., Street, L. and Walsh, A. (1992) *HBJ Mathematics*, London: Harcourt, Brace & Jovanovitch.

Monaghan, F. (2005) '"Don't think in your head, think aloud": ICT and exploratory talk in the primary school mathematics classroom', *Research in Mathematics Education* 7: 83–100.

Mosley, F. (1986) *Count Me In*, London: HarperCollins.

NCTM (National Council of Teachers of Mathematics) (1981) *Teaching Statistics and Probability*, London: Jonathan Press.

Ofsted (Office for Standards in Education, Children's Services and Skills) (1995) *Recent Research in Mathematics Education 5–16*, London: HMSO.

—— (2008) *Mathematics: understanding the score; messages from inspection evidence*, London: Ofsted.

Pengelly, H. (1985) *Mathematics: Making Sure*, Adelaide: Department of Education, University of Western Australia.

Pinczes, E. (1993) *One Hundred Hungry Ants*, Houghton Miffin.

Pinel, A. (1994) *Loop Cards, available from* www.adri.pinel.btinternet.co.uk (accessed 25 January 2009).

Pratt, N. (2006) *Interactive Maths Teaching in the Primary School*, London: Paul Chapman Publishing.

Pratt, N. (2002) 'Mathematics as Thinking', *Mathematics Teaching* 181, Derby: Association of Teachers of Mathematics.

PRIME (Primary Initiatives in Mathematics Education) (1991) *Calculators, Children and Mathematics*, Hemel Hempstead: Simon & Schuster.

Rousham, L. (2003) 'The empty number line: a model in search of a learning trajectory', in I. Thompson, *Enhancing Primary Mathematics Teaching*, Maidenhead: Open University Press.

Schaeffer, B., Eggleston, V. H, and Scott, J. L. (1974) 'Number development in young children', *Cognitive Psychology* 6: 357–79.

Vygotsky, L. (1978) *Mind in Society*, Cambridge, MA: MIT.

Wegerif, R., & Mercer, N. (1997). 'A dialogical framework for researching peer talk', in R. Wegerif & P. Scrimshaw (eds.), *Computers and Talk in the Primary Classroom*, Clevedon: Multi-lingual Matters.

Wheeldon, I. (2006) 'Peer Talk', *Mathematics Teaching* 146, Derby: Association of Teachers of Mathematics.

Wigley, A. (1994) 'Teaching number', *Mathematics Teaching* 199, Derby: Association of Teachers of Mathematics.

Williams, Sir P. (2008) *Independent Review of Mathematics Teaching in Early Years Settings and Primary Schools – Final Report from Sir Peter Williams* (Williams Review). Nottingham: DCFS.

Young Loveridge, J. (1987) 'Learning mathematics', *British Journal of Developmental Psychology* 5: 155–67.

Index

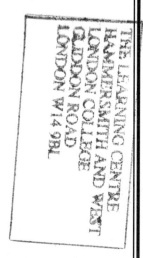

Lightning Source UK Ltd.
Milton Keynes UK
UKOW021923150312

189049UK00004B/8/P